JASON AND
THE GOLDEN FLEECE
(THE ARGONAUTICA)

RICHARD HUNTER is a Fellow of Pembroke College and
University Lecturer in Classics at the University of
Cambridge.

THE WORLD'S CLASSICS

APOLLONIUS OF RHODES

Jason and
The Golden Fleece
(*The* Argonautica)

Translated with an Introduction and Explanatory Notes by
RICHARD HUNTER

Oxford   New York
OXFORD UNIVERSITY PRESS

Oxford University Press, Walton Street, Oxford OX2 6DP

Oxford New York
Athens Auckland Bangkok Bombay
Calcutta Cape Town Dar es Salaam Delhi
Florence Hong Kong Istanbul Karachi
Kuala Lumpur Madras Madrid Melbourne
Mexico City Nairobi Paris Singapore
Taipei Tokyo Toronto

and associated companies in
Berlin Ibadan

Oxford is a trade mark of Oxford University Press

First published by the Clarendon Press 1993
First published as a World's Classics paperback 1995

British Library Cataloguing in Publication Data

Data available

Library of Congress Cataloging in Publication Data
Apollonius, Rhodius.
[Argonautica. English]
Jason and the golden fleece: the Argonautica / Apollonius of
Rhodes ; translated, with introduction and explanatory notes by
Richard Hunter.
xxxiii. 175 p. : maps ; 23 cm.
Includes bibliographical references (p. [xxxii]–xxxiii) and index.
1. Argonauts (Greek mythology)—Poetry. 2. Jason (Greek
mythology)—Poetry. 3. Medea (Greek mythology)—Poetry.
I. Hunter. R. L. (Richard L.) II. Title.
PA3872.E5 1993   883'.01—dc20   93–1935
ISBN 0-19-814757-0 (Hbk.)
ISBN 0-19-282461-9 (Pbk.)

3 5 7 9 10 8 6 4

Printed in Great Britain by
BPC Paperbacks Ltd
Aylesbury, Bucks

PREFACE

The *Argonautica* is a difficult poem: the Greek is often obscure, and understanding the poem's aesthetic framework and meaning requires coming to terms with poetic traditions which are alien (and sometimes alienating) to many modern readers. Nevertheless, its importance within ancient literary history is not in doubt, even for those who do not actually like it; more significantly, perhaps, its particular literary and intellectual qualities are now attracting much more serious critical attention than ever before. The aim of the present volume is to fill a perceived gap in what should be available if the *Argonautica* is in fact to reach as many readers as possible, and if appreciation of it is going to continue to make headway. I have tried to convey both the stylistic variety of the poem, and the fact that all of it is written in a language very far from the everyday; where the translation seems forced or imprecise, this *may* be because I have seen these qualities in the Greek. The *Argonautica* was never an 'easy read'. No one, on the other hand, is more conscious than I am of the failings of my translation; I can only hope that it will be judged sufficiently *utile* for the absence of the *dulce* to be excused.

The basis of the translation has been Vian's Budé text, and in the Notes I have signalled doubts about the text only where even the general sense is unclear.

I am much indebted to Hilary O'Shea for encouragement when it was badly needed, to OUP's editors and readers for their criticisms and suggestions, and to John Donaldson for his invaluable help with the maps. My largest debts—ones I share with all modern students of this poem—are to Hermann Fränkel and, above all, to Francis Vian whose Budé edition was the *sine qua non* of this volume.

R. L. H.

Cambridge
October, 1992

CONTENTS

References to the *Argonautica* are to Francis Vian's Budé edition of the Greek text (Paris, 1974–81). The shoulder-heads in the Translation refer to lines of the text in that edition, the running heads in the Notes to pages of the Translation in this book.

INTRODUCTION

1. *Apollonius of Rhodes*

The details of the life of Apollonius, like so many problems in the
chronology of post-classical Greek poetry, are fraught with un-
certainty; nevertheless, we possess just enough evidence to make
speculation both tempting and potentially fruitful, and modern
scholarship has certainly not resisted that temptation.[1] The medieval
manuscripts of the *Argonautica* transmit two 'Lives' containing
biographical information which can probably be traced back at least
to the late first century BC; there is also a Byzantine 'Life' (in the
lexicon known as the *Suda*), and a fragmentary list, dating from the
second century AD, of the Librarians of the Royal Library at
Alexandria. The information which these sources contain is lacunose
and contradictory, but there is enough common ground to create at
least a plausible framework.

Our sources are almost unanimous that Apollonius came from
Alexandria itself, and if this is true, he will have been something of
an exception among that city's leading literary figures who tended to
be outsiders attracted by the wealth and prestige of the court of the
Ptolemies.[2] The standard designation of Apollonius as 'the Rhodian'
seems then rather odd, but it may perhaps be explained by a period
of time spent on the island, as a gossipy story in the two extant
'Lives' suggests, or because his family had connections there.
Whatever the truth, it seems clear that Apollonius held the post of
Royal Librarian under Ptolemy II Philadelphus during the central
years of the century (perhaps *c*.270–245 BC), and was perhaps also
tutor to the future Ptolemy III Euergetes. He was thus at the very
centre of the Ptolemaic institutionalization of culture and learning to
which we owe so much of what we still possess of Greek literature.[3]
It is very likely that the *Argonautica* was composed in Alexandria

---

[1] My account here must be necessarily brief; for a fuller discussion with
bibliography cf. Hunter (1989), 1–9.

[2] Thus Callimachus and Eratosthenes came from Cyrene, Asclepiades from
Samos, Zenodotus from Ephesus, etc.

[3] Cf. further below pp. xi–xii.

during these years, though the exact chronology of the poem remains a matter of fierce debate among scholars.

The *Argonautica* is the only extant work of Apollonius, but we hear also of hexameter poems on the foundation legends of various Greek and Egyptian cities; this interest in the preservation and poeticization of stories of the establishment of Greek civilization is clearly visible also in the *Argonautica* and corresponds to central concerns of much of the scholarly work of cataloguing and recording which we associate with the Alexandrian Library. It is perhaps particularly unfortunate that we have lost Apollonius' *Foundation of Alexandria*, for this poem probably mingled 'mythical' and 'real' time in ways which might have shed much light on the genesis of Virgil's *Aeneid*.[4] There is also evidence that Apollonius wrote in metres other than the hexameter. As a scholar, he wrote prose works on, among others, Homer, Hesiod, and Archilochus; these works were largely concerned with explicating interpretative problems and with questions of authenticity, the two central concerns of all literary scholarship at this time. In these concerns there is an important relationship between Apollonius the scholarly poet and Apollonius the scholar of poetry. His poems and his prose works must often have engaged with the same archaic texts, but the mode of engagement will have differed significantly. As a scholar he was concerned to express views on important literary topics and subjects of current debate; as a poet he could use those debates as part of an imaginative interpretation of his literary heritage.

2. *Apollonius and Alexandrian Poetry*

The Greek citizens of Alexander's new foundation on the western edge of the Nile delta had much more in common with Greeks in other centres of the Hellenistic world than with the native Egyptian population which surrounded them. They were regulated by Greek law, and enjoyed the traditional cultural and cultic life of the Greek city.[5] It is natural to suppose that the special position of the city, both geographically and, as a new foundation without a mythic past upon which to build, historically, strengthened the internal solidarity

[4] Cf. below p. xxxi.
[5] On all of these matters the basic modern account is Fraser (1972).

and communality of the Greek population, particularly as Egypt
had long since been fashioned by the Greek consciousness into a
prime example of what was strange, barbaric, 'other'.[6] Be that as it
may—and it is as easy as it is dangerous to speculate on the
psychological pressures which weighed upon the Alexandrian
Greeks—it is clear that the first two Ptolemies, Soter and Philadelphus,
actively promoted Greek culture and the Greek heritage in part, at
least, to bolster their prestige within the wider Greek world and their
claims to be, not just Alexander's obvious Macedonian successors,
but also the natural heirs to his position of undisputed supremacy in
that wider world. Whereas on one hand the Ptolemies took over and
adapted Pharaonic ceremonial and institutions for the sake of
presenting themselves to their native subjects, on the other they
sought to show themselves to the Greeks as quintessentially Greek.
At times in the poetry of third-century Alexandria we can sense the
ironies and the unease which resulted from this two-edged programme,[7] but the mere fact of this extraordinary flowering of Greek
poetry is testimony to the success of this Ptolemaic initiative. The
very subject of Apollonius' epic, a voyage to distant lands and
strange peoples (cf. Alexander's eastern conquests), bringing the
Argonauts into contact with areas of considerable political interest
to the Ptolemies (the Black Sea, Cyrenaica, the Aegean islands),
gives this poem a contemporary dimension which should not be
overlooked; too often the 'Alexandrian-ness' of the *Argonautica* has
been seen merely in the apparatus of scholarly learning which the
poem displays.

Central to the self-projection of the Ptolemies to Greeks both in
Egypt and outside was a drive to attract Greek intellectuals and
poets to the city, and central to that drive was the famous Museum
('place of the Muses') and Library, established by Soter as a place
where scholars could work under royal protection and patronage.[8] It
seems to have been an integral part of this project to seek to collect
in the Library as many texts as possible of as much of Greek
literature, broadly defined, as possible. Our sources paint a
colourful, anecdotal picture of Ptolemaic agents scouring the world

[6] Our main text here is Herodotus, bk. 2.
[7] Cf. Hunter (1993), 154–9.
[8] On these institutions see Pfeiffer (1968), 96–104 and Fraser (1972), 312–35.

to secure books by fair means or foul; best known is the story of how Ptolemy III secured the official Athenian texts of Aeschylus, Sophocles, and Euripides by returning copies, rather than originals, to the Athenians and happily forfeiting his surety. The genesis of this institutionalization of learning has been much debated—it certainly owed something to Aristotle's school, the *peripatos*, in Athens—but this is less important here than the effects of this institutionalization upon the poetry which was produced under it.

In the archaic and classical periods poetry was very often a public matter, performed on festal or cultic occasions by choirs supported by the state; Attic tragedy and comedy are obviously special cases here, but they are, so to say, quantitatively rather than qualitatively different. The fact of oral performance was crucial for the nature of the composition, and our ignorance of the performance is a major stumbling-block in the path of our appreciation of, say, archaic lyric. Even the hexameter poetry of Homer achieved at Athens a public, 'semi-official' status as early as the sixth century when, according to the traditional account, the tyrant Peisistratos introduced regular Homeric recitations at the Panathenaia.[9] A broad, but not misleading, generalization is that in the archaic and classical periods poetry was produced with a specific context of performance in mind—even if that context was as commonplace as a symposium—and that context often determined much about the poetry (e.g. metre, dialect, stylistic level, etc.). In the Museum and Library of Ptolemaic Alexandria, however, many of these contexts no longer existed in the same way, and so poets were no longer constrained as before— though archaic and classical poets would not, of course, have viewed their conditions as constraining—and were freed to appropriate traditional forms and modes, now released from their traditional social contexts, for the exploration of new areas of sensibility. The 'artificial' and bounded nature of poetic life in Alexandria, coupled with the fact of intensive scholarly interest in the poems of the past, produced a crop of new poetic forms[10] which reflected intellectual reconstructions of, rather than being direct products of, those

---

[9] Cf. S. West in *A Commentary on Homer's Odyssey: Volume I* (Oxford, 1988), 35–9.

[10] I use 'forms' here in a broad sense, to cover both what are often called 'genres', and also particular poetic expressions which use familiar shapes in quite new ways, e.g. the *Hymns* of Callimachus.

traditional social contexts for poetry. The new predominance of the hexameter and the elegiac couplet is one major symptom of this.

As always, there is a danger of overstatement. Many of these contexts for poetry—the cultic performance with its accompanying hymns, the symposium where gnomic and erotic poetry entertained the guests—continued as before. Of particular importance for the *Argonautica*, hexameter narrative poetry continued to be written and to be recited publicly at the ever-increasing number of state festivals and games held all over the Greek world. There is no reason to assume that the great poets of Alexandria never left the confines of the Library or that their poetry was read or heard by only a very small circle of like-minded scholars; what little evidence there is on these questions in fact seems to point in the other direction, and we must be wary of treating all 'Hellenistic' poets alike—Theocritus, for example, seems a clear case of a poet whose work took him all over the Mediterranean. Nevertheless, although our evidence here is pitifully small, there do seem to be clear differences between the surviving examples of 'performed', sometimes called 'popular', poetry—such as cultic hymns inscribed on stone and the few fragments of 'non-Alexandrian' epic—and high Alexandrian poetry. It is not merely that the latter, including the *Argonautica*, is marked— and here again it is necessary to generalize broadly—by certain recurrent interests which have obvious counterparts in the work of the scholars in the Museum—the aetiology of local cults and rituals, the poeticizing of arcane stories largely preserved in written prose texts, etymology, and verbal experiment; there is also in Alexandrian poetry an extreme self-consciousness, an overt sense of itself as poetry, and a constant willingness to comment upon itself and its function. One manifestation of this self-consciousness is a detailed engagement with archaic and classical literature, in which 'meaning' is created by the dismantling and reconstruction of the great texts of the past, rather than by simple borrowing from them. Attic tragedy too, of course, had used the audience's knowledge of Homer to map out its own, and different, vision of the world, but it did not, for obvious reasons, engage constantly with these texts at the level of verbal and stylistic detail. When reading Callimachus or Apollonius it is necessary constantly to have Homer 'beside' you, in a way which is not necessary when reading (or watching) tragedy, and, for different reasons, also not necessary for the appreciation of what remains of these 'non-Alexandrian' texts; in Alexandrian poetry, however, the written text has now come into its own.[11] At one level, this is one manifestation of the increasing separation in the Hellenistic age of popular and élite culture, and specifically it is reasonable to associate this aspect of Alexandrian poetry with the fact that these poets were also scholars of past poetry and constantly concerned with the textual details of Homer and his successors. Nevertheless, it is important not to dismiss this 'textuality' of Alexandrian poetry as merely the cerebral games of over-learned men. The creative use of the literature of the past is an open recognition that poets and readers were no longer, if they ever had been, innocent; whether or not Homer was explicitly written into the text of your poems, he was part of the 'mental furniture' with which these poems would be read: better then to make a virtue out of necessity and engage openly with him by guiding the way in which your readers used him in their reading.

A particular mode for the expression of this textual self-consciousness is irony and humour; where the poet is constantly also a commentator on his poetry, the anticipation of reading and reception is inscribed in the text itself, and the poet becomes not just a creator but also a reader, himself surprised by his own creation. Thus, a very noticeable feature of the *Argonautica*, particularly in comparison to the Homeric poems, is how often the narrator speaks 'in his own voice' to comment upon the events of the story. When, for example, Medea puts the evil eye on Talos, Apollonius reacts as a particular kind of reader of the *Argonautica* might react:

Father Zeus, my mind is all aflutter with amazement, if it is true that death comes to us not only from disease and wounds, but someone far off can harm us, as that man, bronze though he was, yielded to destruction through the grim power of Medea, mistress of drugs. (4. 1673–7)

The poet stands outside his poem and contemplates it, almost as though he had nothing to do with it. This ironic gap is particularly prominent in the *Argonautica* where the poet exploits our expectations which are founded upon our (and his) knowledge of the epic tradition—in invocations to the Muses (cf. e.g. 4. 1381–7), in regret

[11] Cf. in general Bing (1988).

for the fate of his characters (cf. 2. 1026–9), in a strikingly ambivalent use of similes (cf. 4. 1337–43).

In choosing to highlight this feature of Alexandrian poetry, there is of course again a danger of imbalance. We are at the mercy of the chances of survival, and it seems clear, even from what survives, that 'Alexandrian' poetry was far from uniform in mode or tone, that there were, for example, significant generic differences between narrative and non-narrative poems.[12] Nevertheless, within a broad range, all of this poetry shows features of the kind outlined, and it may be taken, along with the reshaping of the traditional, inherited poetic forms, as a hallmark of third-century Alexandrian poetry.

Later ages looked to Callimachus of Cyrene as the leading poetic force of the age, and there seems no reason to dispute this verdict. Resident at the royal court during roughly the same period as Apollonius, he produced, among a vast scholarly output, the *Pinakes*, a kind of *catalogue raisonné* of the whole of Greek literature, based upon the holdings of the Ptolemaic Library.[13] Here is the systematic scholarly work to which the more random ransacking of earlier literature by the poets forms a counterpart. As a poet, Callimachus wrote epigrams, numerous occasional pieces for the royal court, a collection of *Iambi* which take their starting-point from the archaic invective of Hipponax, a narrative hexameter poem, the *Hecale*, concerning the story of Theseus and the bull of Marathon, but treated from a radically new perspective,[14] six hymns which take off from the *Homeric Hymns*, and four long books of elegiac *Aitia* which concern the legendary origins of institutions and cults from all over the Greek world. The *Aitia* was a very influential poem among the Roman 'Callimacheans', and recent papyri have considerably increased our knowledge of its scope and structure.[15] Two aspects only need be mentioned here. In various places through the *Aitia* Callimachus concerned himself with Argonautic stories, and there are close enough verbal, contextual, and structural parallels with the *Argonautica* to exclude the possibility of chance. Thus, for example, Callimachus dealt with the foundation of the cult of Apollo Aigletes

---

[12] Cf. Hunter (1993), 113–16.

[13] Cf. Pfeiffer (1968), 127–32; Blum (1991).

[14] See the edition by A. S. Hollis (Oxford, 1990).

[15] For a survey and the now orthodox position cf. Bulloch (1985), 553–7.

at Anaphe during the Argonauts' return in the second *aition* of book 1,[16] whereas Apollonius places it where chronology demanded, at the very end of the voyage (cf. 4. 1694–730), followed only by the origins of the Aeginetan festival of the Hydrophoria, which Callimachus described in another poem (*Iambus* 8). Examples of this close intertextual relationship could easily be multiplied. Most scholars see Apollonius as borrowing constantly from Callimachus, and this may often be a correct assessment and is in accord with the statement in the 'Lives' that he was Callimachus' pupil; we must remember, however, that it is very likely that poets read and discussed each other's work in a constant process of dialogue and revision before 'publication', and so to see the problem as merely one of establishing 'priority' may well convey a misleading impression of what was actually happening. There is indeed some evidence that at least part of the text of the *Argonautica* circulated at some time in a version rather different from the vulgate presented by our manuscripts, and it is not improbable—though it is far from certain—that this version was an early draft of parts of the poem.[17] It is, moreover, worth stressing that, whether we prefer to see a situation of straight borrowing or a process of mutual reading and revision, the fact of the relationship points to shared poetic ideals and interests, not to hostility.

It was necessary to make this last point because the supposed 'quarrel' between Callimachus and Apollonius is one of the best-known clichés of discussions of Alexandrian poetry. Little space need be devoted to it here. The 'Lives' present a confused story of Apollonius retiring in chagrin to Rhodes after his poetry met an unsuccessful reception in Alexandria, but they do not associate Callimachus with this lack of success. Later scandal-mongers identified Apollonius as the object of Callimachus' riddling and abusive poem, the *Ibis*, but it is unlikely that they had any good grounds for this.[18] In the extant prologue of the *Aitia* Callimachus defends his poetry against the attacks of (real or alleged) opponents

---

[16] Argonautic stories in fact seem to frame the four-book version of the *Aitia*, cf. Pfeiffer's edn., i. 111.

[17] This is the so-called *proekdosis*, cf. Hunter (1989), 5–6.

[18] On the *Ibis* see L. Watson, *Arae: The Curse Poetry of Antiquity* (Leeds, 1991), 121–30.

whom he calls Telchines, 'malicious slanderers', and a surviving papyrus gives us what is probably one scholar's guess, which may or may not be based on 'good' information, as to the identity of those opponents; Apollonius is not among them. We are therefore not going to get very far with the biographical sources. More interesting is the relationship between the *Argonautica* and the poetic programme sketched out by Callimachus in a number of poems, but most notably in the prologue to the *Aitia*:

. . .] the Telchines mutter at my song—they who are ignorant and were not born dear to the Muses—because I have not accomplished one continuous song in many thousands of verses about kings [. . .] heroes, but like a child I roll out my verse, little by little, while the decades of my years are not few. [. . .] to the Telchines this is my reply: ' . . . Off with you, deadly offspring of Spite! [Judge] poetry by artfulness, not by the Persian chain. Do not look to me for a loud-resounding song; thundering is not my job, but Zeus'. When I placed the writing-tablet upon my knees for the first time, Lycian Apollo said to me: '[. . .] singer, [. . .] the fatter sacrifice the better, but, my friend, a fine (*leptaleos*) Muse. [. . .] this too is my instruction: proceed along paths which wagons do not traverse, and do not drive along the same tracks as others nor on the broad highway, but along [fresh] ways, even if your course will be narrower . . . (Callimachus, fr. 1, vv. 1–7, 17–28)

Nearly every verse of this famous passage has prompted a vast scholarly discussion but, in general terms, it would appear that Callimachus here (and elsewhere) promotes shorter poems on original subjects ('the untrodden path')[19] and in non-traditional styles; 'fine' or 'thin' (*leptaleos*) poetry is poetry which is subtly crafted and intellectually challenging, poetry which is not padded out with bombast and repetition. Here then there would appear to be a more solid basis for seeing a difference of aesthetic programme between Apollonius and Callimachus. Whether or not the *Argonautica* is subtly crafted and intellectually challenging may be a matter of opinion, but it is certainly not a short poem and it is devoted to a very traditional subject of Greek myth; the four books of *Aitia* may have been as long, but they were episodic and variegated in a way which Apollonius' epic certainly is not. If, however, Apollonius was swimming against the prevailing tide in the form of his poem, the

[19] That this image was itself borrowed from an earlier poet (Pindar) was an irony which would not have been lost on Callimachus.

manner of it, in tone, voice, and the deployment of learning, has much in common with the manner of Callimachus. Apollonius is not as radical as Callimachus—his language and metrical practice, for example, are closer to Homer than are Callimachus'—but these differences, which are more of extent than direction, are in fact less surprising than identity of practice would be, and there are good reasons for believing that Callimachus too moderated some of the more familiar aspects of his manner in his 'short epic', the *Hecale*. In short, a considerable body of evidence points towards both poets as reflecting similar aesthetic trends, even though Apollonius' choice of the long narrative epic remains something of an anomaly in the range of cultivated poetry of the third century. For what it is worth, the fate of the *Argonautica* in Rome strongly suggests that Apollonius was there seen as 'a Callimachean', and certainly not as a purveyor of the rejected, bombastic epic.[20]

The *Argonautica* also has an obvious relationship with the poetry of Theocritus, who is for us the other great figure of the third century. Two of Theocritus' poems, *Idylls* 13 and 22, deal with incidents of the Argonautic voyage, the loss of Herakles and Hylas to the expedition and the boxing-match between Polydeukes and Amykos, which Apollonius juxtaposes at the end of Book 1 and the opening of Book 2; this structural coincidence, together with many parallels of expression and thought, is more than sufficient to establish again that we are not dealing with a chance accident. The matter has been endlessly debated, with most scholars assigning priority to Apollonius; these stories are, after all, Argonautic ones which he was very likely to include. Too frequently, however, a view of Apollonius' chronological priority has been accompanied by the assumption that Theocritus' purpose in writing his versions was to correct the earlier poet by showing how these stories should properly be treated in the modern style, and the arguments with which that assumption is usually supported have amounted to little more than impressionistic assertions of artistic superiority. Whatever the details of Apollonius' relationship with Theocritus, we see again that the epic poet was at the centre of poetic life in the third century; without the *Argonautica*, our sense of the whole period of Hellenistic poetry would be vastly diminished.

[20] Cf. below pp. xxx–xxxi.

3. *The Argonautic Story and the* Argonautica

The story of the quest of Jason and the Argonauts for the Golden Fleece and of Jason's relations with the Colchian princess Medea clearly belong to the very early strata of Greek myth. Homer's Kirke mentions it as a story which is known to all:

'The blessed gods call these rocks the Wanderers; even things that fly cannot pass them safely, not even the trembling doves that carry ambrosia to Father Zeus; even of those the smooth rock always seizes one, and the Father sends another in to restore the number. Nor has any ship carrying men ever come there and gone its way in safety; the ship's timbers, the crew's dead bodies are carried away by the sea waves and by blasts of deadly fire. One alone among seagoing ships did indeed sail past on her way home from Aeetes' kingdom—this was Argo, whose name is on all men's tongues; and even she would have been dashed against the great rocks had not Hera herself, in her love for Jason, sped the ship past.' (*Od.* 12. 61–72, trans. Shewring)

Throughout the *Argonautica* Apollonius alludes to details of the 'pre-history' of the story, and a brief summary may therefore be helpful.[21] The story concerns the intertwined fates of two branches of the descendants of Aiolos, the eponymous hero of the Aeolians. Athamas, king of Boiotia had two children, Phrixos and Helle, by his wife Nephele. After Nephele, Athamas married Ino, who plotted against her stepchildren by tricking Athamas into believing that he had to sacrifice his children to Zeus in order to save the land from famine. Phrixos and Helle were, however, saved from the altar by Hermes and Zeus, and flew eastwards on a magical, golden-fleeced ram; Helle fell off over what became the Hellespont, but Phrixos landed in Aia in the extreme east, where he sacrificed the ram and hung the fleece in a grove sacred to Ares. The king of Aia, Aietes a son of Helios, gave Phrixos his daughter Chalkiope in marriage. The other Aeolian family is located in Thessalian Iolkos, where Jason's grandfather, Kretheus, was king. After Kretheus' death the throne passed not to Jason's father, Aison, but to Pelias, the son of Kretheus' wife Tyro by Poseidon. In some versions Jason was brought up in the countryside in order to be safely out of the way of Pelias who saw in Jason a threat to his throne. Pelias, who had

[21] See also the Genealogical Table, p. xx.

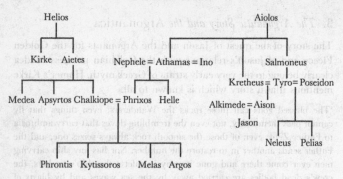

FIG. I. The Families of Jason and Medea

already incurred the anger of Hera by killing his stepmother at the goddess's altar and constantly refusing her honours, received an oracle that he should beware of a man wearing only one sandal, and when Jason one day arrived dressed in this way, Pelias dispatched him to recover the Golden Fleece in order to assuage Zeus' anger for the attempted sacrifice at his altar, offering to give up the throne after the successful completion of the mission. It is at this point that Apollonius' poem opens. We are also expected to know the subsequent history of Jason and Medea. Whereas in the *Argonautica* Medea's brother Apsyrtos is older than she is, and he is treacherously murdered by Jason and Medea in the northern Adriatic (4. 452–81), in the most common version of the story he was still a baby at the time of Jason's expedition, and Medea delayed Aietes' pursuit in the Black Sea by killing the child and throwing his body in pieces into the sea. On returning to Iolkos, they persuaded Pelias' daughters that Medea could rejuvenate their father if they chopped him up and boiled him in a cauldron; thus was the tyrant punished. The subsequent history of Jason and Medea, most notably her vengeful killing of their children to which Apollonius' poem clearly looks forward, is best known from Euripides' *Medea*.

The story of Jason falls into a familiar pattern of 'initiation quest' in which a young man must succeed in terrible challenges before claiming his rightful inheritance; Jason thus resembles Orestes, who must also carry out a horrible killing, and Theseus, to whom he is explicitly compared (3. 997–1004). The central role played by the sorceress Medea, who reflects several aspects of Greek ideas of the dangerous female, is of a piece with this pattern of generational passage: in acquiring the Fleece, Jason also acquires knowledge of the female, a crucial 'other' for the construction of Greek heroism and masculinity. Whereas the story of the Golden Fleece was originally associated with a fabulous 'kingdom of the sun' in the extreme east, at least as early as the seventh century BC this kingdom was identified with Colchis in modern Georgia, where the River Phasis formed the traditional eastern boundary of the known world. Colchian civilization flourished during the classical and Hellenistic periods, and there were many trading contacts with the Greek world; Apollonius' description of the city will therefore have been recognizably 'literary' to much of his readership. Although the Argonautic story was essentially located in the eastern part of the Greek world, there were Argonautic legends and 'remains' all over the Mediterranean and very varied versions of the route taken; Apollonius constructs the voyage in such a way as to encompass as much of the known world as possible, and his mixture of 'scientific' and fabulous geography is very typical of his age.[22] An important influence here was the *Odyssey*, as one ancient tradition placed Odysseus' wanderings in the western Mediterranean. It is this tradition which Apollonius follows in placing Kirke's home on the west coast of Italy.

Aspects of the Argonautic story had been told many times in Greek poetry before Apollonius,[23] and if more non-Homeric archaic epic had survived, we would doubtless know much more about the raw material from which the *Argonautica* was moulded. Two extant poems are, however, of particular importance. One is the *Fourth Pythian Ode* of Pindar, written for the chariot victory in 462 of Arkesilas IV of Cyrene. This poem, much the longest of Pindar's victory odes, tells the Argonautic story in considerable detail, and is echoed at significant points by Apollonius; of particular interest is the importance Pindar attaches to Medea's love for the Greek hero (vv. 213–23). Pindar tells the story because during the return from Colchis Medea prophesied the foundation of Cyrene by Battos, and

---

[22] Cf. below p. xxiii–xxiv, and see the maps.
[23] For a fuller account cf. Hunter (1989), 14–20.

it is this foundation which is alluded to in the account of Euphemos'
dream at the very end of the *Argonautica*. The other crucial extant
text for the appreciation of the *Argonautica* is the *Medea* of Euripides;
the epic shows us why the action of the tragedy was inevitable and
the central events of that tragedy—Jason's perfidy, Medea's
supplication and scheming, and the murder of the children—are
foreshadowed both in the general shape of the epic and, more
specifically, in the language and images of its text.[24] This tragic
depth in the poem is strengthened by the shaping of the central
scenes of Book 3, the book set in Aia, in ways very reminiscent of
classical drama; it is very likely that there is an important debt in
this book to the lost *Colchian Women* of Sophocles, for the relationship
between Medea and Chalkiope strikingly recalls that of Antigone
and Ismene and of Elektra and Chrysothemis. Be that as it may, this
appeal to the world of tragedy is both a literary marker of continuity
between the epic and Attic tragedy, a continuity expressed for us
most famously in Aristotle's *Poetics*, and opens up the events of the
poem to the dark ambivalences of tragic drama. Tragedy has, as we
shall note presently, also had an important influence on the divine
element in the poem. This aspect of the *Argonautica* was clearly an
important formative influence upon Virgil when he came to shape
the story of Dido very much after the fashion of a tragedy.

   The nearly 6,000 verses of the *Argonautica* are divided into four
books, and this division works in tandem with a division into three,
marked by invocations at the head of Books 1, 3, and 4. Books 1 and
2 concern the outward voyage from Iolkos to Aia, closing with the
first night spent in Colchis immediately after arrival; the division
between these books is marked by the great sequence which leads to
the loss to the expedition of Herakles, a loss to which attention will
constantly be drawn through the remainder of the epic. The opening
scene of Book 3 takes place on Olympos, but the human characters
remain in Colchis through all of Book 3 and the first 240 verses of
Book 4. Book 3, however, closes with a strong sense of both
completion and foreboding, for Jason has successfully completed the
challenge set before him, but Aietes is angered and planning

---

[24] Crucial scenes here are the meetings of Jason and Medea (3. 975–1145, 4. 355–
420), the murder of Apsyrtos, and Medea's pleas to Queen Arete and the Argonauts
(4. 1014–52).

vengeance. These simple methods of structuring the poem are supported by two further broad designs.

One is the straightforward linearity imposed by the voyaging structure. On the outward voyage, and on those parts of the return which are not located in the frighteningly indeterminate landscapes of central Europe, Apollonius carefully plots the day-by-day progress of his heroes in such a way that modern scholarship has even been able to reckon the length of time 'spent' on the voyage (about six months).[25] This marking of time is neither the product of a desire to be different from the *Odyssey* nor merely a quasi-naïve device of 'realism', but is central to the poet's vision of his story: the Argonauts' voyage is emblematic for all (past and future) sea-voyages, in which the careful and repetitive marking of time is crucially important, and the whole poem may analogously be conceived of as an *aition* for universal Greek culture. Moreover, the steady security of the passage of the days makes even more terrifying those times—such as the voyage through central Europe and the scene of the impenetrable blackness on the Aegean (4. 1694–705)—when we do not have that security to which to cling.

The second structuring device to be noted here is the very clear set of similarities and oppositions between the outward voyage and the voyage home;[26] events on Lemnos are picked up by events on Drepane, Phineus' guide to the Black Sea contrasts with Argos' narrative from the mists of time, the Symplegades are paralleled by the Planktai, the crew's despair at the death of Tiphys by their despair when caught in the Libyan Syrtis, Apollo's saving appearance at the end recalls his epiphany on the island of Thynias, and so on. More generally, there is an obvious contrast between the detailed and generally accurate geography of the outward voyage which follows a standard trading route along the south coast of the Black Sea and the more 'literary' and imaginative route of the return. This remains true even if it is also the case that the central European geography of Book 4 was that to be found in many prose authorities;[27] Alexandrian scholars were well aware of the potentially

---

[25] Vian's edn. of bk. 4, pp. 12–13.

[26] Cf. e.g. Hutchinson (1988), 121–41.

[27] Of particular importance for the return route were the works of Timaios of Tauromenion (c.356–260) and the obscure Timagetos, who is known largely from

great difference between a story's or description's being textually attested and its being true. Before Apollonius the tradition, broadly speaking, offered three return routes for the Argonauts: the same route as the outward voyage (cf. 4. 1000–3), a return via the encircling stream of Ocean with which the Phasis was originally imagined to connect and then through Libya, and a journey along the Istros (Danube) and Ocean into the extreme west of the Mediterranean. The extraordinary route of Apollonius' Argonauts is a synthetic amalgam which is not only terrifying and bewildering as it is meant to be, but also allows Apollonius to include traditional Argonautic sites in the Adriatic as well as in Libya and the western Mediterranean. Both voyages are, moreover, excellent illustrations of the Alexandrian concern to weld 'modern science' on to traditional poetic frameworks; it is almost as though the contrast between the two voyages is designed to illustrate what has become an important theme of modern research, namely that the distinction between 'science' and 'paradoxography' is not an easy one to draw.

The central poetic technique of the *Argonautica* is the creative reworking of Homer, which is visible in every aspect of the poem, the details of language, large-scale narrative patterns, and also the material and technological world of the poem, which for the most part seeks to reproduce the technological world of Homer;[28] this is perhaps most notable in sailing descriptions which use the 'technical terms' of Homeric navigation, even where these were long outmoded. That there are structural similarities between the stories of Jason and Odysseus was noted in antiquity, and some modern scholars believe that Homer 'borrowed' from Argonautic legends in shaping his story. Be that as it may, Apollonius makes fruitful use of the quasi-paradox that the Homeric texts are both anterior to the *Argonautica* and therefore part of the experience of all readers, and also subsequent to it, in the sense that the Argonauts belong to the generation before the Trojan War; thus, for example, when Medea wishes 'children' for Queen Arete (4. 1028), we recall that she is to

the excellent scholia to Apollonius' poem. On Apollonian geography see Delage (1930), L. Robert, *A travers l'Asie mineure* (Athens/Paris, 1980)—indispensable for the Black Sea voyage—and the introductions to Vian's editions of bks. 1–2 and bk. 4.

[28] There are, as we would expect, exceptions: the palace architecture in Aia (3. 215–46) is a mixture of the fabulous, the Homeric, and the Hellenistic.

have one famous daughter at least, Nausicaa, whose Homeric portrayal is an important model for Medea herself.

The dialogue with the Homeric texts begins at the very opening of the epic which structurally, and by the prominence of Apollo, recalls the opening of the *Iliad*, but in such a way as to make clear that this is going to be a very different kind of poem, both acknowledging the complex temporal construction of the Homeric poems and imposing a sequential linearity upon the narrative which is foreign to the Homeric manner. Apollonius 'begins at the beginning' with Pelias' devising of the expedition and a catalogue of those who came to join Jason; this catalogue refers to a number of places also found in Homer's Catalogue of Ships and thereby clearly marks itself as a descendant of that catalogue. The borrowing of forms and frameworks from illustrious predecessors was normal in the ancient literary tradition, and we may suspect that this was nowhere so true as in hexameter epic. It was not this which determined whether or not the later poem was to be damned as 'slavish imitation', but rather what was done with those borrowed frameworks.

Thus the description of the embroidered cloak which Jason wears to Hypsipyle's palace (1. 721–67) is obviously a descendant of Homer's description of the Shield of Achilles, but not only is the cloak totally different from the shield, it is that difference which is an important conveyor of meaning: the 'warfare' which Jason must conduct is of an altogether more private, nuanced, and sensuous kind than that of Achilles. The long speech of Phineus in Book 2 in which he advises the Argonauts on their route to Colchis forms the counterpart to the speeches of advice and prophecy by Kirke and Teiresias (another blind prophet) in the *Odyssey*, but in contrast to them Phineus speaks the language of 'scientific' geography and ethnography; the gifts of Apollo are now to be found in the knowledge contained in books. The scenes in Aia in Book 3 contain an elaborate set of echoes of the Phaeacian scenes of the *Odyssey*; just as Jason is the Greek stranger arriving unexpectedly, so Medea is cast in the role of Nausicaa, and Aietes in that of Alkinoos. Whereas, however, Alkinoos was generous and welcoming to the point of wishing the stranger to marry his daughter (*Od.* 7. 311–16), Aietes is treacherous and scheming. Whereas Odysseus' arrival briefly brought Nausicaa into contact with another world, but his departure allowed her to retreat safely from that glimpse, the ultimate outcome for Medea will be disastrous: she will flee in terror with the Greek stranger to find, not marital happiness and the 'like-mindedness' (*homophrosyne*) of which Odysseus spoke in glowing terms to Nausicaa (*Od.* 6. 180–5), but misery and abandonment. The return voyage in Book 4 makes free use of the geography of the *Odyssey* as the Argonauts sail to or past many of the places which had traditionally been identified with Odyssean sites, most notably Sicily, Corcyra (Drepane), the standard location of the Homeric Phaeacia, and Libya where later ages had placed Homer's lotus-eaters (cf. Herodotus 4. 177). The island of Kalypso passes by in the distance (4. 574–5), but the land of Kirke—here placed, in accordance with one view of *Odyssean* geography, on the western coast of Italy—is the site for a major scene, the purification of Jason and Medea. Medea's aunt, Kirke, however, is no longer simply the mysterious and controlling hostess of the *Odyssey*; on one side she remains dangerous and threatening, like Talos a remnant of an earlier age, but on the other she scolds her errant niece from a firm sense of propriety and family solidarity.

Another part of the Homeric inheritance were the gods of epic,[29] which had been the subject of a lively intellectual and philosophical debate for more than two centuries before the composition of the *Argonautica*. These gods had been attacked as unworthy or amoral, and defended as being merely examples of particular kinds of figured and rhetorical speech, whether we label those figures 'literary discourse', 'metaphor', or even 'allegory'. It is clear that Apollonius has designed his gods not to conceal the problems that the presentation of the divine in epic raised, but precisely to foreground those problems as an integral part of the self-conscious text. It is, however, also true that the relative prominence of the divine has been considerably reduced in his epic. It is not that the gods are no longer crucial in the lives of the human characters, but that this importance is much more briefly and allusively expressed. Only two major scenes are actually set on Olympos—the confrontations between Hera, Athena, and Aphrodite and between Aphrodite and her son, Eros, with which Book 3 opens, and the conversation between Hera and Thetis which leads to safe passage through the

[29] On this subject in general see Feeney (1991); Hunter (1993), ch. 4.

Planktai for the Argonauts in Book 4 (4. 781–841). Both of these scenes are characterized by the wry ironies we associate with Homer's Olympians and contain detailed reworkings of specific Homeric scenes. When, however, these divinities appear on earth, they do so in ways which differ considerably from their Homeric counterparts: Athena travels on a cloud to shove the *Argo* through the Symplegades (2. 537–606), the crew sees Apollo pass by without apparently taking an interest (2. 669–84), Thetis and the nymphs pass the *Argo* through the Planktai like young girls tossing a ball from one to another (4. 939–69). Otherwise when the poet casts his glance upwards, he may note what has happened without letting the divine characters speak for themselves:

When the tall body of Apsyrtos crashed to the ground in death, Zeus himself, the king of the gods, was no doubt seized by anger at what they had done. He devised that they should be cleansed of the blood of the murder . . . Hera realized Zeus' plans for them . . . (4. 557–9, 577)

It is human action which is foregrounded, and the gods work in the background, powerful, but merely guessed at; it is reasonable to see Apollonius here as the heir of Attic tragedy, in which the characters often suspect the hand of the divine at work, but must act in doubt and fear.

To some extent the diminution of the full Olympian 'apparatus' is compensated for by an array of minor and somewhat exotic divinities who cross the Argonauts' path: sea-creatures such as Glaukos and Triton (1. 1310–28, 4. 1551–619), the 'heroines' of Libya (4. 1305–36), the Hesperid maidens (4. 1393–460), and the Harpies who are chased away by the sons of Boreas (2. 262–300). These 'wonders' may in part be seen as exemplifying the poem's interest in the human confrontation with the strange and the magical. It has often been noted that, even in the *Odyssey*, Homer seems to have played down the potential of his narrative for magical and fantastic elements; Apollonius, however, is centrally concerned with the various 'irrational' powers which affect our lives—*eros*, rhetorical persuasion, baneful magic. This is not simply a question of 'Hellenistic taste' for the exotic, but rather of the conditions under which we must carve out our lives and make terrible mistakes in so doing. At one level these 'wonders' and others like them, such as

Aietes' earthborn warriors, are deliberately 'epic' and beyond the range of possible human experience; at another, mythopoeic level, they embody terrors and doubts which are only too familiar.

It is from this angle also that we may approach the question of Apollonius' central character, Jason. As a young man facing a terrible ordeal, he is prone to doubt and despair, not unlike some presentations of Orestes when facing the awful fact of having to kill his mother. Much modern criticism of him as too weak and insipid to be the convincing 'hero' of an epic—by which is meant an Achilles or an Odysseus—fails to take account of the nature of the story of which this character is a part, and of the aesthetic principles of the poem in which he finds himself. In other words, Apollonius has often been criticized for failing to accomplish what there is good reason to believe he had no desire to do. Jason is indeed driven by events rather than driving them—he after all did not choose to undertake the expedition for the sake of heroic glory—and is willing to do anything necessary to achieve his safe return, whether this be enlisting Medea's aid or murdering her brother in a treacherous ambush. Like Odysseus, he is figured as reliant upon planning and schemes, what the Greeks called *metis*, rather than frontal assault and brute force (cf. 3. 171–93), but, unlike Odysseus, he must often rely upon others for those schemes (cf. e.g. 4. 1330–79). Like Homeric heroes (Paris, Odysseus), but also like the young Hylas (1. 1207–39, Theocritus 13), he is attractive to women, and his *aristeiai* are as much his meetings with Hypsipyle and Medea as his victory over the earthborn; his only two other victims, Kyzikos (1. 1030–9) and Apsyrtos (4. 452–81), are both killed at night, the former the victim of a ghastly mistake. Clearly Jason is quite unlike the central characters of the Homeric poems, but there are good reasons for this, beyond the nature of the quest in which he is involved.

Jason is not as dominant in his poem as Odysseus is in his, or even Achilles in his absence is in his. This is partly because of the extraordinary, in some cases (the Boreads, the Dioskouroi) supra-natural, crew which surrounds him, and partly because Apollonius chooses to be interested in other Argonauts as well as Jason (Herakles, Orpheus, Peleus). Guiding aesthetic principles of diversity and discontinuity are as visible in this facet of the poem as in all others. This is not to seek to play down the obvious ironies which surround Jason, though these have often been looked for in the wrong places. He clearly *is* contrasted with the violent Idas, but this latter was a notorious blasphemer to whom Zeus finally put an end. He is also contrasted with Herakles, but any such contrast is bound to be multi-faceted because of the nature of Herakles himself: the long-suffering tragic hero and ancestor of the Ptolemaic dynasty was also the gluttonous comic buffoon. When Jason urges the Argonauts to choose the best available leader, they immediately look to the greatest among them, indisputably Herakles, who however imposes the leadership of Jason. This scene is not designed to make us laugh at Jason, but its focus is rather the nature of leadership itself: Herakles is 'the best man' absolutely, but he is not the most appropriate leader, and not just because he does not have the same personal stake in the expedition as does Jason. The central Argonautic virtue is group solidarity and communality (note 1. 336–40); Herakles' virtues, like the journeys he must undertake (4. 1481–2), are inimitable and personal to him. His path crosses that of Jason briefly, but his imperatives and his destiny are quite different (cf. 1. 865–74).

In general, we may observe that the basic unit in Apollonius' composition is the individual scene, and that any overarching notion of consistent or plausible 'character' is subordinated to the particular concerns of individual scenes. Thus the figure of Jason, seen in despair on the outward voyage or devising the murder of Apsyrtos in a hurried plan to calm Medea's fury, can appear vacillating and unattractive to modern readers, but he must be viewed within the overall context of Apollonius' apparently revolutionary aesthetic scheme.[30] Some modern readers may not 'like' what they find, but that is simply a matter of taste; understanding is what is important.

Finally, we may note that Apollonius also dismantles the Homeric ancestor texts on a stylistic level. The stylistic range of the *Argonautica* is very varied,[31] and in particular long passages can appear at first glance to be little more than versified prose (if we

---

[30] I say 'apparently' because of the virtually total loss of epic poetry between Homer and Apollonius.

[31] The translation seeks to catch this variety, but I have little confidence that I have succeeded.

omit morphology from consideration); this results from the much freer use of enjambment and complex syntax (particularly indirect speech) than is found in Homer. This—like the avoidance of repeated passages and scenes—is not simply a 'natural' difference between oral and written epic, but must be seen as part of Apollonius' whole poetic project, to renew the epic tradition by creating what would pass in third-century Alexandria as an intellectually respectable way of writing in the same genre as Homer. Similarly, at the level of morphology and vocabulary, the language of Apollonius is an artifical amalgam, firmly based in the language of Homer, but drawing from many registers of high literature, here renewed and expanded by the extensive use of analogical formation and linguistic experimentation. It is utterly unlike the Greek which was spoken in third-century Alexandria, and this effect of distance, often hard to appreciate in translation, is an important aesthetic effect to which we must give due weight in assessing Apollonius' creation.

4. *The Argonautica in Rome*

When the Roman neoteric poets enthusiastically took over Alexandrian techniques and models in the middle of the first century BC, the *Argonautica* became a centrally important text. It was translated into Latin by Varro of Atax, a contemporary of Catullus, but unfortunately only a very few fragments survive. More importantly for us, it was clearly an important model text for Catullus in Poem 64, the 'epyllion' which tells the stories of Peleus and Thetis and Ariadne and Theseus, and which opens with the scene of the *Argo* setting sail as the very first ship. It is instructive to find clear echoes of it in a poem which sets such store upon a new aesthetic of narrative; it is tempting to use this as evidence that Catullus at any rate was not in any doubt about the place of the *Argonautica* in the general scheme of Alexandrian poetry.

Similar conclusions may be drawn from the extensive use of the *Argonautica* in Virgil's *Aeneid*.[32] The Roman epic is shot through with echoes of Apollonius' poem, although of course it did not have for Virgil the status of principal model which unquestionably belongs to

---

[32] On this subject see Briggs (1981); Clausen (1987); Hunter (1993), ch. 7.

Homer. Most famously, the scenes set in Carthage owe a considerable
debt to Apollonius and, in particular, Dido owes much to Medea; as
if to reinforce the association, Aeneas' final sight of Dido in the
Underworld (*Aen*. 6. 450–66) combines Medea's plea to Queen
Arete with Lynkeus' distant vision of Herakles as the great hero
passes out of Apollonius' poem. Thus the *Argonautica* is associated
with what threatens Aeneas' safe journey and the destiny of Rome;
Virgil establishes a dialogue between Homer and Apollonius, in
which the Alexandrian aesthetic of the latter, which is so powerfully
attractive, threatens the Homeric march of history. The other large-
scale debt of Virgil to Apollonius may perhaps be seen in the mixing
of temporal levels which is such a feature of the *Aeneid*; events and
institutions of the time of the Trojan arrival in Italy foreshadow and
anticipate the events and institutions of Virgil's own time. A related
interplay of time-frames is a significant feature of Apollonius' poem,
a feature enhanced of course by the prominence of aetiology in the
epic, and in this the ideological rhetoric of the two poems may be
closer than is usually recognized.

Echoes of the *Argonautica* are not rare in the works of Ovid and
post-Ovidian poets; particularly noteworthy is Lucan's description
of Cato's army in Libya in the ninth book of the *Bellum Ciuile* which
clearly borrows from Apollonius' Libyan narrative. The Argonautic
story is the subject of the extant, but unfinished, epic of Valerius
Flaccus written during the reigns of Titus and Domitian. Valerius'
principal models are Apollonius and Virgil, but the poem is in no
sense a translation of the Greek epic, and its scope and aesthetics are
entirely different.[33]

---

[33] For a recent assessment cf. P. R. Hardie, *The Epic Successors of Virgil* (Cambridge,
1993).

LIST OF REFERENCES AND
FURTHER READING

This bibliography contains (i) works referred to in the footnotes to the Introduction, and (ii) some other works for 'further reading'. It has no claims to completeness; for a fuller bibliography see Hunter 1993.

BEYE, C. R. (1969), 'Jason as Love-Hero in Apollonios' *Argonautika*', *Greek, Roman and Byzantine Studies*, 10, 31–55.

—— (1982), *Epic and Romance in the Argonautica of Apollonius* (Carbondale, Ill.).

BING, P. (1988), *The Well-Read Muse. Present and Past in Callimachus and the Hellenistic Poets* (Hypomnemata 90, Göttingen).

BLUM, R. (1991), *Kallimachos: The Alexandrian Library and the Origins of Bibliography*, trans. H. Wellisch (Madison, Wis.).

BRIGGS, W. W. (1981), 'Virgil and the Hellenistic Epic', in H. Temporini and W. Haase (eds.), *Aufstieg und Niedergang der römischen Welt* ii. 31. 2 (Berlin/New York), 948–84.

BULLOCH, A. W. (1985), 'Hellenistic Poetry', in P. E. Easterling and B. M. W. Knox (eds.), *The Cambridge History of Classical Literature I: Greek Literature* (Cambridge), 541–621.

CAMPBELL, M. (1983), *Studies in the Third Book of Apollonius Rhodius' Argonautica* (Hildesheim).

CARSPECKEN, J. F. (1952), 'Apollonius Rhodius and the Homeric Epic', *Yale Classical Studies*, 13, 33–143.

CLAUSEN, W. (1987), *Virgil's Aeneid and the Tradition of Hellenistic Poetry* (Berkeley/Los Angeles).

DELAGE, E. (1930), *La Géographie dans les Argonautiques d'Apollonios de Rhodes* (Bordeaux).

FEENEY, D. C. (1986), 'Following after Hercules, in Virgil and Apollonius', *Proceedings of the Virgil Society*, 18, 47–85.

—— (1991), *The Gods in Epic* (Oxford).

FRASER, P. M. (1972), *Ptolemaic Alexandria* (Oxford).

GENETTE, G. (1980), *Narrative Discourse* (Ithaca, NY).

GOLDHILL, S. (1991), *The Poet's Voice* (Cambridge).

HUNTER, R. L. (1989), *Apollonius of Rhodes; Argonautica Book III* (Cambridge).

—— (1993), *The Argonautica of Apollonius: Literary Studies* (Cambridge).

HUTCHINSON, G. (1988), *Hellenistic Poetry* (Oxford).

NYBERG, L. (1992), *Unity and Coherence: Studies in Apollonius Rhodius' Argonautica and the Alexandrian Tradition* (Lund).

PFEIFFER, R. (1968), *History of Classical Scholarship from the Beginnings to the End of the Hellenistic Age* (Oxford).

WILLIAMS, M. F. (1991), *Landscape in the Argonautica of Apollonius Rhodius* (Frankfurt am Main).

ZANKER, G. (1987), *Realism in Alexandrian Poetry* (London).

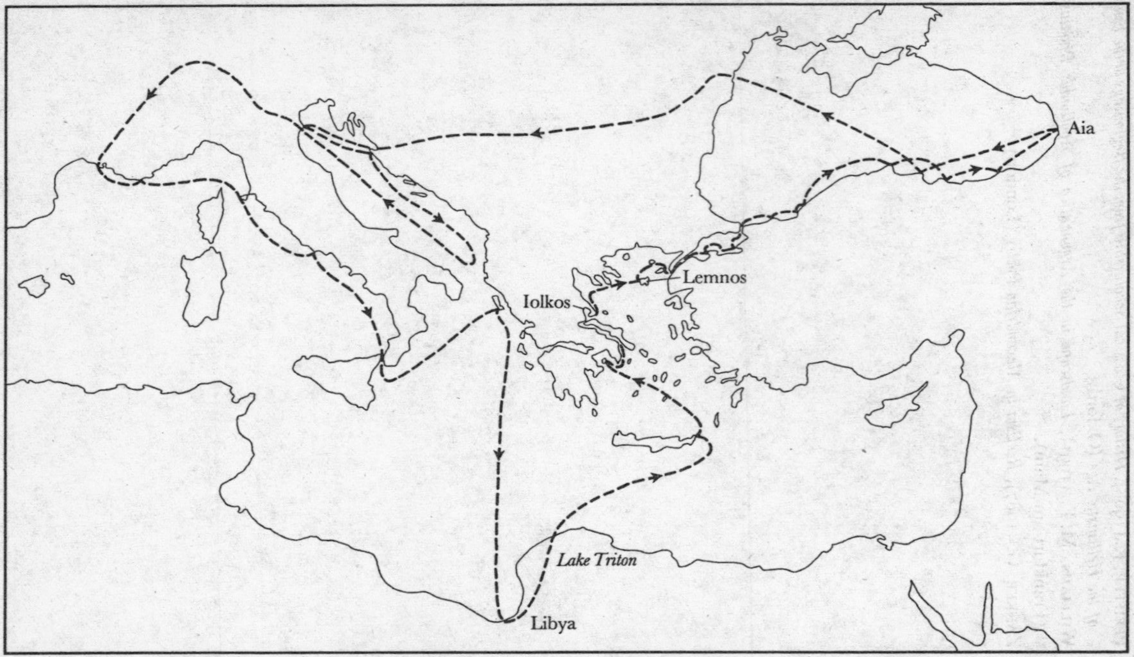

MAP I. The Voyage of the Argonauts

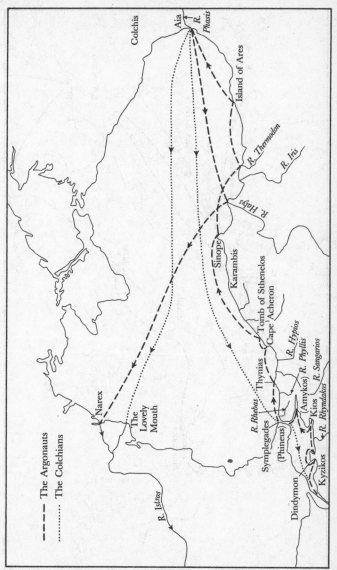

MAP 2. The Black Sea

——— The Argonauts
··········· The Colchians

Colchis

Aia

R. Phasis

Island of Ares

R. Thermodon

R. Iris

R. Halys

Sinope

Karambis

Tomb of Sthenelos

Cape Acheron

R. Hypios

R. Phyllis

R. Sangarios

Thynias

R. Rhebas

(Amykos)

Kios

R. Rhyndakos

Symplegades

(Phineus)

Narex

The Lovely Mouth

Kyzikos

Dindymon

R. Istros

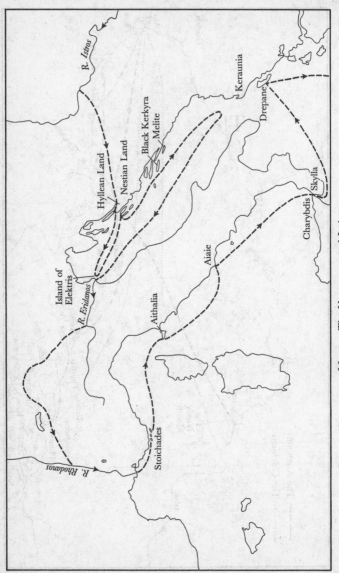

MAP 3. The Voyage around Italy

Jason and
The Golden Fleece
(The *Argonautica*)

BOOK 1

Taking my start from you, Phoibos, I shall recall the glorious deeds of men of long ago who propelled the well-benched *Argo* through the mouth of the Pontos and between the Dark Rocks to gain the golden fleece. For such was the oracle which Pelias had received, that a hateful fate awaited him in the future—destruction caused by a country man* whom he should see wearing only one sandal. Not long after, in accordance with your prophecy, as Jason was crossing on foot the streams of the Anauros* in winter, he saved one sandal from the mud but the other was caught by the current and he abandoned it to the depths. He hurried straight on to Pelias' palace, to take part in a sacred feast which the king was offering to his father Poseidon and all the other gods—except Pelasgian Hera to whom he paid no regard. As soon as Pelias saw Jason he realized, and devised for him the challenge of a voyage which would be full of suffering, so that either on the sea or among a foreign people he might lose all chance of safe return.

The ship is celebrated in the surviving songs of earlier poets who tell that it was built by Argos with the advice of Athena.* I now shall recount the lineage and names of the heroes, their voyages over the vast sea and all they achieved on their wanderings. May the Muses be the inspirers of my song!

First let us recall Orpheus to whom Kalliope herself is said to have given birth near the Pimpleian height,* after she had shared the bed of Thracian Oiagros. Men say that the sound of his songs bewitched the hard rocks on the mountains and the streams of rivers. As signs of his music, the wild oak trees which flourish on the Thracian coast at Zone* stand to this day in close-set ranks; he brought them all the way down from Pieria by the bewitching music of his lyre. Such then was Orpheus, lord of Bistonian Pieria,* whom in obedience to the urgings of Cheiron the son of Aison welcomed as a helper in the challenges to be faced.

Without delay came Asterion, whose father was Kometes; he dwelled by the waters of the swirling Apidanos, at Peiresiai* near Mount Phylleion, where the great Apidanos and the noble Enipeus flow together, their streams uniting after distant journeys.

After these came Polyphemos son of Eilatos, leaving Larisa behind. In former times, when the Lapiths* took up arms against the Centaurs, he fought as a young man among the sturdy Lapiths. Now his limbs had grown heavy, but his spirit was still ready for war as before.

Nor was Iphiklos left behind for long in Phylake.* He was uncle to the son of Aison, for Aison had married his sister, Alkimede, the daughter of Phylakos; this kinship and bond compelled him to be included in their number.

Nor did the ruler of Pherai,* rich in flocks, Admetos, remain under the peak of Mount Chalkodonion.

Nor did Erytos and Echion, the sons of Hermes, possessors of rich crops and skilled in trickery, remain at Alope.* As a third, their brother Aithalides came with them as they set out. The daughter of Myrmidon, Phthian Eupolemeia, gave birth to him beside the streams of the Amphryssos, but the other two were the children of Antianeira, daughter of Menetes.

There came too Koronos, son of Kaineus, leaving behind rich Gyrton;* he was a good warrior, but did not surpass his father. For poets tell that, though destroyed by the centaurs, Kaineus was still alive. Alone and cut off from the other heroes he drove the centaurs off; they charged back but as they advanced they had not the strength to push him back or to kill him. Unwounded and unbending he passed beneath the earth, knocked down by a storm of heavy fir-trees.*

There came too Titaresian Mopsos* whom the son of Leto had taught better than anyone else to understand the divine messages of birds.

Eurydamas, son of Ktimenos, also joined. He dwelled in Dolopian Ktimene near Lake Xynias.*

Moreover Aktor sent his son Menoitios from Opous,* so that he could travel with the heroic men.

In the group too were Eurytion and bold Erybotes, one was the son of Teleon, the other of Iros son of Aktor; glorious Erybotes was the son of Teleon, Eurytion of Iros. Oileus made up their number to three: he was outstanding in courage and skill at rushing upon the enemy from behind, once he had turned their lines.

From Euboia came Kanthos; Kanethos son of Abas had acceded

to his desires in sending him forth. He was not destined to return safe to Kerinthos, for it was his fate to perish in the course of their wanderings on the boundaries of Libya; this was also the fate of the skilled prophet Mopsos. There is thus no final boundary of men's wretchedness, since these men too they buried in Libya, as far from the Colchians as the distance visible between the setting and the rising of the sun.

Next gathered Klytios and Iphitos, the guardians of Oichalia, sons of cruel Eurytos, the Eurytos whose bow was given to him by the Far-Darter; but he gained no profit from the gift, for he tried to rival the giver himself.*

After them came the two sons of Aiakos, though not together nor from the same place. After they had unwittingly killed their brother Phokos, they fled to settle far from Aegina: Telamon settled on the Attic island,* but Peleus made his home far away in Phthia.

After them from the land of Kekrops* came the warrior Boutes, son of noble Teleon, and with him Phaleros of the sturdy spear. His father Alkon had sent him out: he had no other sons left to care for him as he lived through old age, but nevertheless he dispatched his dearest and only son to win glory among the bold heroes. Theseus, however, the greatest of all the sons of Erechtheus, was held back beneath the land of Tainaron* by an unseen bond; he had accompanied Peirithous—a fruitless journey!* Both of these would certainly have made the accomplishment of the task easier for all.

Tiphys, son of Hagnias, left the region of Siphai,* peopled by the Thespians. He was skilled at foretelling when the waves of the broad sea would rise up, skilled too at foretelling wind-storms, and at guiding a voyage by the sun and the stars. Tritonian Athena* herself roused him to join the band of heroes, and his arrival accorded with their hopes. Athena herself it was who had constructed the swift ship, and Argos the son of Arestor had joined her in building it to her instructions, and thus it surpassed all other ships whose oars made trial of the sea.

After them arrived also Phleias from Araithyrea,* where he dwelled beside the springs of the Asopos, rich thanks to his father Dionysos.

From Argos came Talaos and Areios, the two sons of Bias, and stout Leodokos. Their mother was Pero, daughter of Neleus; it was

for her that Melampous of the family of Aiolos endured grim
suffering in the stalls of Iphiklos.*

Not even the mighty Herakles, whose heart was never daunted,
not even he, so we learn,* scorned the needs of the son of Aison.
When he heard the report of the gathering of the heroes, he had just
crossed from Arkadia into Lyrkeian Argos* on the journey on which
he carried alive the boar which grazed in the glades of Lampeia
across the great Erymanthian marsh.* In front of the market square
at Mykenai he shook the boar wrapped in bonds off his great back,
and set off of his own volition contrary to Eurystheus' intentions.
With him came Hylas, an excellent squire in the first blush of youth,
to carry his arrows and guard his bow.

After him came the descendant of divine Danaos, Nauplios. He
was in fact the son of Klytoneos, the son of Naubolos, and Naubolos
in turn was the son of Lernos; Lernos we know* was the son of
Proitos son of Nauplios. Once upon a time Amymone, the maiden
daughter of Danaos, had lain with Poseidon and then given birth to
Nauplios who surpassed all men in the arts of sailing.

Of those who dwelled in Argos Idmon* came last of all. Though
he knew of his own fate from studying birds, he came so that his
people should not begrudge him his glorious reputation. He was not
in truth the son of Abas, but his father was the son of Leto* himself
who placed him among the glorious descendants of Aiolos, and
taught him prophecy, to pay attention to birds, and to observe signs
in burnt-offerings.

Aitolian Leda roused mighty Polydeukes and Kastor, skilled in
handling swift-footed horses, to come from Sparta. These beloved
sons had been borne to her in a single labour in the house of
Tyndareos.* She did not scorn their entreaties, for she was
planning a future worthy of the product of Zeus' bed.

The sons of Aphareus, Lynkeus and violent Idas, came from
Arene,* both mightily confident in their great strength. Lynkeus had
the sharpest eyes of any mortal, if the report is true that without
trouble he could see even down beneath the earth.

Periklymenos son of Neleus also set out on the journey, the oldest
of all the sons born at Pylos to divine Neleus. Poseidon had given
him boundless strength, and the ability in battle to become whatever
he prayed to be when in the tight corners of war.*

Moreover Amphidamas and Kepheus came from Arkadia, the two sons of Aleos, who dwelled in Tegea and the territory of Apheidas.* Ankaios joined them as a third; he was sent by his father Lykourgos, the elder brother of the other two, who, now growing old, remained behind in the city to care for Aleos, but sent his own son to go with his brothers. Ankaios came in the skin of a Mainalian bear,* brandishing in his right hand a great, two-edged axe. His grandfather Aleos had hidden his weapons in the deepest recess of a granary in the hope of preventing him too from setting out.

There came too Augeias who was said to be the son of Helios. Proud of his prosperity, he ruled over the Eleans. Greatly did he desire to see the Colchian land and Aietes himself, lord over the Colchians.

Asterios and Amphion, sons of Hyperasios, came from Achaean Pellene which once their grandfather Pellen had found on the brow of Aigialos.*

After them came Euphemos, leaving Tainaron* behind. He was the fastest of all men, and Europa, daughter of mighty Tityos, had borne him to Poseidon. Euphemos could run even over the swell of the grey sea: his swift feet did not get wet, for he passed on his watery journey dipping only the very tips of his toes.

Two more sons of Poseidon came, Erginos who left behind the city of glorious Miletos, and scornful Ankaios from Parthenia, seat of Imbrasian Hera.* Both vaunted their skill in sailing and war alike.

After them came bold Meleager, son of Oineus, who set out from Kalydon,* and Laokoon; Laokoon was the brother of Oineus, but they did not have the same mother, as Laokoon's mother was a serving-woman. Though he was already aged, Oineus sent him to look after his son who was still a boy when he joined the valiant band of heroes. He, I believe, would have surpassed all the others but for Herakles, if he had remained to develop for one more year among the Aitolians. He was accompanied on this voyage by his maternal uncle, Iphiklos son of Thestios, a man skilled in fighting with the javelin, skilled too in hand-to-hand combat.

With him came Palaimonios, son of Olenian Lernos;* he was called son of Lernos, but in fact by descent was the son of Hephaistos, and for this reason lame in both feet. But no one could scorn his stature or his courage, and so he too was included among all the heroes and brought greater glory to Jason.

From among the Phocians came Iphitos, of the lineage of Naubolos son of Ornytos. Of old he had been host to Jason, when he came to Pytho seeking oracles about his voyage, and Iphitos had received him in his home.

There came also the two sons of Boreas, Zetes and Kalais; the daughter of Erechtheus, Oreithyia, had once borne them to Boreas on the remote edge of wintry Thrace. There Thracian Boreas had carried her after snatching her up from the land of Kekrops* where she was whirling in the dance beside the Ilissos. He brought her from far away and, wrapping her in murky clouds, bedded her at the place which men call the Rock of Sarpedon, beside the stream of the river Erginos.* On their temples and on both sides of their feet black wings glittered with golden scales and fluttered as they rose in the air—a great marvel to behold! In the wind the dark hair which fell from their heads and necks shook over their backs.

Not even the mighty Pelias' own son, Akastos, wished to remain in his father's house, nor Argos, workman-assistant of the goddess Athena. These two also were to be included in the crew.

Such then was the number of those who gathered to aid the son of Aison. The people of the area called all the heroes Minyans, since the majority of them and the best among them proudly claimed descent from the daughters of Minyas.* Indeed the mother of Jason himself was Alkimede, daughter of Klymene the daughter of Minyas.

When the servants had made ready everything with which oared ships are equipped when men are forced to voyage over the sea, then the heroes went through the city towards their ship which lay at the place where the coast* is called Magnesian Pagasai. As they hastened on their way a great crowd of the citizens ran with them, but the heroes stood out among them like bright stars among clouds. This is what each citizen would say as he saw them rushing forward with their weapons:

'Lord Zeus, what does Pelias have in mind? Where is he hurling such a great band of heroes, out from the Panachaean land? The very day they arrive they will raze Aietes' palace with the fire of destruction if he does not consent to give them the fleece. They must go; there is no way out from this terrible labour.'

This was the talk throughout the city. The women constantly raised their arms to the sky in supplication of the immortals, praying them to grant the safe return their hearts desired. As she wept one would say to another in lamentation:

'Wretched Alkimede, to you too has misery come, late though it may be, and your life has not finished in splendour. Very bitter indeed is Aison's fate! Better for him would it have been if he were already wrapped in the shrouds of death and lay beneath the earth, still unaware of this awful challenge. When the virgin Helle perished, would that Phrixos too, and his ram, had been covered over by the dark waves! But that grim marvel spoke with a human voice—to store up countless pains and grief for Alkimede in the future!'

Thus the women spoke as the heroes moved forward.

The slaves and maidservants had already assembled in great numbers in the house, and each felt the wound of sharp pain. With them was Jason's despairing mother; his father, gripped by deadly old age, lay wrapped in the covers on his bed. Jason sought to soothe their pain with words of encouragement. He told the servants to pick up his armour, and this they did in silence, heads bowed in depression. Just as his mother had at the very first thrown her arms around her son, so now she clung to him weeping bitterly. As a lonely young girl falls with relief upon her grey-haired nurse and cries—she has no longer anyone else to care for her, but drags out a wearisome life at the beck and call of a stepmother. Just now she has been battered by the lady's many reproaches, and as she grieves her heart within her is held fast in the bonds of its misery, and she has not the strength to sob forth all the sorrow that throbs within—just so did Alkimede weep bitterly as she held her son in her arms. In her pained yearning she addressed him as follows:

'If only on that day, when to my sorrow I heard King Pelias announce his terrible command, I had on the spot given up my life and found oblivion from care, so that, my child, you could have buried me with your own dear hands. This alone was all I had left to hope from you—all the other rewards of my nurturing I have long since received. But now I, who before was admired among Achaean women, like a slave shall be left behind in the empty palace, wasting away in my wretchedness and longing for you, who before brought

me great renown and glory, you, the first and only child for whom I
undid the girdle of motherhood; for to me more than other women
did the goddess Eileithyia* begrudge the pleasure of many children.
What misery is mine! Never, not even in a dream, did I imagine that
Phrixos' escape would bring me disaster.'

Thus did she complain among her tears, and her serving-women
bewailed in response to her lament. Jason sought to comfort her with
gentle words:

'Please, mother, do not cause yourself too much bitter pain, since
your tears will not prevent the suffering, but you will merely add
grief upon grief. To mortal men the gods allot woes which cannot be
foreseen: despite the pain in your spirit, have the courage to bear
your share of these. Take courage from the assistance of Athena and
the favourable oracles of Phoibos, and moreover from the present
help of the heroes. Remain here quietly in the house with the
servants, and do not act as a bad omen for the ship. My friends and
slaves will accompany me on my way there.'

With these words he left the house and set out. As Apollo proceeds
from his fragrant shrine and travels through holy Delos or Klaros or
Pytho or broad Lykia beside the streams of the Xanthos; just so did
he pass through the great crowd of the people and a loud shout arose
as they all urged him on. Into his path came the aged Iphias,
priestess of Artemis protectress of the city, and she kissed his right
hand; as the crowd pressed foward she could not speak to him
though she wished to, but was left behind there beside the path, an
old woman deserted by the young, and he departed on his way far in
the distance.

He left the well-built streets of the city and reached the coast of
Pagasai where the group of his companions waited for him beside
the *Argo*. He stopped at the entrance to the port and they all
gathered round him. Then they noticed Akastos and Argos coming
down together from the city, and were struck with amazement at the
sight of these two hurrying to join them contrary to Pelias' wishes.
Argos, son of Arestor, wore a bull's hide covered with dark hair which
stretched from his shoulders to his feet, while the other was wrapped
in a gorgeous cloak which his sister Pelopeia had given him. Jason
refrained from questioning them in detail, but he bade the crew sit
down together in assembly. They all took their seats there in due

order on the rolled sails and the lowered mast, and the son of Aison
addressed them in his concern for what was best:

'All the equipment which the ship should carry on our voyage is
now properly ready and stowed; this then will not cause us long to
put off our sailing once favourable winds blow. But, my friends,
common is our hope for return to Hellas in the future, and common
our paths to Aietes' palace—therefore now without other thoughts
choose the very best man as your leader—the man who will be
concerned with every detail in conducting both our quarrels and our
agreements with men of foreign lands.'

So he spoke, and the young men immediately turned their eyes to
the bold Herakles who was sitting in their midst, and with one voice
they all urged him to take command. He, however, remained sitting
where he was, raised his right hand, and said:

'Let no one offer me this honour—I shall not accept it, and I shall
not allow anyone else to put himself forward: let he who gathered
our band together lead us on our way.'

Such were Herakles' high-minded words, and they approved his
instructions. The warrior Jason himself leapt up joyfully to address
his enthusiastic crew:

'If you grant me the honour of being in charge of our expedition,
let nothing, as before, stand in the way of our journey. Now at last
let us propitiate Phoibos with sacrifice and straightaway prepare a
feast. While we are waiting for the arrival of the servants in
command of my animal yards who are charged with carefully
selecting cattle from the herd and driving them here, let us draw
down the ship to the sea, place all the equipment on board and
assign the rowing-benches by lot. Let us while we wait also build an
altar on the shore to Apollo, God of Embarkation, whose oracle
promised that he would provide signs and reveal the routes over the sea
if I should begin my tasks for the king with sacrifices in his honour.'

With these words he was the first to turn to the tasks in hand, and
the others stood up in obedience to him. They piled up their clothes
in a heap on a smooth rock which lay out of range of the sea's waves
but which had long since been washed clean by the storm's spray.
Following Argos' instructions they first of all firmly wrapped a
twisted cable around the ship, pulling it taut on both sides, so that
the planks would remain held securely in place by the bolts and

would be able to withstand the force of the swell which opposed them. Then they quickly dug out a channel wide enough for the ship, leading from the prow down to the sea; along this their arms would pull the ship, and as they proceeded they hollowed it out to a depth lower than the bottom of the keel. In this channel they placed polished rollers, and then manœuvred the ship onto the topmost rollers, facing down to the sea, so that it could be transported by sliding over them. On both sides of the ship they placed the oars upright, so that they projected a cubit above the side of the ship, and secured them fast around the pins. They then positioned themselves between the oars on both sides of the ship and with their arms gripped it firmly against their chests. Tiphys went on board to give the signal to the young men to pull at the appropriate time. He urged them on with a great shout, and they at once put all their weight into the task and with one heave they pushed the ship off the frame in which its base rested. Their feet danced as they pushed ever forward, and the *Argo* from Pelion followed them with a rush, and on both sides they cried out as they leapt forward. Beneath the stout keel the rollers screeched as the ship scraped over them, and all around rose murky smoke caused by the pressure of its weight. So it slipped into the sea, and they pulled back on the cables to check its further progress. They fixed the oars to the pins, and placed on board the mast, the well-made sail, and the stores.

When they had carefully attended to every detail, they first of all drew lots for the rowing-benches, with two men occupying each bench. The middle one, however, they reserved for Herakles and, as an honour above the other heroes, Ankaios who lived in the city of Tegea; to these alone they gave over the middle bench, without bothering to draw lots. Without argument they entrusted Tiphys with the task of guiding the rudder of the stout-built ship. After this they carried stones down to the water's edge and there on the shore heaped up an altar to Apollo under the names of 'god of the shore' and 'god of embarkation'. Over it they quickly laid branches of dried olive-wood. In the meantime the herdsmen of the son of Aison had brought down two oxen chosen from the herd; these the younger companions dragged to the altar while the others made ready the lustral water and sacred barley-grains. In his prayers Jason invoked his ancestral Apollo:

'Hear me, lord who dwells in Pagasai and the city of Aisonis,*
named for my father. When I consulted your oracle at Pytho, you
promised to guide my journey safely to its completion, for it is you
who are responsible for the challenge which confronts us. Guide the
ship, I beseech you, both as we sail out and on the return to Hellas,
and keep my comrades safe. As many of us as return, so will be the
number of bulls which we will place upon your altar in glorious
sacrifice. Countless other offerings will I take to Pytho, countless to
Ortygia.* For the present, come, Far-Darter, and receive this
sacrifice of ours which, as our very first act of acknowledgement, we
offer as we embark upon this ship. May it be to a destiny free
from disaster, lord, that I loose the cables as you have planned.
May a kindly breeze blow and may we travel with it over a calm
sea.'

With these words of prayer he threw the barley-grains. The two
heroes responsible for the oxen, mighty Ankaios and Herakles,
girded themselves in preparation. The latter crashed his club down
on the middle of the forehead of one ox; in one movement its heavy
body fell to the ground. Ankaios cut the other's broad neck with his
bronze axe, slicing through the tough tendons; it fell sprawling over
its two horns. Their comrades quickly slaughtered and flayed the
oxen, chopping and cutting them up and removing the thigh pieces
for sacrifice. These they covered all over with a thick layer of fat and
burnt them on spits, while the son of Aison poured libations of
unmixed wine. Idmon rejoiced as he gazed at the flame, which burnt
brightly all around the sacrifices, and the favourable omen of the
murky smoke, darting up in dark spirals. Swiftly he revealed to them
without concealment the mind of the son of Leto:

'Your fate ordained by the gods is to return here with the fleece.
Numberless are the challenges which lie before you on your journey
there and on the return. I, however, am destined by the hateful
allotment of a divinity to perish far away from here, somewhere on
the Asian continent. Even before today birds of ill-omen had
instructed me as to my fate, but I left my homeland to embark upon
the ship, so that a glorious reputation might thus be left behind in
my home.'

So he spoke. On hearing his prophecies the young heroes rejoiced
in their return, but the fate of Idmon brought them grief.

The sun had now passed the top point of its journey and the ploughlands were beginning to grow shady from the rocks as the sun slipped down towards the evening twilight. The Argonauts had all laid a thick bed of leaves on the sand the length of the grey shore and were reclining in due order. Beside them lay food in great abundance and sweet wine which the wine-pourers drew out with jugs. They swapped stories of the kind young men always do when taking their pleasure over a meal and wine, and all excess which is never satisfied has been banished. There, however, the son of Aison pondered upon everything helpless and absorbed, like a man in despair. Idas observed him with scorn and abused him in a loud voice:

'Son of Aison, what is this plan which you are turning over in your mind? Tell us all what you are thinking! Has fear come over you and crushed you with its weight? It is this which panics men who are cowards. Be witness now my rushing spear with which above all other men I achieve glory in wars—for Zeus is not the source of so much strength as is my spear—that no grief shall destroy us nor shall our challenge be left unachieved while Idas travels with you— no, not even should a god confront us, so powerful a helper am I whom you have brought from Arene.'

With these words he took a full cup in both hands and drank the unmixed, sweet wine, soaking his lips and dark beard with the juice. All the others murmured together among themselves, but Idmon answered him openly:

'Poor fool, have your thoughts always been your undoing, or is it the neat wine which causes the heart in your breast to swell with recklessness and leads you to spurn the gods? There are other words of consolation with which a man might encourage his comrade; what you say is utterly outrageous. This is the kind of bluster with which we are told the sons of Aloeus* used to attack the blessed gods: you are nothing like their equal in courage, but they were both destroyed, strong though they were, by the swift arrows of the son of Leto.'

So he spoke, but Idas son of Aphareus burst into laughter and with scorn in his eyes replied abusively:

'Come now! Tell me this through your prophetic skill: will the gods destroy me in the way that your father bestowed destruction upon the Aloiadai? Take thought for how you will escape safe from my hands if you are found to have uttered empty prophecies!'

So he attacked him angrily, and the quarrel would have gone further, had not their companions and the son of Aison himself restrained their dispute with words of rebuke. Moreover Orpheus took up his lyre in his left hand and began to sing.

He sang* of how the earth, the heavens, and the sea—once upon a time united with each other in a single form—were sundered apart by deadly strife; and how a position fixed for eternity in the sky is held by the stars and the paths of the moon and the sun; how the mountains rose up, and the origin of sounding rivers with their own nymphs, and all creatures on the ground. He sang how first Ophion and Eurynome,* daughter of Ocean, held power over snowy Olympos, and how a violent struggle caused them to yield their positions of honour, he to Kronos and she to Rheia, and to fall into the waves of Ocean. Kronos and Rheia then ruled over the blessed Titan gods, while Zeus was still a young boy, still with the thoughts of an infant, and lived in the Diktaian cave;* the earth-born Kyklopes* had not yet armed him with his blazing bolts, his thunder, and his lightning—the weapons which guarantee Zeus his glory.

This was his song. He checked his lyre and his divine voice, but though he had finished, the others all still leaned forwards, ears straining under the peaceful spell; such was the bewitching power of the music which lingered amongst them. Not long afterwards they mixed libations to Zeus as ritual demanded, and as they stood they poured these over the burning tongues of the sacrifices; then their thoughts turned to sleep in the dark of night.

When the shining eyes of gleaming Dawn beheld the steep ridges of Pelion and under a clear sky the headlands were washed by a sea stirred up in the breeze, then Tiphys awoke. At once he roused his comrades to go on board and to make ready the oars. The harbour of Pagasai and Pelian *Argo* itself, eager to be underway, gave a great shout; fitted in the middle of the keel was a divine plank of Dodonan oak placed there by Athena. The heroes went to their places on the rowing-benches, in due order just as they had previously drawn lots for the rowing, and they all calmly took their proper seats beside their weapons. In the middle position sat Ankaios and the mighty Herakles—near him was his club, and beneath his feet the hull of the

ship sank low in the water.* Already the cables were being pulled in
and libations of wine poured over the sea; Jason, however, turned
his eyes away from his homeland as he wept.

Like young men who set up the dance in Phoibos' honour at Pytho
or perhaps Ortygia or by the waters of the Ismenos,* and to the
music of the lyre beat the ground around the altar with the rhythmic
tap of their swift feet, just so did their oars slap the rough water of
the sea to the sound of Orpheus' kithara. Waves rose and on both
sides the dark ocean seethed with foam as it churned over at the
strength of these powerful men. As the ship advanced, their armour
shone in the sun like flame; the long wake showed ever white, like a
path standing out over a green plain.

On that day all the gods looked from heaven upon the ship and
the generation of demi-gods who sailed the sea, best of all men.* On
the highest peaks the nymphs of Pelion gazed in wonder at the
handiwork of Itonian Athena* and at the heroes themselves whose
arms plied the oars mightily. From the top of the mountains Cheiron
son of Phillyra came down to the sea and dipped his feet where the
waves broke white; with his great hand he bade them farewell and
wished them a safe return from their journey. With him came his
wife, and in her arms Achilles, son of Peleus, to be held up to his
dear father.

They cleared the curving shore of the port, thanks to the
knowledge and skill of wise Tiphys, son of Hagnias, who held the
well-planed rudder expertly in his hands to guide their route truly;
then they set the great mast into the central cavity and secured it
with the forestays which they pulled tight on both sides. They drew
the sail up to the top of the mast and then let it drop down to be
filled out by a stiff breeze. On the deck they threw the cables one by
one around the polished bollards, and sped peacefully on their way
past the long headland of Tisaia. The son of Oiagros played upon
his lyre and sang for them in sweet song a hymn to the Protector of
Ships, she of the noble father, Artemis who haunted those peaks by
the sea as she watched too over the land of Iolkos. From out of the
deep sea darted fish, large and small together, which followed their
path through the water and leapt around them. As when a flock of
sheep which have filled themselves full of grass follow to the stall in
the steps of their rustic master, and he goes in front playing a lovely

shepherd's tune on his shrill pipe; just so did the fish accompany the
boat which the strong breeze pushed ever forwards.

Soon the rich grainlands of the Pelasgians disappeared in the
mist; as they swiftly pressed ever onwards they went past the crags
of Pelion, and the headland of Sepias* disappeared. Skaithos set in
the sea came into view, and they saw too in the distance Peiresiai
and, in clear weather, the coast of the Magnesian land and the tomb
of Dolops.* There in the evening they put in, since the winds were
against them. In the gloom they offered burnt sacrifices of sheep in
Dolops' honour, as the swell of the sea rose. Two days they remained
idly there on the coast. On the third day they pushed out the boat
and drew up the huge sail high on the mast. That coast men still call
Aphetai Argous ['Sailing of the *Argo*'].*

From there they ran further, past Meliboia, as they gazed at the
coast and the beach exposed to storms.* At dawn they saw at once
Homole hard by the sea as they sailed past, and very soon they were
to rush past the stream of the river Amyros.* Next they looked upon
Eurymenai and the ravines of Ossa and Olympos which are battered
by waves. During the night that followed, the wind's breeze carried
them swiftly past the hills of Pallene as they sailed out beyond Cape
Kanastron. In the morning the Thracian peak of Athos rose up
before the travellers. Athos is as far from Lemnos as a properly
equipped ship can travel in a morning, but the shadow of its topmost
peak reaches even as far as Myrine.* All that day until the evening
they were favoured by a very stiff breeze which stretched tight the
sail of the ship; but the wind dropped as the rays of the sun faded,
and it was by rowing that they reached rocky Lemnos, the Sintian
island.*

There, in the year just passed, the whole people had been
pitilessly killed at one stroke by the wickedness of the women.
Spurning their lawful wives whom they had come to hate, the men
conceived a violent desire for slave-girls whom they had brought
over after their pillaging raids on the Thracian mainland opposite.
The cause was the terrible anger of the Kyprian goddess, because
they had for a long time denied her due honours. O wretched women
whose grim jealousy knew no bounds! They destroyed not only their
husbands together with the slave-girls in their beds, but also the
entire male population with them, so that there could be no requital

in the future for the awful murder. Alone of all the women, Hypsipyle spared her aged father Thoas who ruled among the people. She set him to drift over the sea in a hollow chest in the hope that he might be saved. He was drawn ashore on the island of Oinoe—as it used to be called, but later it was named Sikinos—by fishermen; the name came from Sikinos whom the naiad Oinoe bore to Thoas.* The Lemnian women all found cattle-grazing, putting on bronze armour, and cutting furrows in the wheat-bearing fields easier than the works of Athena* with which they had always busied themselves in former times. Nevertheless, often indeed did they scan the wide sea in dread fear as to when the Thracians would come.

Thus, when they saw the *Argo* being rowed towards the island, they straightaway put on the armour of war and rushed out of the gates of Myrine on to the shore, like bacchants who devour raw flesh. They no doubt imagined that the Thracians were approaching. With them Hypsipyle, daughter of Thoas, donned her father's armour. Not knowing what was happening, they poured out in silence, so great was their fear and suspense.

For their part, the heroes sent forth from the ship Aithalides,* the swift herald, to whom they had entrusted the carrying of messages and the sceptre of his father Hermes. The god had provided him with an unperishing memory of all things, and not even now when he has passed to the unforeseeable whirlpools of Acheron* has forgetfulness overtaken his spirit; in a constant alternation fixed by fate it is at one time numbered among the dead beneath the earth, and at another it emerges to the light of the sun to be among the living. But why should I tell at length these stories concerning Aithalides? As the day waned and gloom spread, he persuaded Hypsipyle to receive the travellers; in the morning the north wind blew, but the Argonauts did not release the mooring-ropes.

The Lemnian women came through the city and sat down in assembly as Hypsipyle their queen had instructed. As soon as they had all gathered in one throng, she addressed them with words of exhortation:

'Dear friends, let us give the men gifts to please them—the sort of things which one should have on a ship, supplies and sweet wine, so that they will continue to remain outside our walls and need will not force them to come among us; otherwise they will learn clearly what has happened and an evil report would spread far abroad, since we have committed an awful deed. They, too, would take no pleasure at all in what we have done, if they should learn about it. This then is where my planning has reached; but if anyone can devise a better plan, let her stand up. It is for this reason that I have called you here.'

With this she sat down on her father's stone seat. Then her dear nurse Polyxo rose up, trembling on feet withered with age and supporting herself with a staff; great was her desire to address them. Beside her sat four unmarried maidens with thick, white hair. She stood in the middle of the assembly, scarcely able to raise her neck from between her hunched shoulders, and spoke thus:

'Let us indeed send gifts to the strangers, as Queen Hypsipyle wishes, since it is better to be generous. But what plan do you have to preserve the value of your lives if a Thracian army or some other enemy force should fall upon us, as frequently happens among men? Look how this group too has now arrived unexpectedly. If some god should turn aside this threat, countless other troubles—worse than warfare—await in the future. When the older women fade away and you younger ones reach hateful old age without having had children, how will you live then, poor fools? Will the cattle yoke themselves in the rich fields and pull the earth-cutting plough through the fallow land? As the seasons revolve, will they gather the harvest as soon as it is ripe? As for myself, I suppose that my clothes will be made of earth within the coming year, even if up until now the Keres* have shuddered at the sight of me. I shall receive my share of customary funeral honours before I see this disaster approaching us; but I urge you younger ones to reflect well upon these things, for now you have a means to save yourselves, right here before you, if you are willing to turn your homes, all your possessions and the care of your glorious city over to the strangers.'

So she spoke and the assembly filled with noise, for her speech delighted them. Straightaway after her Hypsipyle rose up again and replied as follows:

'If this plan is approved by everyone, I shall without delay dispatch a messenger to the ship.'

With these words she turned to Iphinoe who was close by:

'Please go, Iphinoe, and ask the man who commands this

expedition to come to my palace, so that I may tell him of a decision of the people which will please him. Bid his comrades, if they so wish, to disembark into our country and city without fear, provided that their intentions are friendly.'

So saying she broke up the assembly and rose to return to her own palace. For her part Iphinoe went to the Minyans, and when they asked her with what intention she had come, she immediately replied to the questions of the whole group:

'Hypsipyle, the maiden daughter of Thoas, sent me here to summon the captain of the ship, whoever he is, so that she may tell him of a decision of the people which will please him; and she bids his comrades, if you so wish, to disembark into our country and city straightaway now,* provided that your intentions are friendly.'

So she spoke, and her words which boded well were approved by all. They imagined that Thoas was dead and that Hypsipyle, his beloved daughter, reigned. Quickly they sent Jason off and prepared to go themselves.

Around his shoulders Jason pinned a double cloak of purple, the work of the Itonian goddess,* which Pallas had given to him when first she set up the stocks for the building of the *Argo* and issued instructions for measuring the cross-beams with the rule. You could cast your eyes more easily towards the rising sun than gaze upon the brilliant redness of the cloak. Its centre was bright red, the border all the way round purple, and along the full length of the edge had been woven many cunning designs in sequence.

Upon it were the Kyklopes* seated at their ceaseless task, fashioning a thunderbolt for Zeus their king. The brilliant object was all finished, but for the lack of a single ray which they were now hammering out with iron mallets; it seethed with the blast of savage fire.

Upon it were Amphion and Zethos,* the two sons of Asopos' daughter Antiope. Beside them lay Thebes, still without its towers, and they were just now eagerly putting down the city's foundations. On his shoulders Zethos raised up the peak of a towering mountain, and he looked like a man struggling hard. After him came Amphion; pure sounds flowed from his golden lyre, and a rock twice as large followed in his steps.

Next in sequence was fashioned the deep-tressed Kytherean

goddess* holding the war-shield of Ares. Her tunic had been unclasped and had slipped down from her shoulder over her left arm to hang beneath her breast. Facing her a perfect reflection was visible in the bronze shield.

Upon it was a thickly grassed pasture where cattle grazed. The Teleboans* and the sons of Elektryon fought over the cattle, the latter trying to defend themselves, the former, Taphian bandits, wishing to plunder them. The dewy meadow was drenched with their blood, as the many thieves overpowered the few herdsmen.

Upon it was worked a contest of two chariots. In front drove Pelops* shaking the reins; alongside him stood Hippodameia. Myrtilos had driven his horses on in hard pursuit, and with him was Oinomaos, his spear stretched out ready in his hand; but the axle broke in the nave and he toppled sideways just as he moved to strike Pelops in the back.

Upon it was the design of Phoibos Apollo, a large boy, not yet full-grown. He was shooting an arrow at the giant Tityos* who was reckless enough to try to drag off the god's mother by her veil. Tityos was the child of noble Elare, but Earth had nourished him and brought him to the light again.

Upon it was Phrixos the Minyan, depicted as though really listening to the ram, and the ram seemed to be speaking. As you looked on this pair, you would be struck dumb with amazement and deceived, for you would expect to hear some wise utterance from them. With this hope you would gaze long upon them.

Such then was the gift of the goddess, Itonian Athena.* In his right hand Jason took the far-travelling spear which Atalanta had once given to him as a mark of friendship when she greeted him in kindness on Mainalos.* Great was her desire to join the expedition, but of his own accord he refused to accept her, as he feared the terrible conflicts which love causes.

He went towards the city like the bright star* whose rising is admired by young brides, shut up in their new-built chambers. Its red brilliance through the dark air bewitches their eyes, and the virgin, too, rejoices in her desire for the young man who lives in a distant city, the future husband for whom her parents are keeping her. Like that star did the hero follow behind the messenger. When they were through the gates and inside the town, the women of the

city thronged behind them, delighted by the stranger. He, however,
kept his eyes fixed on the ground and took no notice all the way to
Hypsipyle's gleaming palace. When they saw him, the servants
opened the splendid panelled doors, and Iphinoe led him quickly
through a beautiful porch and bade him sit on a bright couch
opposite her mistress. Hypsipyle turned her eyes away and a blush
came over the maiden's cheeks. Nevertheless, despite her coy
reserve, she addressed him with winning words:

'Stranger, why do all of you thus wait for so long outside the
walls? Our men do not live in the town, but they have moved to the
Thracian mainland where they plough the wheat-bearing fields. I
shall give a truthful account of the whole story of our misfortune so
that you, too, may know it well. While my father Thoas ruled over
the citizens, our men launched raids from their ships on the homes of
the Thracians who live opposite and brought back here a geat haul
of booty together with young girls. However, the wrath of Kypris, a
deadly goddess, was at work, for she cast mind-destroying folly upon
them. They rejected in loathing their lawful wives and, giving way to
their lust, chased them from their homes, preferring—poor fools!—
to sleep with slaves acquired in war. For a long time we put up with
this, in the hope that eventually they would change their minds, but
the trouble multiplied and got ever worse. Our legitimate children
were shown no honour in their homes, and a bastard race was
placed above them. Unmarried girls and their deserted mothers
wandered aimlessly through the city with no one to care for them. A
father had not the slightest concern for his daughter, even if before
his very eyes outrage was done to her by the violent fury of a
stepmother. Children no longer as before protected their mothers
from shameful insults, and brothers no longer cared about sisters.
Our men were interested only in the slave-girls, whether it be at
home, in the public dances, in the market-place or at feasts. Finally,
some god gave us the strength and courage to refuse to receive the
men within our towers on the return from Thrace, until they should
either come to their senses or go off to live somewhere else with their
slave-girls. With our permission they then took all the male children
who remained in the city and went back to the snowy ploughlands of
Thrace where they still live now. Therefore, come and live with us in
the city. If you are willing and would find it pleasant to dwell here,

you could take over the honoured position of my father Thoas. I do not think that you will find fault with the land, for its crops are richer than those of any other inhabited island in the Aegean sea. Now go and report to your comrades what I have said, and do not stay outside the city.'

These were her words as she glossed over how the men had been murdered. Jason answered her as follows:

'Very welcome to us, Hypsipyle, is the help which you offer in our need. I shall return again to the city when I have given my comrades a detailed report of everything in order. As for the kingship of the island, you yourself must look to this. I do not refuse your offer because I think it a small thing, but because I am driven on by grievous challenges.'

With this he touched her right hand and straightaway turned to go back. Around him as he went countless young girls thronged joyfully on all sides until he had passed through the gates. When he had left, the women mounted on swift-running chariots to bring many gifts of friendship to the Argonauts, and they reached the shore after Jason had already given his men a full account of all Hypsipyle had told him when he answered her summons. Then the women invited the Argonauts to be entertained in their homes, and the men did not resist, as Kypris roused sweet desire in them; she did this for the sake of Hephaistos, the god of many wiles, so that once again his island of Lemnos might be duly populated by men. The son of Aison set off for the palace of Hypsipyle, and all the others went where chance led them, with the exception of Herakles. From his own choice he remained by the ship, together with a few comrades who stayed away from the merry-making. Soon the city was full of joyful dancing and the rich smoke of feasting; in their hymns and sacrifices they paid honour above all other immortals to the glorious son of Hera* and to Kypris herself.

The sailing was now continually deferred from one day to the next. They would have wasted a great deal of time remaining there, had not Herakles summoned his comrades together, without the women, and reproached them as follows:

'Poor fools, does the shedding of kindred blood prevent us from returning home? Have we left our homes to come here in search of brides, scorning the women of our own cities? Do we want to live here and cut up the rich ploughland of Lemnos? We will not win glory shut up here interminably with foreign women. No god is going to hand over the fleece to us in answer to our prayers; we will have to work for it. Let us all return to our own countries and leave him to wallow all day in Hypsipyle's bed until he has won great renown by filling Lemnos with his sons!'

So did Herakles upbraid the crew. No one dared look up to meet his gaze or say anything in answer to him, but without discussion the meeting broke up and speedily they made preparations for departure. As soon as the women learned of this they came running out. As when bees pour from a hive in the rocks to surround the beautiful lilies with their buzzing, and the dewy meadow rejoices as the bees flit from place to place gathering their sweet crop, so did the women press around the men, weeping and embracing them as they said good-bye, and they prayed to the blessed gods to grant them a safe return home. Hypsipyle, too, took the son of Aison's hands and made this prayer, as her tears of regret at his departure fell in streams:

'Go now, and may the gods keep you and your comrades safe and sound as you bring the golden fleece to the king. This is what you want and what your heart desires. This island and my father's throne will be waiting, if after your return you ever wish to come back here again. You will find no trouble gathering a very large population from the other cities. But you will not want to do this, nor do I imagine that these things will be fulfilled. On your voyage and when you have returned, please remember Hypsipyle, and leave me now some instructions which I shall happily carry out with all my heart, should the gods grant me a child.'*

Deeply moved, the son of Aison answered thus:

'Hypsipyle, I hope that all these things will be rightfully accomplished by the blessed gods. Do not ask me to stay,* since it is enough for me to be allowed by Pelias to live in my homeland; my only prayer is that the gods deliver me from my trials. But if I am fated not to return to Greece from this distant voyage and you should bear a male child, send him when he is grown to my father and mother in Pelasgian Iolkos. If he finds them still alive he will console their grief, and far from King Pelias they will be cared for, safe in their own home.'

After these words he was the very first to board the ship, and the other heroes followed. They sat down in their rows and grasped the oars, and Argos released the mooring-ropes which had been attached to a sea-battered rock. Then they began to beat the water powerfully with their long pinewood oars. On Orpheus' instructions they put in at evening at the island of Elektra,* daughter of Atlas, so that through reverent initiations they might learn secrets which cannot be revealed and thus sail in greater safety over the chilling sea. I shall say nothing more about this: hail to the island itself and to its indigenous gods, guardians of the mysteries of which I may not sing!

From there they rowed eagerly across the deep stretches of the 'Black Sea'* with Thrace on one side and, on the open side, the coast of Imbros. They reached the point of the Chersonnese just after sunset. There a stiff southerly wind came up, and they raised the sail and entered the dangerous stream of Athamas' daughter.* In the morning they had left behind an open sea, and at night they travelled through another, having passed within the Rhoiteian headland* with the territory of Ida on their right. Leaving Dardania behind they proceeded to Abydos and then sailed past Perkote, the sandy shore of Abarnis and holy Pityeia.* In the course of the night they completed their passage through the Hellespont which eddied and surged as the ship sliced through its waters.

Inside the Propontis there is a steep island* sloping down into the sea; it is joined to the rich grainfields of the Phrygian mainland by a low isthmus over which the waves wash. The island lies above the mouth of the Aisepos and its shores offer harbours on both sides; inhabitants of the area call it Mountain of the Bears. Violent and savage were those who lived on the island, children of the Earth—an extraordinary sight for their neighbours. Each had six mighty arms, two coming out from their stout shoulders and the other four attached lower down on their terrible sides. The isthmus and the plain were inhabited by the Doliones whose king was the hero Kyzikos, son of Aineus and Ainete, the daughter of noble Eusoros. Thanks to Poseidon, the earth-born, awful though they were, did not harm the Doliones, as they were originally descended from the god.

The Thracian winds carried the *Argo* swiftly to the island and they put in to the 'Beautiful Harbour'.* There Tiphys advised them to untie their small anchor-stone and to abandon it below the spring Artakie; in its place they chose another, heavier one appropriate to the task. Later, in accordance with an oracle of the Far-Worker,* the Ionian sons of Neleus* duly set up the abandoned stone as a sacred relic in the temple of Athena, Protector of Jason.

All the Doliones and Kyzikos himself came in friendship to greet the Argonauts hospitably when they learned of the purpose of the expedition and of the glorious families to which the heroes belonged. They urged the Argonauts to move further along the coast to moor their ship in the city harbour. There they set up on shore an altar to Apollo, the protector of those who disembark, and then prepared sacrifice. The king himself supplied their need for sweet wine and flocks, as he had been advised by an oracle that when a god-sent expedition of heroic men should come to his country he should give it a friendly welcome and not think of making war. He, too, was just showing the first beard of manhood, and had not yet been blessed with children. His wife, the lovely-tressed Kleite, daughter of Merops of Perkote, remained in the palace untouched by the pains of child-bearing. He had recently brought her from her father's house on the coast facing the city, after paying a wondrous bride-price for her. Even so, he left his chamber and his bride's bed to feast with the Argonauts, casting all fear out of his heart. The two sides questioned each other in turn. Kyzikos asked them about their voyage and about Pelias' orders, and the Argonauts made enquiries about the neighbouring cities and the whole gulf of the broad Propontis. Beyond that point the king was unable to satisfy their curiosity.

In the morning some of the Argonauts set off to climb the high peak of Dindymon to view the sea-routes for themselves, while the others rowed the ship from its earlier mooring into the 'Closed Harbour'.* The route which those on land followed is now called 'Jason's Path'. From the other side of the mountain the earth-born rushed down and tried to block off the mouth of the 'Closed Harbour' by throwing countless rocks to the bottom, as though trapping a large sea-creature in the port. But Herakles had remained there on the ship with the younger heroes and he quickly bent his bow at them and brought many down to the ground, one on top of the other, as they hurled the large boulders which they had broken off. No doubt these terrible monsters, too, had been kept by Zeus's wife Hera as a labour for Herakles. The other warrior heroes returned before reaching the lookout-point on Dindymon and joined in the slaughter of the earth-born. They attacked with arrows and spears until they had wiped out all of them, despite their repeated violent assaults. As when carpenters cut long planks with the axe, and place them in a line along the shore so that strong bolts may be driven into them when they have been soaked, so the giants were stretched out in a line at the narrow point of the foam-white harbour. A group lay with their heads and chests in the salt sea and their lower limbs stretched out on the dry land; others had their heads on the sands of the shore and their feet out in the sea. Both were a prey for the birds and fish simultaneously

When they could proceed without fear and the wind had come up, they untied the ship and journeyed further across the sea's swell. The *Argo* ran on under sail all day long. As night drew on, however, the wind did not remain constant, but gusts from the opposite direction seized the ship and blew her back until they once again reached the land of the hospitable Doliones. There they disembarked during that same night, and the rock around which they hurriedly threw the mooring-ropes is still called the 'Sacred Rock'. No one, however, was clever enough to realize that they had landed on the same island. In the darkness the Doliones, too, failed clearly to understand that the heroes had returned; they no doubt imagined instead that a Pelasgian war-force of Makrians* had landed, and therefore they put on armour and joined battle with them.

With spears and shields they clashed together like a fierce blast of flame which shoots up as it seizes upon dry scrub. A terrible and violent struggle fell upon all the Doliones. The king himself was not destined to escape his fate by returning from the battle to his marriage-chamber and his wife's bed. Leaping forward the son of Aison struck him through the centre of the chest as Kyzikos turned to face him; his breast-bone shattered on the spear and he rolled over in the sand to meet his fated end. This mortals may never escape, and all around us is spread a great net of doom. Thus Kyzikos no doubt believed that he was now beyond the reach of any grim disaster that the heroes could inflict, but fate caught him on that same night as he fought with them. Many of the king's helpers were also killed.* Herakles slew Telekles and Megabrontes. Sphodris was slaughtered by Akastos; Peleus destroyed Zelys and the bold Gephyros, while Telamon of the strong spear killed Basileus. Promeus was Idas' victim, and Hyakinthos Klytios', while Megalossakes and Phlogios fell to the two sons of Tyndareus. Next to them the son of Oineus* destroyed bold Itymoneus and Artakes, leader of men. All of these are still glorified by the inhabitants with the honours due to heroes. The Doliones who survived yielded their position and fled, as flocks of doves flee before swift hawks. In a disordered throng they rushed inside the gates, and straightaway the city was full of lamentation because the men had returned in flight from this grievous war.

At first light both sides realized the fatal error which could no longer be undone. Violent grief seized the Minyan heroes when they saw Kyzikos, son of Aineus, lying in front of them in the blood-filled dust. For three full days they and the Doliones lamented and tore their hair. Then they put on bronze armour and circled the king's body three times before burying him in a tomb. Afterwards, in accordance with custom, they conducted funeral games on the Leimonian Plain, where to this day the tomb rises up, clearly visible to later generations.

Nor did Kleite survive after her husband's death, but she added even worse misery to what had gone before by fitting a noose around her neck. The very nymphs of the groves mourned her death, and from all the tears which dropped to the earth from their eyes the goddesses fashioned the spring which men call Kleite, the everrenowned name of the unhappy bride. Zeus made that day the most wretched of all for the men and women of Kyzikos. No one could bring themselves to taste food, and for a long time afterwards grief prevented them from working at the mill, so they lived simply on uncooked food. Therefore, still today, when the Ionian inhabitants of Kyzikos pour annual libations in honour of the royal pair, it is at the public mill that they always grind meal for the sacred cakes.

After this, strong, blustery winds blew continuously for twelve days and nights and prevented them from sailing. On the following night most of the heroes had long been sunk in sleep when the third watch came; as the others slept deeply, Akastos and Mopsos, son of

Ampykos, kept guard. Over the blond head of the son of Aison flew a halcyon,* and its shrill voice foretold that the winds would drop. When he heard it, Mopsos understood the happy omen in the cry of the shore-bird. The god* then changed the course of the bird's flight and it darted up to settle on the sternpost of the ship. Without delay Mopsos shook Jason awake on his bed of soft sheepskins and spoke as follows:

'Son of Aison, you must climb to this holy place on rugged Dindymon to appease the Mother of the whole company of the blessed gods, the lady of the fair throne; if you do this, these harsh winds will drop. For this is the message I have just now heard in the cry of the sea-dwelling halcyon which fluttered above you as you slept, revealing all that must be done. Upon the Mother depend the winds, the ocean, the whole earth beneath and the snowy seat of Olympos; whenever she leaves the mountains and climbs to the great vault of heaven, Zeus himself, the son of Kronos, makes way, and all the other immortal gods likewise show honour to the dread goddess.'

So he spoke, and his words were very welcome to Jason. He leapt joyfully from his bed, quickly roused all his comrades and told them how Mopsos, son of Ampykos, had interpreted the divine bird. Quickly the younger heroes drove cattle from their stalls up to the steep peak of the mountain, while the others unmoored the ropes which were attached to the 'Sacred Rock' and rowed to the 'Thracian Harbour'.* They too then climbed the mountain, leaving only a few comrades behind on board ship. From the top, the Makrian peaks and the whole coastline opposite Thrace were as clear as if they held them in their hands; they saw too the misty entrance to the Bosporos and the Mysian heights and, on the other side, the river Aisepos and the city and Nepeian plain of Adrasteia.*

There was a tough vine-stump, old and withered, which had grown in the forest. They cut this down to make a holy image of the mountain-goddess, and Argos carved it skilfully; they set the image on a rocky outcrop under the branches of the oaks which grew on the summit high above all other trees. Beside it, they heaped up an altar of stones and crowned themselves with oak leaves to perform the sacrifice. In their worship they called upon the mother of Dindymon, mistress of all, the dweller in Phrygia, and with her Titias and

Kyllenos,* who alone of the many Cretan Daktyls of Ida are called 'guiders of destiny' and 'those who sit beside the Idaian Mother'. The nymph Anchiale once brought forth the Daktyls in the Diktaian cave as she clutched with both hands at the Oiaxian* earth. As he poured libations upon the burning victims, the son of Aison many times implored the Great Mother to turn aside the storm-winds, and taking their cue from Orpheus, all the young heroes leapt and danced an armed dance and beat their swords on their shields so that the ill-omened sound of the continuing lamentations of the people for their king should be lost in the air. For this reason the Phrygians still worship Rheia with tambourines and drums. The goddess was no doubt well disposed towards the holy sacrifices, as became clear from obvious signs. Trees poured forth fruit in abundance, and around their feet the earth spontaneously sent up flowers amidst the soft grass; wild animals left their dens and lairs in the forest and came fawning with their tails. The goddess caused another marvel as well. Before this, there had been no flowing water on Dindymon, but in their honour she now caused an endless stream to gush down from the thirsty summit. The inhabitants of the area have ever since called that source 'Jason's Spring'. Then the heroes prepared a feast in the goddess's honour on the Mountain of the Bears and sang of Rheia, mistress of all. At dawn the winds dropped and they rowed away from the island.

Then the heroes engaged in keen competition to see who could keep rowing the longest, for there was now no breath of wind and the surface of the sea was perfectly still. Trusting to this calm, the Argonauts rowed their ship forward with great force, and not even the storm-footed horses of Poseidon could have caught it as it darted over the sea. As the swell increased, however, with the fierce winds which first rise up from the rivers towards evening, the heroes yielded to tiredness and began to give up. Then when all the others were worn out and exhausted, Herakles' strong arms pulled the boat along; his efforts shook the well-fitted planks of the ship. But when they had seen the mouth of the Rhyndakos and the great tomb of Aigaion* as they travelled not far out from the Phrygian coast in their eagerness to reach the land of the Mysians, then Herakles' oar broke in the middle while he was ploughing long furrows in the rough water. He fell sideways; one piece was left in his hands and

the other was carried away by the eddying sea. He sat up again
and glared around in silence, for his hands were not used to idle-
ness.

At the hour when a gardener or a ploughman, hungry for supper,
is glad to return from the fields to his hut and, filthy with dust,
squats down on his weary knees in the entrance to pour curses on his
belly and stare at his worn hands, at that hour the heroes reached
the land of Kios near Mount Arganthoneion and the mouth of the
Kios. The Mysians who inhabit the land received them hospitably,
as they came in friendship, and supplied their need for provisions,
sheep, and wine in great quantity. Some of the heroes gathered
firewood, others collected piles of grass in the meadows for bedding,
others made fire with sticks or mixed wine in bowls and prepared
dinner. First, however, they sacrificed in the evening gloom to
Apollo, protector of those who disembark.

Herakles, son of Zeus, told his comrades to get on with the meal
and went off into the forest to cut himself a suitable oar. In his
wandering he came across a fir-tree which was neither weighed
down by too many branches nor too far grown, but resembled rather
a slender poplar in both height and width. Quickly he placed his
quiver and bow on the ground and took off his lion-skin. He hit the
tree with his bronze-covered club, and shook it to its very roots in
the ground. Then, confident of his strength, he placed both arms
around the trunk and, feet well apart, leant in with his broad
shoulder and lifted the deep-rooted tree right out of the ground,
together with all the earth which had held it in. As when at the
winter setting of grim Orion a sudden, violent wind-squall strikes
down upon a ship's mast and tears it off the forestays, wedges and
all, so did Herakles lift up that tree. Then he picked up his bow and
arrows, his lion-skin and club, and hurried back.

Meanwhile Hylas had gone off away from the others with a
bronze pitcher to look for a sacred spring, so that he would have
water ready for dinner when Herakles returned and so that
everything else would be carefully and properly prepared. These
were the habits in which Herakles had trained him ever since he had
taken him away as a young child from the house of his father, the
excellent Theiodamas, whom Herakles had pitilessly slain in the
land of the Dryopes when Theiodamas opposed him in the matter of

a ploughing-ox.* In his distress Theiodamas was ploughing fallow-land when Herakles told him to hand over his ox and Theiodamas was unwilling to do so. Herakles in fact wanted an excuse to bring destructive war upon the Dryopes because they gave no heed to justice in their lives. But these things would lead me far from the path of my song.

Soon Hylas reached the spring which those who live close by call Pegai.* He arrived just as the nymphs were arranging their dance, for all the nymphs who inhabited that lovely ridge were accustomed every night to honour Artemis with songs. Some were nymphs of the mountain peaks and the glades; others were forest-nymphs who had come from far away. The nymph of the spring, however, was just rising from the fair-flowing water when Hylas came, and she saw close at hand how the sweet grace of his beauty blushed red in the rays of the full moon which shone from the sky. The Kyprian goddess set her heart racing and only with difficulty could she gather herself together in her helpless amazement. But as soon as Hylas leant over to dip the pitcher in the stream and the water gurgled loudly as it swept into the echoing bronze, the nymph placed her left arm on his neck and with her right hand on his elbow she drew him down towards her, desiring to kiss his soft mouth. He fell into the middle of the eddying water.

The only one of the crew to hear his cry was the hero Polyphemos, son of Eilatos, who had come along the path to await the return of the towering Herakles. He rushed to Pegai, like some wild animal which has heard from afar the noise of sheep and, burning with hunger, goes after the flocks but does not reach them before the shepherds have put them away safe in their stalls. Just as that beast moans and roars terribly until it has no strength left, so did the son of Eilatos groan loudly, rushing around and shouting out, until his cries grew faint. Suddenly he drew his great sword and went off at a sprint in case wild animals had taken Hylas or bandits had ambushed the unprotected boy and were carrying off such an easy prey. As he ran along the path, drawn sword in hand, he met Herakles himself; he had no trouble in recognizing the hero hurrying through the darkness towards the ship. Panting and distressed, he immediately relayed his grim message of disaster:

'I must be the first to tell you, poor friend, of a terrible grief. Hylas has not returned safe from his trip to the spring, but bandits have seized him and are carrying him off, or wild beasts are tearing him. I heard his cries.'

When Herakles heard this, sweat poured down over his temples and deep in his body the dark blood boiled. In a rage he threw the fir-tree to the ground and ran wildly wherever his feet led him. As when a bull is stung by a gadfly and rushes off, abandoning the meadows and the marshes, and has no thought for the keepers or the herd, but runs without resting or sometimes stops and lifts its broad neck to bellow in distress at the bite of the cruel fly, so in his rage did Herakles' legs move swiftly and without pausing, but sometimes he would break off his labour and in a loud voice give off cries which reached far into the distance.

When the dawn star had just appeared over the highest mountain-peaks, the breeze got up and Tiphys at once told the crew to go on board to take advantage of the wind. Straightaway they embarked in haste, pulled up the anchor-stones and hauled the ropes tight. The sail swelled out in the wind and, far out from the shore, they were carried happily along the Cape of Poseidon. But when the shining brightness of dawn spread from the horizon over the sky and paths were clearly picked out and the dewy plains glittered in the bright gleam, then they realized that by mistake they had left Herakles and Polyphemos behind. They began to quarrel fiercely and squabble bitterly amongst themselves because they had abandoned the best of all the heroes; the son of Aison was so struck by helplessness that he could not speak in favour of any proposal, but sat gnawing at his heart because of the grim disaster which had occurred. Telamon, however, was gripped by anger and spoke out:

'Sit there at your ease, since it was you who arranged to abandon Herakles. This was your plan. You didn't want his glory to overshadow yours throughout Greece, if the gods ever allow us to return safe. But why waste time on words? I shall go after him, even without these friends of yours who helped you plan this treachery!'

So saying he rushed at Tiphys, son of Hagnias; his eyes flashed like sparks from a raging fire. The Argonauts would indeed have gone back to the land of the Mysians, struggling against the sea and the ceaseless blast of the wind, had not the two sons of Thracian Boreas restrained the son of Aiakos with harsh words. A rash act!

Herakles later exacted a terrible and violent revenge because they
had prevented a search being made for him. As they returned from
the funeral games in honour of Pelias, he killed them on sea-girt
Tenos. Over them he piled earth and set up two pillars; when noisy
Boreas blows, one of the pillars sways—an extraordinary marvel to
behold! This was what was destined to happen in due time.

From the depths of the sea Glaukos,* the wise spokesman of
divine Nereus, appeared to them. His shaggy head and chest
emerged out of the water as far as his waist, and grabbing hold of the
stern of the ship with a firm hand he called out to them in their
excitement:

'Why do you seek to take bold Herakles to the city of Aietes
against the will of great Zeus? It is his destiny to accomplish at
Argos all twelve labours for cruel Eurystheus, at the cost of great
suffering, and then to share the feasts of the immortals when once he
has achieved the few labours which remain. Waste no regrets upon
him. Polyphemos too is destined to found a glorious city for the
Mysians at the mouth of the Kios and then to end his days in the
vast land of the Chalybes. As for Hylas, on account of whom these
two wandered off and were left behind, a divine nymph has out of
love made him her husband.'

With these words he dived down and disappeared in the vast
cloak of the waters. Around him eddies seethed and foamed, and the
ship was driven through the waters which the god had parted. The
heroes rejoiced, and Telamon, son of Aiakos, went straight to Jason
and, taking hold of his fingers, embraced him and said:

'Do not be angry with me, son of Aison, if I have committed a
foolish mistake; great grief made me say terrible things which had
been better left unsaid. But let us remain friends as before, and let
the winds carry my error away.'

With good sense did the son of Aison reply:

'Good friend, harsh indeed were your wounding words when, in
front of all these men, you said that I had wronged an excellent hero.
But though I felt pain then, I shall not nurse a bitter wrath, since it
was not for flocks of sheep or possessions that you raged in anger,
but rather for a man who was your comrade. I hope that you would
fight like this with another for my sake, should such an occasion ever
arise again.'

After these words they both sat down, reconciled as before.

As for the two who were left behind by the plans of Zeus, Polyphemos, son of Eilatos, was destined to build a city for the Mysians which would bear the name of their river,* and Herakles to return to complete the labours of Eurystheus. He threatened to lay waste at once to the Mysian land unless they could bring him news of whether Hylas was dead or alive. As a pledge of good faith, they gave him as hostages the finest sons chosen from among the people and they swore never to abandon their efforts to find Hylas. For this reason the Kians still to this day search for Hylas, son of Theiodamas, and they take an interest in well-built Trachis.* For it was there that Herakles settled the young hostages whom the Mysians gave over to him.

All day and all night a strong wind carried the *Argo* on, but as first light appeared the wind had dropped completely. When they made out a coastline which apparently projected a long way into the gulf, they rowed towards it and put in there at sunrise.

BOOK 2

There were the cattle-stalls and pens of Amykos, proud king of the Bebrykians, whom a nymph, Bithynian Melie, had borne to Poseidon Genethlios with whom she had lain.* He was the most outrageous of men, and even upon strangers he had imposed a shameless ordinance: no one might depart before trying his luck against the king in boxing, and many men from neighbouring territories had thus met their end. On this occasion, too, when he came down to the ship he arrogantly scorned to enquire of their mission and their identity, but at once addressed them as follows:

'Listen, you sea-wanderers, to things which it is proper for you to know. It is the law that no stranger who has come to the land of the Bebrykians may depart until he has lifted up his hands in combat against mine. Therefore choose the best man* from among you all and set him to box against me here and now. If you choose to ignore and trample upon my laws, you will find that the consequences will be grim and violent.'

So he spoke in his haughtiness. Wild anger seized the Argonauts when they heard, and the threats struck Polydeukes most of all. At once he stood as his comrades' champion and replied:

'Enough! Do not practise your wretched brutishness upon us, whoever you claim to be. We shall fall in with your laws, as you have stated them. I myself now willingly undertake to fight you.'

So he spoke without hesitation. Amykos turned his eyes and stared at him, like a lion which has been wounded by a spear and is surrounded by hunters on the mountain; it has no interest in them though pressed by a great throng, but its eyes stare only at that man alone who struck first without killing.

Then the son of Tyndareos took off his robe; it was finely woven, of delicate work; one of the Lemnian women had given it to him to mark their friendship. For his part, Amykos threw down his dark double cloak, together with its brooches, and the staff of rough mountain-olive which he carried. In a moment they had found a suitable place nearby, and made all their companions sit down in two groups on the sand. To look upon, Amykos and Polydeukes were quite different in physique and stature. One was like the monstrous offspring of awful Typhoeus* or even one of the children whom Gaia herself once bore in her anger against Zeus. But the other, of the line of Tyndareos, was like that star in the heavens whose sparkling rays are brightest as it rises through the darkness of evening.* Such was the son of Zeus, his first beard still soft, his eyes shining; but his strength and might swelled like those of a wild beast. He moved his arms to test whether they were still supple as of old and had not been completely wearied by toilsome rowing. Amykos for his part carried out no tests, but stood some distance away, silently staring at Polydeukes; his heart throbbed in his desire to make the blood flow from his opponent's chest. In the space between them Amykos' servant, Lykoreus, placed two sets of raw leather thongs which had been dried to a terrible hardness. Then Amykos addressed his opponent with words of disdain:

'I willingly grant you whichever you want, without the need for a lot, so that you will have no cause to blame me afterwards. Put them on your arms! When you have learned your lesson, you will be able to tell others of my surpassing skill at cutting the dried hide of bulls and smearing the cheeks of men with blood.'

So he spoke. The other made no abusive retort, but smiling calmly, he at once picked up the thongs which lay by his feet. Kastor and mighty Talaos, son of Bias, came up to him and quickly tied the thongs, offering many words of encouragement for the battle ahead. Aretos and Ornytos did the same for Amykos: poor fools, they did not know that that was the last time an evil fate would allow them to tie on the thongs.

When they had each separately been equipped with thongs, they put up their heavy fists in front of their faces and came fiercely to meet each other. Then the king of the Bebrykians—like a jagged sea-wave which rears up to confront a swift ship, and the ship barely manages to survive, thanks to the skill of the clever steersman, as the sea surges to break over the deck—just so did Amykos ceaselessly harry the son of Tyndareos and allowed him no respite, while Polydeukes used his cleverness to escape unhurt from all the rushing attacks. Quickly he sized up Amykos' crude method of fighting, both its strengths and weaknesses, and he stood his ground, swapping blow for blow. As when carpenters hit their mallets against ship timbers which resist as the sharp pegs are driven into them and countless ringing blows sound out over each other, just so on both sides was heard the thud of cheeks and jaws and a terrible shattering of teeth. They did not call a halt to the exchange of wounds until both were overcome by breathlessness and exhaustion. Standing a little distance apart, they wiped the pouring sweat from their faces, panting with weariness. Then they rushed at each other again, like a pair of bulls angrily disputing for a grazing heifer. Amykos stretched himself up on his toes like a man going to slaughter an ox, and crashed his heavy fist down on his opponent; Polydeukes, however, withstood the assault by tilting his head to one side, and the blow just struck his shoulder. He then stepped close to his opponent by swinging his leg forward, and with a sudden assault struck him above the ear, shattering the bones inside his head. Amykos fell forward on his knees in pain; the Minyan heroes gave a shout of triumph, and Amykos' life-spirit dissolved in an instant.

   The Bebrykians did not neglect their king, but in a great mass they advanced upon Polydeukes brandishing hard clubs and hunting-spears. His comrades drew their sharp swords from their scabbards and placed themselves in front of Polydeukes. First Kastor struck Aner* in the head as he rushed to attack; his head was split in two and the halves dropped down onto his shoulders. Polydeukes himself faced the monstrous Itymoneus and Mimas. The latter he charged and knocked into the dust with a swift kick under the chest; as the other approached, he hit him with his right fist above the left eye, tearing off the lid and leaving the eyeball exposed. Oreites, Amykos' grim and violent attendant, wounded Talaos, son of Bias, in the side. He did not kill him, however, as the bronze spear pierced his belt and grazed only his skin without entering the vital parts. So too Aretos wielded his solid club against Iphitos, the steadfast son of Eurytos, who was not yet doomed to a wretched end. Indeed Aretos himself was very soon to fall to the sword of Klytios. Ankaios also, the bold son of Lykourgos, snatched up his mighty axe and leaped to the attack in the midst of the Bebrykians; in his left hand he held out his dark bearskin as protection. With him rushed the sons of Aiakos, and with them too raced the warrior Jason. As when on a winter's day the sudden attack of grey wolves causes panic among countless sheep in their stalls; the wolves have slipped by the keen-scented dogs and the shepherds also, and as they search for the first victim their gaze roams everywhere, while the sheep stumble over each other as they are hemmed in on every side—just so did the Argonauts cause grim panic in the insolent Bebrykians. As when herdsmen or beekeepers smoke out a great swarm of bees from a rock, and for a while the bees buzz furiously in confusion in the hive, but finally, overcome by the murky smoke, they dash out of the rock—just so the Bebrykians did not stand their ground for long, but scattered throughout their territory, bearing the news of Amykos' death. The poor fools did not know what other unexpected misfortune was close at hand! On that day their fields and villages were ravaged by the hostile forces of Lykos and the Mariandynoi who took advantage of the king's absence; for they were constantly in dispute with the Bebrykians about the iron-bearing land. The heroes now raided the stalls and cattle-pens, and rounded up a great flock of sheep and drove them off. This was how they talked among themselves:

'Imagine what these cowards would have done, if by chance the gods had brought Herakles here with us! If he had been here, there would, I think, have been no boxing-match. As soon as Amykos came to announce his laws, Herakles' club would have made him forget both his laws and his arrogance! Ah, thoughtlessly did we leave him on land when we set off over the sea; without him, each and every one of us will come to know grim destruction.'

So they spoke, but everything had come to pass through the plans of Zeus. As darkness came on, they remained where they were, tending the wounds of the injured; after sacrificing to the immortals, they prepared a great feast, and the pleasures of the mixing-bowl and the burning victims did not allow anyone to sleep. On the shore the boat was tied to a laurel tree;* they plucked its leaves to crown their fair brows, and in harmony sang a hymn to the accompaniment of Orpheus' lyre. All around in the windless air the coast rejoiced in their song. It was the Therapnaian son of Zeus* whom they celebrated.

When the rising of the sun from the horizon had lit up the dewy peaks and caused the shepherds to stir, the Argonauts untied the ropes from the base of the laurel tree, put on board as much booty as was needed, and set off under sail through the eddying Bosporos.

There a monstrous wave rears up in front of a ship like a soaring mountain; it threatens to crash down as it towers high over the clouds.* You would imagine that there was no escape from a miserable fate, as the violent wave hangs like a cloud over the middle of the ship; the wave drops, however, when confronted by an excellent steersman. So it was that the Argonauts proceeded by the skill of Tiphys, unharmed though terrified. On the following day, they tied their ropes to the Thynian coast across from the Bebrykians.

On the coast there dwelt Phineus, son of Agenor, who of all men had endured the most grievous sufferings because of the power of prophecy which the son of Leto had once bestowed upon him. He had not the slightest thought even for Zeus himself as he unerringly revealed to men the god's holy mind. Therefore Zeus sent a long old age upon him and took away the sweet light of his eyes. Nor did he allow Phineus to enjoy the innumerable good things which neighbours always brought to his house when they came to ask for oracles, but without warning the Harpies* would ever swoop down through the clouds and with their claws snatch the food from his mouth and hands. Sometimes they left behind nothing at all, sometimes just a little so that he could stay alive in his wretchedness. Moreover, they poured a foul stench over his food, so that no one could bear even to stand a long way off, let alone bring it to their mouths, so powerful was the rank smell of what was left of the meal.

As soon as Phineus heard the crew's voices and the sound of their approach, he realized that the men who were passing were the very ones at whose arrival it was decreed by Zeus that he should enjoy the food set before him. Like a ghostly dream he got up from his bed, and supporting himself on a staff, made his way to the door on withered feet, feeling along the walls. His limbs shook with the feebleness of old age, his dessicated flesh was caked with filth; there was nothing behind his skin but bones. He came out of his dwelling, and sank down on his weary knees at the threshold of the court. A dark dizziness enveloped him, the earth beneath seemed to him to revolve, and he sank into a helpless torpor, unable to speak. When the Argonauts saw him, they gathered round in amazement. Gasping and struggling for breath, he spoke to them in prophecy:

'Hear me, most glorious of the Panhellenes, if indeed you are the ones who, at the chilling command of a king, are led by Jason on the ship *Argo* in search of a fleece—it is certainly you. In its prophetic wisdom my mind still knows every detail; even in the midst of grim troubles, O lord, son of Leto, I bestow thanks upon you. By Zeus, protector of suppliants, who is most terrible to men who sin, in the name of Phoibos and for the sake of Hera herself, who of all gods is most protective of you in your journey, I beg you, help me, save an unfortunate man from outrage and do not in scorn sail away and abandon me. The Fury has trampled upon my eyes and my old age drags out with no prospect of an end. But this is not all. On top of all my miseries another misery, most bitter of all, hangs over me. The Harpies swoop down from some invisible lair and snatch the food from my mouth. I can think of no device which would help, but when I desire to eat I could more easily deceive my own mind than them—so quickly do they dart through the air. If ever they do leave me a scrap, the power of its stench is foul and unendurable. No mortal could bear to come near it even for a moment, not even if his heart was forged with adamant. But bitter, insatiable necessity compels me to remain and thus feed my wretched stomach. It is decreed by the gods that the sons of Boreas will chase them away. It will not be as total strangers that they will act to protect me, as certainly as I am Phineus, once famous among men for my prosperity and powers of prophecy; my father was Agenor, and when I ruled over the Thracians I won their sister Kleopatra with a bride-price and brought her to my home as my wife.'

The son of Agenor fell silent, and each of the heroes was seized by a deep grief, but particularly the two sons of Boreas. Wiping away their tears, they drew close to him in his grief; Zetes grasped the old man's hand, and addressed him as follows:

'Poor man, no mortal, I think, has suffered more terribly than you. Why have you been afflicted with so many woes? It was wretched thoughtlessness which led you to sin against the gods through your knowledge of prophecy: it is for this that they are greatly angered. As for us, however—if a god has certainly set this honour before us, then we are eager to help, though our minds within us tremble; for the ways in which the immortals rebuke mankind are clear to all. Despite our strong desire, we shall not chase off the Harpies when they come until you swear that in so doing we will not incur the displeasure of the gods.'

So he spoke. The old man opened wide his useless eyes and raising them towards Zetes answered in the following words:

'Silence! Let not your mind imagine such things, my child. Be witness the son of Leto who in his kindness taught me the art of prophecy; be witness the grim Fate to which I have been allotted, this black cloud over my eyes, and the spirits below—may they show me no kindness after death if I break my oath—that no divine anger will arise from the help you give.'

These oaths fired their desire to rid him of the Harpies. Without delay the younger heroes prepared a feast for the old man—it was to be the Harpies' final prey. The Boreads stood nearby so that they could drive them away with their swords when they swooped down. At the very moment the old man touched the meal, the Harpies leapt down from the clouds without warning, like sudden storms or flashes of lightning, and attacked with a rush, screaming in their lust for food. The heroes cried out at the sight of them, but the Harpies devoured everything and with a cry flew off far away over the sea, leaving behind an intolerable stench. In pursuit of them raced the two sons of Boreas, their swords drawn. Zeus granted them unwearying strength, for without Zeus' help they could not have followed after the Harpies who would always outstrip the blasts of the Zephyr on their journeys to and from Phineus. As when on mountain-sides dogs skilled in hunting race along as they track horned goats or deer, and straining just behind their prey gnash together the teeth at the front of their jaws, but to no effect; like this did Zetes and Kalais sprint very close to the Harpies, just touching them vainly with the tips of their fingers. Against the gods' wishes they would have torn the Harpies apart when they caught them far away at the Floating Islands ['*Plotai*'],* had not swift Iris seen and leapt down through the sky from heaven. She checked them and turned aside their anger thus:

'Sons of Boreas, it is not permitted by the gods to kill the Harpies, the dogs of great Zeus, with your swords. I myself shall swear that they will never visit Phineus again.'

So saying she swore by a libation of Styx water,* which for all the gods is the most terrible and most sanctified, that the Harpies would never again approach the dwelling of Phineus, son of Agenor. This too was decreed by fate. The Boreads were satisfied with the oath and turned around to hurry back to the ship. For this reason men now call those islands the Turning Islands ['*Strophades*'], whereas previously they had been called the Floating Islands. The Harpies and Iris parted: they entered a deep cave on Minoan Crete, and she sprang aloft on swift wings to return to Olympos.

In the meantime the heroes had washed all the filth off the old man's body and had sacrificed sheep chosen from among the plunder from Amykos. Then they prepared a great feast in the hall, and sat down to dine. Phineus dined with them—greedily, satisfying his desire as we do in dreams. When they had had enough of eating and drinking, they stayed awake through the night waiting for the sons of Boreas. The old man himself sat in their midst by the hearth, and told them about the paths they must sail and how to accomplish the journey:

'Listen to me now. It is not permitted by the gods that you should know everything accurately, but what they wish you to know, I shall not conceal from you. On a previous occasion I thoughtlessly committed a foolish act by revealing the mind of Zeus in all its particulars through to the end. It is his wish that prophecy should reveal the decrees of the gods only incompletely, so that men are always ignorant of some part of the gods' purpose.

'When you depart from me, you will first see the Dark Rocks, two of them, where the sea narrows. I tell you that no one has ever succeeded in passing through them. They are not firmly fixed with deep roots, but clash together constantly, and above them a great mass of sea-water seethes and boils, while all around the rocky shore resounds with a harsh roaring. Therefore follow my advice, if indeed you are travelling with prudence and respect for the blessed gods. Do not thoughtlessly rush on in the enthusiasm of youth to bring death upon yourselves. I bid you first of all let a dove fly far from the ship to test the way as a sign. If on her wings she passes safely through these rocks and reaches the Pontos, then hold back no longer from making the journey yourselves. Grasp the oars in the strong grip of your hands and cut through the narrow channel of the sea, since success will depend not so much on your prayers as on the strength of your arms. Abandon all other concerns and exert yourselves to the utmost, and with confidence. Up until this point I do not forbid you from calling upon the gods. If, however, the dove perishes between the rocks as she flies through, turn back, as it is much better to give way before the gods: you could not then escape from grim destruction by the rocks, even if the *Argo* were made of iron. Unhappy men, do not recklessly ignore my god-sent advice, even if you believe me to be thrice as accursed and hateful—or even more—to the gods of heaven than I am. Do not recklessly ignore the bird-sign and travel further in your ship.

'This then will turn out as it may. If you succeed in escaping from the clash of the rocks and reach the Pontos safe and sound, then proceed* with the land of the Bithynians on your right—taking care to avoid reefs—until, after passing the mouth of the swift-flowing Rhebas and the Black Promontory,* you reach the harbour of the island Thynias.* Continuing from there a short distance over the sea, you will put in at the land of the Mariandynoi on the opposite coast. There is a path which descends to Hades, and the Acherousian headland* rears aloft; down below, the swirling Acheron cuts through the headland itself and disgorges its waters from a gaping cavern. Not far from here you will pass by the many mountain-peaks of the Paphlagones; Enetean Pelops* was their first king, and they boast of being his descendants. There is a headland opposite the Bear Helike, sheer on all sides, and men call it Karambis;* above it the gusts of Boreas split apart, for on the sea side it reaches the sky. When one has rounded this, the Great Shore stretches out. At the end of the Great Shore there is a headland beside which the stream of the river Halys* empties out with a terrible roar. Not far away the stream of the Iris,* a smaller river, rolls into the sea in white eddies. Further on from there the great 'Elbow' rises up and juts out from the mainland. After that comes the mouth of the Thermodon,* lying in a calm bay under the headland of Themiskyra; the river has reached that point after its journey through a vast land. There is the plain of Doias, and nearby are the three cities of the Amazons; after this come the most toilsome of men, the Chalybes, labourers who own a harsh and unyielding land where they mine and work iron. Not far away, beyond the Genetaian headland of Zeus, protector of guests, live the Tibarenoi who are rich in flocks. Their immediate neighbours are the

Mossynoikoi who dwell in the adjoining wooded plain and the hills. They build wooden houses on structures made of planks and solid towers called 'mossynai'; this is the source of their name.

'Pass by these people and put in at a rugged island,* using a cunning ploy to drive off the awful birds which haunt that deserted place in their countless thousands. While on campaign the Amazon queens, Otrere and Antiope, built a stone shrine to Ares on the island. There help will come to you from the grim sea—help about which I must remain silent. So it is with kindly intention that I tell you to halt at the island. But why must I sin again by prophesying every detail in full sequence?

'Beyond the island and the mainland opposite live the Philyres; beyond them are the Makrones, and after that the vast tribes of the Becheires. In order after them come the Sapeires, whose neighbours are the Byzeres, and beyond them finally are the warlike Colchians themselves. Continue in your ship until you reach the furthest recess of the Pontos where the swirling Phasis empties its broad stream into the sea through the Kytaian land* as it arrives from the Amarantian mountains far away and the plain of Kirke. On entering the mouth of that river, you will see the towers belonging to Kytaian Aietes and the shaded grove of Ares, where the fleece hangs on the top of an oak tree and is guarded on all sides by a watchful dragon—a monster terrible to behold! Neither by day nor in the darkness are its awful eyes overcome by sweet sleep.'

Such was his speech, and fear at once gripped his audience. For a long time they were downcast and unable to speak. Finally, seeing no way out of this terrible situation, Aison's heroic son spoke:

'Aged sire, you have related the paths we must sail and the sign we must obey in order to pass through the hateful rocks and reach the Pontos. But I would gladly know from you also whether we will be able to return back again to Greece once we have escaped from these rocks. How can I accomplish this? How can I make such a long sea-journey for a second time? I have no experience, and neither do my companions, and Colchian Aia lies pressed against the very edge of Pontos and of the earth.'

So he spoke, and the old man addressed him in answer:

'Once you have safely passed through the deadly rocks, my child, have confidence: god will guide you on a different route back from

Aia, and there will be escorts enough on your way there. But, my friends, look to the Kyprian goddess* for cunning help: upon her rests the glorious success of your trials. Now ask me about these things no more!'

So spoke the son of Agenor. Just then the two sons of Thracian Boreas darted down through the air and landed with their swift feet on the threshold. The heroes leapt up from their seats when they saw that they had returned. Breathing heavily from his efforts, Zetes answered their eager enquiries by telling them how far they had driven the Harpies, how the goddess Iris had prevented them from killing them and had sworn an oath out of goodwill, and how in fear the Harpies had gone down into the great cave on the Diktaian crag.* All the comrades in the house and Phineus himself rejoiced at the news; full of kindness towards the old man, the son of Aison quickly addressed him:

'There was indeed then some god caring for you, Phineus, in your grim wretchedness, and he brought us here from afar, so that the sons of Boreas might help you. If he would also grant light to your eyes, then I think that I would rejoice as much as if I had succeeded in returning back to my home.'

So he spoke, but the other, his eyes lowered in despondency, replied:

'Son of Aison, what has happened cannot be undone, nor will there be any remedy in the future, for my empty eyes are slowly wasting away. But rather I ask god to grant me death now, and in death I will find complete happiness.'

So the two of them spoke, one with another, until soon, while they were still conversing, the Early-Born appeared.* Phineus' neighbours gathered around him. Before this they would visit him regularly every day and always bring him a portion of their food; to all of them, even the most humble, he gave his prophecies kindly, and his skill put an end to the troubles of many. Therefore they used to come to look after him. Among them was Paraibios, who was dearest of all to Phineus, and he was glad to find the Argonauts in the house; in earlier times Phineus had once told him that an expedition of heroes which had set out from Hellas to make for the city of Aietes would tie its ropes to the Thynian land and, by Zeus' will, would put an end to the assaults of the Harpies. The old man satisfied his visitors with

his wise counsel and then sent them away, but Paraibios alone he
bade remain there with the heroes. Soon, however, he sent him off to
bring back the very best sheep from his own flocks, and when he had
left the hall, Phineus addressed the assembled company with gentle
words:

'My friends, not everyone tramples on others and forgets
kindnesses: such a one is this man who came here to learn of his fate.
For he laboured and toiled to his very limit, but his poverty ever
rapidly increased and ground him down; day upon day his situation
grew worse, and there was no respite to his labours. In fact he was
paying a wretched penalty for his father's mistake. Once upon a
time when his father was alone in the mountains cutting down trees,
he paid no heed to the pleas of a Hamadryad nymph who wept as
she sorrowfully tried to persuade him not to cut the trunk of the
coeval oak in which she had always lived her long life. But in the
insolence of youth he thoughtlessly felled it, and so the nymph sent a
joyless fate upon him and his children for the future. When he came
here, I realized the nature of the offence, and told him to build an
altar to the Thynian nymph and on it to perform sacrifices of
expiation, asking her to release him from his father's doom. After
escaping the fate which the gods had decreed for him, he has never
forgotten or neglected me. I have difficulty in getting him to go
away, as he wants always to stay to help me in my distress.'

So spoke the son of Agenor, and at that moment Paraibios
reappeared bringing two sheep from the flock. At the old man's
bidding, Jason and the two sons of Boreas stood up to assist, and as
the day drew to a close they sacrificed at the hearth, calling on
Apollo, god of prophecy. The younger men among the crew
prepared a splendid meal, and when they had dined well, they all
retired to bed, some beside the cables of the ship, and some right
there in Phineus' house.

In the morning the Etesian winds* had got up; these blow equally
over every land, as a result of assistance which Zeus once sent.
Among men of an earlier age, it is said, a girl called Kyrene grazed
her flocks beside the marshes of Peneios.* She wished to remain a
virgin and to keep her bed undefiled, but once when she had her
flocks beside the river Apollo snatched her up and, carrying her far
from Haimonia, handed her over to the protection of the nymphs of

the land who lived beside the Hill of Myrtles* in Libya. There she bore Phoibos a son, Aristaios, whom the inhabitants of Haimonia, rich in grain, call Agreus and Nomios.* In his affection for her, the god made her there a long-lived nymph and huntress, but he took her baby son to be brought up in the cave of Cheiron. When the child had grown up, the divine Muses sought out a wife for him, and taught him the arts of healing and prophecy; they also made him keeper of their flocks which grazed the Athamantian plain of Phthia, around sheer Othrys and the sacred stream of the river Apidanos. When Sirius was burning the islands of Minos* with its fire from heaven and for a long time the inhabitants had found no relief, then the Far-Darter advised them to summon Aristaios to save them from the pestilence. At his father's bidding Aristaios left Phthia and settled in Keos, having gathered together the Parrhasian people who are descended from the race of Lykaon.* He built a large altar to Zeus, god of rain, and in due order performed sacrifices on the mountains to Sirius and to Zeus himself, son of Kronos. For this reason, the Etesian winds which Zeus sends cool the earth for forty days, and to this day on Keos priests make offerings before the rising of the Dog-Star. This is the story which men tell. The heroes were thus constrained to remain where they were, and every day the people of Thynia showed gratitude to Phineus by sending him countless gifts.

After this they built an altar to the twelve blessed gods on the sea-coast opposite, and sacrificed upon it; they then embarked on the swift ship to row further. They did not forget to take a timid dove with them; Euphemos caught it and held it cowering in fear in his hand. They untied the double cables from the land, and their departure did not go unnoticed by Athena. Without delay she leapt on to a light cloud which could bear her great weight swiftly, and hastened towards the Pontos to bring welcome help to the rowers. As when a man who wanders far from his own land*—as indeed we wretched men often do wander, and no land seems distant, but all paths are spread before us—can picture his own home, and as he sees in a flash the path there over land and sea, his thoughts dart quickly and his eyes grasp one place after another, just so did the daughter of Zeus swiftly leap down and place her feet on the Thynian coast of the Inhospitable Sea.*

When they had reached the narrow opening of the winding strait, tightly formed by harsh rocks on both sides, the swirling rush of water surged around the ship as it proceeded, and they voyaged in great fear, for the roar of the rocks crashing together was already a constant din in their ears and the sea-battered cliffs echoed with the noise. Then Euphemos took a position on the prow with the dove in his hand, and the others, taking their instructions from Tiphys son of Hagnias, rowed at a quiet pace in order that they might afterwards have the strength to force the boat through the rocks. As they rounded the last bend, they suddenly caught sight of the rocks opening up, and all their spirits ebbed away. Euphemos sent off the dove to race on its wings, and all of the Argonauts lifted their heads to watch. The bird flew between the rocks which came together again with a great crash; a huge body of spray was thrown up like a cloud, the sea gave a terrible roar, and all around the limitless sky resounded. As the sea surged around the harsh rocks, hollow sea-caves boomed within, and the white foam from the thundering wave was hurled high above the cliffs.

Then the current around it took hold of the ship. The rocks caught the end-feathers from the dove's tail, but it escaped safe and the rowers gave a great shout. Tiphys himself screamed at them to row with all their might, for the rocks were opening up again. They rowed in trembling fear until the back-wave on its return washed them into the midst of the rocks. Then the most awful terror seized all of them, for unavoidable destruction hung over their heads. Beyond the rocks they could now see all around the broad expanse of the Pontos, but suddenly a huge, arching wave like a sheer mountain-peak reared up in front of them. When they saw it they lowered their heads and turned away, for it seemed certain to crash down and cover the whole ship; Tiphys, however, eased off on the ship which was struggling under the oars, and the brunt of the wave's force rolled under the keel. It then seized the stern and dragged the ship far from the rocks, carrying it aloft on its surge. Euphemos went among all the companions shouting at them to put all their force into their oars, and they gave a cry as they beat the water. Whatever progress the rowers made, the ship was thrown back twice as far by the surge; as the heroes laboured, their oars bent like curved bows. Then suddenly a wave rushed upon them from the

opposite direction, and like a runaway boulder the ship was tossed
on the wild wave ever further through the hollow sea. The eddying
current held her in the midst of the Clashing Rocks; on both sides
the Rocks shook and thundered, and the timbers of the ship could
not move. Then Athena took hold of a mighty cliff with her left
hand, and with her right she shoved the ship between the Rocks.
Like a feathered arrow it shot through the air, and as the Rocks
clashed violently together they broke off the tip of the stern-
ornament. Athena leapt up to Olympos, after the safe escape of the
crew, but the Rocks were firmly locked together and rooted in one
spot forever; for it was fated by the blessed gods that this would
happen whenever any man had survived the voyage through them.

After their release from chilling fear, the Argonauts no doubt
breathed more easily as they gazed at the sky and the broad expanse
of sea spread out before them, for it seemed that they had been saved
from Hades. Tiphys was the very first to speak:

'I believe that it is due to our ship that we have come safely
through this danger at least. The responsibility is none other than
Athena's, who breathed divine strength into the *Argo* at the time
when Argos fitted her together with bolts; thus the gods do not
permit her destruction. Son of Aison, no longer have such fear of
your king's order now that a god has granted us safe passage
through the rocks; Phineus, son of Agenor, said that after this we
would successfully accomplish our challenges.'

As he spoke he drove the ship forward through the middle of the
sea, following the Bithynian coast. But Jason answered him with soft
words:*

'Tiphys, why do you offer me these consolations in my grief? I
have erred; my wretched folly offers no remedy. When Pelias gave
his instruction, I should have immediately refused this expedition
outright, even if it meant a cruel death, torn apart limb from limb.
As it is I am in constant terror and my burdens are unendurable; I
loathe sailing in our ship over the chill paths of the sea, and I loathe
our stops on dry land, for all around are our enemies. Ever since you
all first assembled for my sake, I have endured a ceaseless round of
painful nights and days, for I must give thought to every detail. You
can speak lightly, as your worries are only for yourself. I have no
anxiety at all for myself, but I must fear for this man and that, for

you no less than for all our other companions, that I shall be unable to bring you back unharmed to Greece.'

So he spoke, testing the heroes, and they all shouted words of encouragement. At their urging, his heart within was warmed and he spoke to them without concealment:*

'My friends, I am given new confidence by your courage. Since you are so steadfast in the midst of grim terrors, I shall no longer be afraid, even if I must journey through the deep pits of Hades. Now that we have sailed through the Clashing Rocks, I think we shall never confront another such terror in the future, as long as we travel in accordance with Phineus' wise advice.'

So he spoke, and ceasing from such talk, they turned to the unremitting labour of rowing. Soon they passed by the swift stream of the river Rhebas and the peak of Kolone,* and not long afterwards the Black Promontory, and after it the mouth of the Phyllis. There in former times Dipsakos received the son of Athamas in his house when he was fleeing on the ram from the city of Orchomenos. Dipsakos' mother was a nymph of the meadows, and he had no liking for wanton violence, but lived quietly with his mother and grazed his flocks on the banks of his father's waters. As the Argonauts went past, they saw his shrine and the broad banks of the river, the plain, and the deep-flowing Kalpe. After the day ended, they laboured no less mightily with unwearying oars all through the windless night which followed. As when working cattle strain to cut a furrow in damp plough-land, and sweat pours in streams from their flanks and necks—their eyes turn to look sideways under the yoke, parched breath snorts ceaselessly from their mouths, and they force their hooves into the ground as they struggle all day long—like this did the heroes drag their oars up through the sea.

At the time when the immortal sunlight has not yet appeared, but it is no longer quite dark and a faint gleam has pierced the night—the time which those waking call *amphilyke**—at that hour they entered the harbour of the deserted island of Thynias and stepped on to the land, completely worn out by their efforts. The son of Leto, travelling afar from Lykia to the countless race of the Hyperboreans, appeared to them. On both sides of his face golden curls like bunches of grapes waved as he proceeded; in his left hand he carried a silver bow, and his quiver was slung around his back from the shoulder. Under his feet the whole island shook and waves washed over the dry land. At the sight of him the Argonauts were struck helpless with amazement; no one dared to look directly into the god's brilliant eyes, but they stood looking down at the ground, and he passed through the air far away out to sea. After a long silence Orpheus finally addressed the heroes as follows:

'Come, let us call this the holy island of Apollo of the Dawn, because he appeared to all of us here on his dawn journey; let us build an altar to him on the shore and make what sacrifice we can. If later he grants us safe return to the Haimonian land, then we shall offer to him the thighs of horned goats. For the moment I bid you seek to please him with savour of sacrifice and libations. Be gracious, O lord, be gracious in your appearance!'

So he spoke. Some of them at once built an altar out of stones, while others scoured the island to see whether they could find any deer or wild goats, such as frequently graze in the deep forests. The son of Leto granted them a successful hunt, and on the holy altar they solemnly burnt two thighs from each animal while calling upon Apollo of the Dawn. As the meat burned, they arrayed a broad dance in celebration of the brilliant Phoibos, the *Iepaiion Iepaiion*.* With them the noble son of Oiagros sang a clear song to the accompaniment of his Bistonian lyre.* He sang how once at the foot of the rocky ridge of Parnassos the god killed the monstrous Delphyne* with his bow, when a young boy still in his nakedness, still rejoicing in long curls—be gracious, please! Eternally, lord, your hair is uncut, eternally it remains unravaged. So does holy law proclaim, for only Leto herself, daughter of Koios, may hold it in her dear hands—and the Korykian nymphs,* daughters of Pleistos, urged him on, shouting '*Hie, hie*'; this is the source of Phoibos' lovely title. When the Argonauts had celebrated the god with dance and song, they poured solemn libations and, laying hands upon the victims, swore that they would forever help each other in concord of mind. Even to this day there stands the shrine of kindly Homonoia which at that time they built to honour the most glorious divinity.

When the third day came, they left the steep island, taking advantage of a strong west wind, and sailed further, observing as they passed the mouth of the river Sangarios* on the coast opposite, the rich and fertile land of the Mariandynoi, and the streams of the Lykos and Lake Anthemoeisis. The cables and all the ship's tackle shook as they proceeded in the breeze. The wind dropped during the night and at dawn they were pleased to reach the harbour of the Acherousian headland,* whose beetling cliffs overlook the Bithynian sea; below it stand rocks beaten smooth by the sea, and around them waves break with a great thundering. High above, spreading plane-trees grow on the very peak. Down from the headland a hollow glade inclines away toward the interior. Here, covered over by foliage and rocks, is a cave of Hades, from whose chill depths a freezing vapour forever rises to create a brilliant white frost which grows warm in the midday sun. Around that dread headland there is never silence, only the unending groan of the beating sea and the sound of leaves rustling in the draughts which rise from deep within the earth. Here too is the mouth of the river Acheron which travels through the headland to be disgorged into the Eastern Sea;* a hollowed ravine is its path from the summit. In more recent times, the Nisaian Megarians* gave the river the name Soonautes* at the time when they were about to settle in the land of the Mariandynoi. The river saved them and their ships when they were taken by a nasty storm, for when the wind dropped they were able to bring their ship to land there by entering the river and the shelter of the Acherousian headland.

The ruler of that area, Lykos, and the Mariandynoi soon realized that the Argonauts had moored in their territory, for their fame as the destroyers of Amykos had preceded them. Indeed for this very reason the Mariandynoi came from all directions to make alliance with them, and they hailed Polydeukes as a god, since they had long been in a state of war with the overbearing Bebrykians. In one body then they quickly proceeded to the city and spent that day in Lykos' palace, enjoying a feast in friendship and taking pleasure in each other's stories. The son of Aison told Lykos of the lineage and name of each of his companions, of Pelias' instructions, of how they had been entertained by the Lemnian women, of all they had done at Dolonian Kyzikos, and of how they reached Mysia and the Kios where they unwittingly abandoned the hero Herakles. He reported Glaukos' prediction and how they had killed the Bebrykians and Amykos, and described Phineus' prophecies and his suffering, and

how they had escaped from the Dark Rocks and encountered the son
of Leto on the island. As Lykos heard Jason's story unfold in due
order, his spirit was bewitched; but he felt grief at the abandonment
of Herakles, and spoke to all of them as follows:

'My friends, what a man it is whose assistance you have lost on
your vast journey to Aietes. I saw him here in the palace of my father
Daskylos and know him well. He came here on foot as he travelled
through the Asian continent to recover the girdle of the warrior
Hippolyte;* at the time my cheeks were just showing the first beard.
He took part then in the funeral games for my brother Priolas who
was killed by Mysians—our people still grieve for him with the most
pitiful lamentations; Herakles boxed against the mighty Titias who
surpassed all our young men in beauty and strength, and beat him,
knocking his teeth on to the ground. He brought under my father's
sovereignty not only the Mysians but the Mygdones, who dwell in
the territory bordering on ours, and he conquered the land and
peoples of Bithynia as far as the river Rhebas and the peak of
Kolone. Moreover the Paphlagonians who are descended from
Pelops and are surrounded by the dark water of the Billaios*
likewise yielded to him. But since Herakles has lived far away, the
Bebrykians and the outrages of Amykos have robbed me of this
territory; for a long time now they have plundered so much land that
they have extended their boundaries to the marshes of the deep-
flowing Hypios.* Now however they have met vengeance at your
hands. It was not, I believe, without divine blessing that I made war
on the Bebrykians on the very day, son of Tyndareos, on which you
slew that man. Therefore I shall now happily offer whatever return I
can, for this is what weak men should do when their betters provide
assistance unasked. I shall send my son Daskylos to accompany all
of you on your voyage, for with him on board you will enjoy a
hospitable welcome all along the coast as far as the very mouth of
the Thermodon. Moreover, high up on top of the Acherousian
headland, I shall build a shrine to the sons of Tyndareos; every
sailor on the sea will see it from afar and greet them reverently. For
the future I will set aside for them, as for gods, a fertile area of good
plough-land on the plain in front of the city.'

In this way they entertained each other all day long as they
feasted. In the morning they hastened to return to the ship; Lykos

gave them countless gifts and himself accompanied them on their way. He also dispatched his son from the palace to travel with them.

Then it was that fated destiny overtook Idmon, son of Abas and excellent prophet; his skill in prophecy did not save him, since necessity led him on to death. In the marshland formed by the reeds of the river lay a white-tusked boar, cooling its flanks and vast belly in the mud; it was a deadly beast which aroused alarm even in the nymphs of the swamp. No mortal knew that it was there, but it grazed alone in the broad wetlands. The son of Abas was walking along the bank of the muddy river, when the boar leapt up from his hidden lair and with a charge gored him in the thigh, cutting right through the sinews and the bone. With a piercing cry Idmon fell wounded to the ground, and all the others shouted in response. Peleus aimed his javelin at the deadly boar which had sped off in flight into the marsh. It rushed back at him, but Idas struck it and, with a terrible snarl, it impaled itself on the swift spear. They left it there on the ground where it had fallen, but Idmon—his life ebbing away—was carried by his grieving companions to the ship, and it was in his companions' arms that he died.

They had no more thought for sailing, but remained there distraught and prepared the funeral. They lamented for three whole days, and on the fourth they buried him with lavish honour; the Mariandynoi and King Lykos himself joined in the rites. Beside his tomb they slaughtered countless sheep as grave-offerings, in the manner appropriate for the dead. This man's tomb rises in that land a little below the Acherousian headland; as a marker visible to men of later generations, it is crowned by a ship's roller made from wild-olive and covered in abundant foliage. If, with the Muses' help, I must also tell without constraint of what follows, Phoibos instructed the Boiotians and the Nisaians* to pay honours to this man under the title 'Protector of the City' and to establish a city around this roller of ancient olive-wood; they, however, to this day glorify Agamestor rather than Idmon, the descendant of god-fearing Aiolos.

Who else died? Once more at that time the heroes raised up a tomb over a lost companion, and two markers of those men may still be seen. The story is that Tiphys, son of Hagnias, died; he was not fated to sail further. He too was laid to rest by a brief illness far from his home, after the crew had buried the corpse of the son of Abas. At this fatal disaster they were overwhelmed by grief beyond bearing. They buried Tiphys without delay, but then they sank down where they were on the shore in helpless despair, wrapped themselves in their cloaks, and lay still without thought for food or drink. Their hearts were depressed with sorrow, because all hope for a successful return seemed very far away. They would have delayed there in distress even longer, had not Hera put overmastering boldness into Ankaios; Astypalaia had borne him to Poseidon beside the Imbrasian waters,* and he was a steersman second to none. Rushing over to Peleus, he addressed him as follows:

'Son of Aiakos, how can it be to our credit to ignore the challenge we have undertaken and to sit idle in a foreign land? It was less as a skilled warrior that Jason brought me far from Parthenia in pursuit of the Fleece than as one knowledgeable about ships. Therefore have no fear at all about our ship. Moreover, there are other skilled men here; we may set any one of them upon the stern, and our sailing will suffer no harm. Convey this message of comfort to them quickly, and urge them with confidence to remember their challenge.'

So he spoke, and Peleus' heart was lifted with joy. Without delay he stood in their midst and addressed them all:

'My poor friends, who do we grieve to no purpose? Nothing will come of it. We may suppose these men to have perished as their allotted fate decreed, but we have many steersmen among our number. Therefore let us not hold back from making the attempt: cast grief aside, and stir yourselves to your task!'

The son of Aison answered him in helplessness:

'Son of Aiakos, where are these steersmen of yours? Those who before we proudly claimed as skilled are now downcast and deeper in despair than I myself. I predict disaster for us no less grim than what has befallen those who have died, if we neither reach the city of deadly Aietes nor return again through the rocks to the land of Hellas. Here a miserable fate will hide us from men's view, without glory, growing old and useless.'

So he spoke. With great eagerness Ankaios undertook to guide the swift ship, for his impulse came from a god. After him Erginos, Nauplios, and Euphemos sprang up, all keen to act as steersman; but the other comrades held them back and entrusted the task to Ankaios.

They embarked on the morning of the twelfth day, for a strong
west wind was blowing in their favour. They swiftly rowed out of the
Acheron and, confident in the wind, opened out the sail; as it
billowed out before them, they cut their way through the water,
blessed by fair weather. Quickly they passed the mouth of the river
Kallichoros, where men say that after leaving the peoples of India
for residence in Thebes, the Nysaian son of Zeus* held his rites and
established dances in front of the cave in which he lodged through
gloomy nights of ritual. From that time those who live in the area
have called the river 'Kallichoros' and the cave 'Aulion'.

Next they saw the tomb of Sthenelos,* son of Aktor, who died
there on the sea-shore from an arrow wound; he was returning from
the bold expedition against the Amazons on which he had
accompanied Herakles. The Argonauts proceeded no further, for
Persephone herself sent up the tearful shade of the son of Aktor, who
had begged her to be allowed to see his compatriots even for a short
while. Stepping upon the crest of the tomb he gazed out at the ship;
he looked as he did when he went to war, and his beautiful four-
horned helmet with its scarlet plumes gleamed afar. Then he
retreated back into the dark gloom, leaving the onlookers full of
amazement. Mopsos, the son of Ampykos, interpreted the divine
sign and told them to beach the ship and to appease the spirit with
libations. They at once furled the sail and moored the ship to the
beach, where they paid honour to Sthenelos' tomb with libations
and ritual burnt sacrifice of sheep. As well as these libations, they
built an altar to Apollo, the Saviour of Ships, and burnt thigh-bones
upon it. There Orpheus dedicated his lyre, and for this reason the
place bears the name 'Lyre'.

As the wind was strongly in their favour they quickly went on
board, let down the sail and stretched it tight by both sheets. The
ship sped powerfully out to sea, like a hawk which rides the breeze
swiftly through the high air as it spreads wide its wings; perfectly
still, it glides on motionless pinions. They passed the stream of the
Parthenios, most gentle of rivers as it flows into the sea; there, as she
climbs again from the hunt up to heaven, the daughter of Leto cools
her body in the lovely waters.* During the night they rushed
constantly forward and sailed by Sesamos and high Erythinoi,
Krobialos, Kromna, and wooded Kytoros.* After this they rounded

Karambis as the first rays of the sun appeared, and then they rowed along the Great Shore all day and all the following night. Soon after this they stepped on to Assyrian territory, where Zeus had settled Sinope, the daughter of Asopos, and had granted her perpetual virginity, after he had been deceived by his own promises. He desired to make love to her, and promised to give her whatever her heart desired; she then cunningly asked that he allow her to remain a virgin. In this same way she also fooled Apollo who wanted to sleep with her, and after them also the river Halys. No man ever took away her virginity in embraces full of desire. There too still lived the sons of noble Deimachos of Trikka—Deileon, Autolykos, and Phlogios—who had become separated from Herakles.* When they saw the expedition of heroic men, they came to them and told them truly who they were; they did not wish to remain on that coast any longer, but they embarked on the *Argo* as soon as the Argestes* blew.

With these men on board, the Argonauts were borne on by a stiff breeze and left behind the river Halys;* behind too fell the Iris which flowed nearby, and the alluvial coast of Assyria. On the same day they rounded at a distance the cape of the Amazons which protects a harbour. There the hero Herakles once ambushed Melanippe, daughter of Ares, when she had come on an expedition, and as a ransom for her sister, Hippolyte gave him her highly coloured girdle; Herakles then sent Melanippe back unharmed. They put in at the bay formed by this cape beside the mouth of the Thermodon,* since the swell was rising as they proceeded. No river is like the Thermodon, nor does any other divide into so many branches to cover the land as it flows into the sea. If someone were to count them all, he would find four short of a hundred. There is, however, in truth a single source, which descends to the plain from the high mountains called, so we are told, 'Amazonian'. From there it scatters through the higher terrain which opposes it, and it is for this reason that its channels are winding. Each one twists its own way, either staying close to the main stream or making a long detour, wherever it can best find low ground; many drain away unseen and unnamed, but the Thermodon itself mingles with a few other branches and in full view empties into the inhospitable Pontos below the curving headland. If they had stayed there long, they

would have mixed in battle with the Amazon women, and the strife
would not have been bloodless, since the Amazons who lived on the
Doiantian plain were far from kindly and did not respect laws; grief-
bringing violence and the works of Ares were what they cared about,
for they were descended from Ares and the nymph Harmonia who
slept with the god in the recesses of the grove of Akmon,* and bore
him warrior daughters. Zeus, however, stirred the breezes of the
Argestes again, and the wind carried them away from the rounded
headland where the Themiskyreian Amazons armed themselves.
The Amazons did not in fact all live together in one city, but were
divided through the land in three tribes. There were these who lived
apart and were at that time ruled by Hippolyte, the Lykastians also
dwelled separately, as did the javelin-hurling Chadesians. For the
next day and the following night they coasted along the land of the
Chalybes. These people neither plough with oxen nor cultivate any
honey-sweet fruits; moreover they pasture no flocks on dewy
grazing-land. Rather they dig in the hard, iron-bearing earth to
exchange the metal for what they need to live. The rising of every
dawn brings them wearisome toil, as they labour in a murky and
smoky blackness.

Immediately after the Chalybes, they rounded the headland of
Genetaian Zeus* and hurried along the coast of the land of the
Tibarenoi. There, whenever the women bear their husbands'
children, it is the men who fall on to the beds and lie groaning, their
heads bound. The women look after them properly with food and
prepare for them the baths due a newly-delivered mother. Next they
passed by the Sacred Mountain and the land where the Mossynoikoi
live in their 'mossunai' throughout the mountains; it is these huts
which give them their name. The customs and ordinances which
rule their lives are quite at variance with what is normal. Everything
that it is proper to do openly, whether in public assembly or in the
market-place, all of this they carry out at home; everything that we
do in our houses, this they do outside in the middle of the streets and
incur no censure for it. There is no public shame about love-making,
but like grazing pigs they enjoy general promiscuity and mate with
the women on the bare earth, paying not the slightest attention to
anyone nearby. The king sits in the highest 'mossune' and
administers fair justice over the large population. Poor chap! If he

makes a mistake in his judgements, they lock him up and keep him hungry for that day.

They passed by the Mossynoikoi and spent the day rowing near the island of Ares* which faced them, as the soft breeze had dropped in the early half-light. Soon they saw darting through the air one of the birds of Ares which inhabited the island; it shook its wings at the ship's path and shot a sharp feather at it. The feather lodged in the left shoulder of noble Oileus; his oar fell from his hands as he was struck. The crew stared in wonder at the feathered arrow, and Erybotes, who was sitting next to Oileus, pulled it out and bound up the wound with the belt by which his own scabbard was suspended around him. Then another bird appeared in flight. The hero Klytios, son of Eurytos, had stretched his curved bow in anticipation, and shot a swift arrow at the bird to bring it down; it twisted around and fell near the swift ship.

Amphidamas, son of Aleos, said to the crew:

'Near us is the island of Ares, as you yourselves know from the sight of these birds. For my part I do not think that arrows will be sufficient to allow us to land. Rather, let us devise some other stratagem that will help us if, mindful of Phineus' instructions, it is your intention to land on the island. Not even Herakles, when he journeyed to Arkadia, was strong enough to use his bow to drive off the birds which floated on the Stymphalian lake; I saw this with my own eyes. Instead he stood on a high peak and shook a bronze rattle in his hands to make a great din; the birds fled away screeching in panic and fear. Therefore let us too now give thought to some similar stratagem. I shall tell you what I myself have already devised. Put your high-crested helmets on your heads; half of you by alternation should row, while the other half fit out the ship with carved spears and shields. Everyone together give out a mighty scream, so that the birds will take fright at the strange racket, the nodding crests and the spears raised aloft. If we reach the island itself, then make a terrible din both with your shields and by yelling aloud.'

So he spoke, and all were pleased with his stratagem to help them. On their heads they placed the bronze helmets with their terrible gleam and the scarlet crests which waved in the air. Every second man rowed while the others concealed the boat beneath their lances and shields. As when a man covers his roof with tiles, both as an ornament for his house and to keep out the rain, and each tile fits exactly beside the next one, so did they cover over the ship by fitting the shields together. As is the noisy din of men moving in war when battle-lines clash, so did the scream rise up into the air from the ship. The birds could no longer be seen, but as the Argonauts drew near to the island and beat on their shields, countless thousands immediately took off in every direction in panicked flight. As when from the clouds the son of Kronos sends down a fierce hailstorm on to a city and its houses, but the inhabitants sit calmly and listen to the clattering on the roofs overhead, since the winter season has not caught them unprepared, for they have already strengthened the roof; just so did the birds send a fierce hail of arrows against the crew as they flashed high up over the sea towards the mountains rising on the horizon.

What was Phineus' intention in making the divine expedition of heroic men put in here? What help would then come to them in their need?

The sons of Phrixos had embarked on a Colchian ship and were travelling from the court of Kytaian Aietes at Aia to the city of Orchomenos in order to recover their father's boundless wealth; he had enjoined this journey upon them as he was dying. On that day they had been very close to the island when Zeus stirred up the blast of the North Wind and his rain signalled the watery passage of Arktouros.* During the day the wind was soft and gently shook the leaves on the topmost branches of the mountain trees, but at night it fell fiercely upon the sea and the roaring blasts roused the waves. Dark mist filled the heavens, no bright stars appeared anywhere through the clouds, and all around a gloomy blackness pressed them. Soaked to the skin and fearful of a miserable end, the sons of Phrixos were carried aimlessly on the waves. The force of the wind tore out the sail and even broke the ship itself in two after it had been battered by the swell. With the help of the gods the four of them clung to one of those mighty planks which had been held together by sharp bolts, but which came loose as the ship broke up; narrowly avoiding death, they were carried in despair towards the island by the waves and the gusts of wind. Suddenly an extraordinary storm broke, and the rain fell on the sea and the island and all the mainland opposite where the insolent Mossynoikoi lived. In the dead of night all four of the sons of Phrixos, together with the strong plank, were thrown by the force of the waves on to the coast of the island. As the sun rose, Zeus' great rainstorm abated, and the two groups* soon met one another. Argos was the very first to speak:

'We beg you, whoever you are, by Zeus the Observer, to show kindness and give assistance to those in distress. Harsh storm winds swept on to the sea and scattered all the planks of the wretched ship, in which we had embarked to cross the sea on necessary business. Therefore we now beseech you to give us merely a covering for our bodies and to tend our needs, taking pity on men of your age who are in trouble. Show respect for suppliants and strangers, remembering Zeus the protector of strangers and suppliants: both suppliants and strangers belong to Zeus, and on our behalf he is also no doubt the observer.'

Believing that the prophecies of Phineus were being fulfilled, the son of Aison questioned him prudently:

'We will in kindness give you all of these things here and now. But come, tell me truly where on the earth you live, what business compels you to travel over the sea, and your own glorious names and family.'

Helpless in his trouble Argos replied:

'That a descendant of Aiolos called Phrixos travelled to Aia from Hellas I have no doubt you yourselves are already aware. Phrixos reached the city of Aietes mounted on a ram, which Hermes made golden, and even to this day you can see its fleece spread out on the thickly leaved branches of an oak. Then on its own instructions,* Phrixos sacrificed the ram to the son of Kronos, Zeus Phyxios*—this chosen from all his titles—and Aietes received him in the palace and, as a gesture of his kindly intentions, gave him in marriage his daughter Chalkiope and asked no bride-price for her. These two are our parents. Phrixos died an old man in Aietes' house and, in accordance with our father's instructions, we are travelling to Orchomenos to recover Athamas' possessions. If, as is natural, you wish to learn our names, this man's name is Kytissoros, this is Phrontis, and this Melas. Myself you may call Argos.'

So he spoke, and the heroes were delighted at the meeting and in wonderment showed them great kindness. Jason again spoke appropriately to them in the following way:

'You are indeed related to me through my father, and those you beg for help in your wretchedness are well disposed towards you. Kretheus and Athamas were brothers and I am Kretheus' grandson; I am in fact travelling with these companions of mine from Hellas to the city of Aietes. But we will talk of these things at a later time; now first put on clothes. I think that it is the gods who have brought you to me in your distress.'

After these words he gave them clothes in which to dress themselves, and then they all hastened to the temple of Ares to sacrifice sheep. Without delay they took their places around the altar of small stones which stood outside the roofless temple. Inside the temple was a sacred black stone to which all the Amazons once used to pray; whenever they came over from the mainland, it was not their ritual custom to burn offerings of sheep or cattle on this altar, but they carved up horses which they had specially nourished for a year. After the sacrifice and the feast which had been prepared, the son of Aison then resumed the discussion as follows:

'In truth Zeus watches over everything, and it is not concealed from him forever who among us respects the gods and who is unjust. Just as he saved your father from death at the hands of his stepmother and gave him very great prosperity in a distant land, just so has he brought you too safe through a deadly storm. On this ship of ours we may go in whichever direction we wish, whether to Aia or to the rich city of divine Orchomenos, for it was Athena who designed it and who with a bronze axe cut the wooden planks from the peak of Mount Pelion; in building it she was joined by Argos. Your ship, however, was scattered by an evil wave, before you could approach the rocks which clash together all day long at the narrow channel of the Pontos. But come—we wish to bring the golden fleece to Hellas: help us and guide our voyage, since my expedition is to atone for the attempted sacrifice of Phrixos, which has brought Zeus' anger on the descendants of Aiolos.'

His words were designed to win them over, but they heard them with horror, for they did not believe that men who wished to take the ram's fleece would meet a kindly reception from Aietes. Argos' reply doubted the wisdom of undertaking such an expedition:

'My friends, you will not lack any help whatsoever that our strength can provide, whenever the need arise. Nevertheless, Aietes is savage and cruel, and so this expedition causes me very great fear. He boasts that he is the offspring of Helios and around him live countless tribes of the Colchians; his terrifying voice and great strength would rival Ares. To take the fleece without Aietes knowing is also no easy task, for all around it is guarded by a deathless and sleepless serpent, the product of Earth itself; the serpent arose on the spurs of the Caucasus, below the Typhaonian Rock, where men say that Typhaon attacked the god with his mighty arms. He was struck by the bolt of Zeus, son of Kronos, and warm blood dripped from his hand. Even so he reached the mountains and the plains of Nysa, where to this day he lies encased in the waters of Lake Serbonis.'*

So he spoke, and at once the paleness of fear came over their cheeks, as they heard of the terrible challenge. Peleus, however, answered him with confidence:

'Do not try to put terror into us with your words, my friend. We are not so short of courage that we will prove Aietes' inferiors when we are tested under arms. This crew too, I think, is knowledgeable in the art of war, for nearly all of us are descendants of the blessed gods. Therefore I am confident that the Colchian tribes will not be of help to him, should he refuse to grant us the golden fleece in friendship.'

In this way they spoke together until they fell asleep, having once again satisfied themselves with a meal.

When they awoke in the morning, a gentle breeze was blowing, and they raised the sail which billowed out in the gusts of wind. Soon they left Ares' island behind, and on the following night they sailed past the island of Philyra,* where Philyra slept with Kronos, the son of Ouranos, when he ruled over the Titans on Olympos and Zeus was still being reared by the Idaian Kouretes in the Cretan cave. Kronos thus deceived Rheia, but the goddess came upon them in the midst of their love-making, and Kronos sprang up from the bed and rushed off in the form of a long-maned horse. In shame the Oceanid Philyra left that place and territory behind and went to the sweeping Pelasgian mountains, where she bore the mighty Cheiron, part of whom resembles a horse and part a god, because Kronos was transformed as he left her bed. After that, the Argonauts travelled past the Makrones, the vast land of the Becheires, the violent

Sapeires, and after them the Byzeres; they cut quickly through the sea, ever pressing onwards, propelled by a soft wind.

The furthest recess of the Pontos came into view as they advanced, and the tall peaks of the Caucasian mountains rose up, where Prometheus' limbs are pressed down against the harsh rock by unbreakable bronze fetters, and his liver feeds an eagle which always returns to him in its flight. In the evening they saw the eagle flying aloft near the clouds over the high point of the ship, and they heard the sharp beat of its wings. Despite its height, it caused the whole sail to shake as its wings carried it quickly past; its appearance was not that of a bird of the air, but it plied its wings like well-planed oars. Soon they heard Prometheus' wretched groans as his liver was torn out; the air resounded to his cries until they saw the flesh-devouring eagle darting back from the mountain along the same path.

It was during the night that Argos guided them to the broad stream of the Phasis and the very boundaries of the Pontos. At once they took down the sail and the yard and stowed them inside the hollow mast-crutch; there too they rested the mast itself after letting it down. Without delay they rowed into the great stream of the river which was churned up as it yielded before them. On their left was the towering Caucasus and the Kytaian city of Aia, on the other side the plain of Ares and that god's sacred grove, where the watchful serpent guarded the fleece which hung on the thickly leaved branches of an oak. The son of Aison himself took a golden beaker and poured out drops of honey-sweet, unmixed wine into the river, as a libation to Earth, the gods who inhabited the land, and the spirits of dead heroes. He beseeched them to offer kindly help without threat and to receive propitiously the ship's mooring ropes. After this Ankaios spoke as follows:

'We have reached the land of Colchis and the stream of Phasis. Now we must consider among ourselves whether we should make a gentle approach to Aietes, or whether some other method will be successful.'

So he spoke. At Argos' urging, Jason ordered them to row into a thick marsh which was close by, and to anchor the ship. There they spent the night, and not long afterwards they were pleased to see the coming of Dawn.

BOOK 3

Come now, Erato, stand beside me and relate to me how it was that
Jason brought the fleece from Colchis to Iolkos through the power of
Medea's love. I invoke you because you also have been allotted a
share of Kypris' power, and young girls, not yet mated, are
bewitched by the cares you bring; for this reason a lovely (*eperaton*)
name has been attached to you.*

So the heroes waited in hiding, out of sight in the dense reeds.
Hera and Athena, however, saw them, and drew away from Zeus
himself and the other immortals to a chamber where they could
make plans. Hera first tested Athena:

'Daughter of Zeus, suggest a plan. What must we do? Can you
devise a trick by which they might take Aietes' golden fleece back to
Hellas? They would not be able to win him over by gentle words of
persuasion, for he is a man of violent excess; nevertheless, it is not
right to reject any possible method.'

So she spoke, and Athena answered her at once:

'I too, Hera, am deep in thought on these matters about which
you ask me. But my mind remains unable to think of a trick which
will bring benefit to the heroes, though I have weighed up many
plans.'

With this reply they both fixed their eyes on the floor before their
feet, each separately reflecting upon the matter. Hera presently
broke the silence with the following scheme:

'Let us go to find Kypris! Let us confront her and urge her to
speak to her son, in the hope that he can be persuaded to fire his
arrows at the daughter of Aietes, the mistress of drugs, and so
bewitch her with love for Jason. With her assistance I think that he
will bring the fleece to Hellas.'

So she spoke. Athena was delighted with the cunning device, and
answered her gently:

'My father, Hera, bore me ignorant of that boy's arrows, and I
know no way to produce desire by bewitchment.* If you are satisfied
with this scheme, I will go along, but please do the talking when we
confront her.'

With this, they hurried off to the great palace of Kypris, which her husband, lame in both feet, had built for her when first he received her as his wife from Zeus. They entered the court and stood in the portico of the bedchamber where the goddess shared her bed with Hephaistos. He had departed early to his forge and anvils in the great recess of the Wandering Island* where he used blasts of fire to create all manner of marvels. His wife was therefore alone in the house, sitting opposite the doors on an embossed chair. She had let down her hair on to her two white shoulders and was grooming it through with a golden comb, preparatory to plaiting long tresses. When she saw the goddesses in front of her she stopped and called them in, and rising from her chair, sat them down on couches. Then she too sat down again, and put up her hair without finishing the combing. She smiled as she addressed them with flattering deference:

'Good ladies, what purpose and business brings you here after such a long time? Why have you come? In the past I saw very little of you, chief among goddesses* as you are.'

Hera replied to her:

'You mock us, but our hearts are shaken by misery. Already the son of Aison and all those who have come with him in pursuit of the fleece have moored their ship in the river Phasis; now that the task is at hand, we are terribly afraid for all of them, but most of all for the son of Aison. Even if he should set sail for Hades to free Ixion* from his bronze chains, I would use all the strength in my body to protect him so that Pelias, whose insolence left me unhonoured in sacrifices, may not escape a miserable end and live to mock me. Even before this Jason has always been very dear to me, ever since I was testing the proper behaviour of men and Jason came across me beside the stream of the flooded Anauros as he returned from a hunt. All the mountains and tall peaks were flecked with snow and down their sides crashed tumbling torrents. I was disguised as an old woman, and he took pity on me and lifted me on to his shoulders to carry me through the swirling water. Therefore I have always held him in the very highest regard; moreover, Pelias will not pay for his outrage unless you grant the means of return.'

So she spoke, and Kypris was struck dumb with amazement. She was filled with awe at the sight of Hera supplicating her, and finally replied with compliant words:

'Gracious goddess, let there be no creature more cursed than Kypris, if I fail to respond to your plea with whatever word I can utter and with any deed which these feeble arms of mine can achieve. I expect no gratitude in return.'

Such were her words, and Hera made this wise reply:

'It is not force or the strength of arms which is the object of our coming. Please simply bid your son bewitch the maiden daughter of Aietes with desire for the son of Aison. If she willingly offers him her aid, I think that he will easily gain the golden fleece and return to Iolkos, for she is full of guile.'

Kypris then addressed them both in reply:

'My son will listen to you, Hera and Athena, much more than to me! Shameless though he is, for you a little shame at least will show in his eyes. To me he pays no heed, but he constantly provokes and disobeys me. Beset as I am on all sides by the misery of it, I have it in mind to break his bow and grim-sounding arrows right before his eyes. When he was angry he even threatened that if I did not keep my hands to myself while he still had his fury under control, I would have reason to blame myself later on.'*

So she spoke, and the other goddesses smiled and looked at each other. Distressed, Kypris spoke again:

'To others my miseries bring laughter—I should not tell everyone; it is enough that I know about them. But since you both desire it, I shall attempt to win him over: he will not disobey.'

So she spoke. Hera took her graceful hand and answered with a gentle smile:

'Act upon your words without delay, lady of Kythera. Do not be upset and do not have an angry quarrel with your son. He will cease this behaviour in the future.'

With this, she got up from her chair; Athena followed, and they both hurried out to return. Kypris too left her chamber. She went down the mountainside of Olympos looking for her son. She found him in a remote spot in Zeus' flourishing orchard; he was not alone, but was with Ganymede, whom Zeus had established in heaven to dwell with the immortals because the boy's beauty filled him with desire. The two of them were playing with golden knucklebones, as young friends will. Greedy Eros' left hand was already full and he held the palm against his chest as he stood upright. The complexion of his cheeks bloomed with a sweet flush. Ganymede, however, squatted nearby, silent and downcast; he only had two knucklebones left, and he constantly threw one after another without achieving anything in his fury at Eros' crackling mockery. Very soon he lost these as well and went off empty-handed and distraught, without seeing Kypris approach. She stood in front of her son, at once touched his chin and spoke to him:

'Why are you grinning, you unspeakable horror? Have you pointlessly deceived him, unjustly getting the better of an innocent child? Please now, willingly do what I say. If you do, I will give you that lovely toy of Zeus which his dear nurse Adrasteia made for him when he was still a babbling baby in the Idaian cave.* It is a round ball,* and you will get no better plaything from the hands of Hephaistos. Its zones are golden, and two circular joins curve around each of them; the seams are concealed, as a twisting dark-blue pattern plays over them. If you throw it up with your hands, it sends a flaming furrow through the sky like a star. This is what I will give you, but first you must shoot at the maiden daughter of Aietes and bewitch her with love for Jason. Do not delay, for that would make my gratitude less.'

So she spoke, and he was delighted with what he heard. He threw down all his toys and with both hands clutched hold firmly to the sides of the goddess' tunic; he begged her to give the ball to him at once, there and then. She spoke softly to him, drew his cheeks towards her and kissed him as she held him. With a smile she said to him:

'Be witness now your own dear head and mine! I swear to give you the gift and not to deceive you, if you shoot your arrow into Aietes' daughter.'

At these words he gathered up his knucklebones, carefully counted them, and threw them into his mother's shining lap. He snatched up the quiver which was leaning against a tree-trunk, strapped it around himself with a golden band, and took up his curved bow. Through the fruitful orchard of the great god he went, to emerge at the celestial gates of Olympos. From this point the road from heaven descends, and two peaks of soaring mountains hold up the sky, heights of the earth, where the risen sun blushes red with its first rays. In his passage through the vast sky, the fertile earth, the cities of men and the sacred streams of rivers opened up beneath him; elsewhere were mountain-peaks, and all around the sea.

In a remote spot the heroes lurked in the river-marshes and held an assembly as they sat on the benches of their ship. The son of Aison himself spoke, and the others sat in due order and listened quietly, each in his own place:

'Friends, I shall tell you the plan I myself favour, but it is for you to give it your assent. Common is our need, and common to all alike the right to speak. The man who holds back his view and opinion in silence should know that he alone deprives our expedition of its chance for safe return. I suggest that you all remain quietly in the ship, your arms at the ready. I shall go to Aietes' palace, together with the sons of Phrixos and two of our comrades as well, and I shall first speak to him to test whether he is willing in friendship to grant us the golden fleece or prefers to refuse and, trusting in his might, reject our quest. In this way we shall learn the depth of our plight and then be able to decide whether to engage with him in war or whether, if we refrain from battle, some other device will help us. Before testing him with words, let us not try simply to deprive him of his possession by force: it is better first to approach him and seek to win him over by arguments. In tight corners arguments have often smoothed the way and achieved what manly strength could hardly accomplish. Even Aietes once received the blameless Phrixos as he fled from his stepmother's deceit and the sacrifice designed by his father; all men, even the most outrageously shameless, always respect and observe the ordinances of Zeus, Protector of Guests.'

So the son of Aison spoke, and the young men all swiftly approved his words; there was no one who sought to persuade them to any other course of action. He then urged the sons of Phrixos to follow him, together with Telamon and Augeias, and he himself took up the sceptre of Hermes.* They wasted no time in disembarking above the reeds in the river on to the dry land where the plain sloped upwards. This area is called the Plain of Kirke. Here rows of elms and willows grow in profusion, and from their topmost branches corpses are hung by ropes. To this day it is an abomination to the Colchians to cremate men who have died; nor is it proper for them to bury the dead in the earth and to raise a mound over them. Instead they wrap corpses in untreated ox-hides and suspend them from trees far away from the city. The earth too receives an equal share with the air, since women are buried in the earth. This is the normal pattern of their custom.*

As they went along, Hera took thought for their protection and spread a thick mist through the city* so that the numberless Colchians might not notice them on their way to Aietes' palace. As soon as they reached the city and Aietes' palace on emerging from the plain, Hera scattered the fog. They stood in the entrance-way, gazing in amazement at the royal court with its broad gates and the lines of pillars which rose up along the walls; above the palace a stone entablature rested upon bronze capitals. In silence they then stepped over the threshold. Near the entrance vines flourished in profusion, their green leaves forming a canopy high overhead. Beneath them flowed four permanent springs which Hephaistos had dug out; one gushed forth milk, another wine, a third flowed with fragrant unguent, and the last streamed water which was said to be hot when the Pleiads set,* but in turn when they rose it bubbled up from the hollow rock as cold as ice. Such then were the divine marvels which the craftsman Hephaistos had devised in the palace of Kytaian Aietes. He had also fashioned for him bulls with bronze feet, and bronze too were their mouths, and they breathed out a terrible blast of flaming fire. Moreover he had forged a plough of tough adamant, all in a single piece; he did this to repay Helios who had received him in his chariot when he was exhausted by the fighting on the Phlegraian plain.*

In the palace was a central door constructed of metal, and radiating from it in both directions were many stout wooden doors leading to bed-chambers. A decorated colonnade ran the length of both sides of the court, and at an angle to the court on both sides stood the taller parts of the palace. The highest of all was occupied by Aietes and his wife, and another by Aietes' son Apsyrtos. The Caucasian nymph, Asterodeia, bore him, before Aietes made Eidyia, the youngest daughter of Tethys and Ocean, his lawful wife. The sons of the Colchians called Apsyrtos by the name of 'Phaethon',* because he stood out among all the young men. The other rooms were occupied by servants and by Aietes' two daughters, Chalkiope and Medea. Jason and his companions* came across Medea as she was going from room to room looking for her sister. Hera had kept her at home, for normally she did not spend much time in the palace, being busy all day at the shrine of Hekate, where she was the goddess's priestess. When she saw them approaching, she screamed. Chalkiope heard it clearly, and the maidservants dropped their wool and spindles to the ground and all rushed out together. Chalkiope went with them and on seeing her sons she threw up her arms with delight. At the sight of their mother they too greeted her with joyful embraces. Weeping, she addressed them thus:

'You were not then after all going to abandon me thoughtlessly and wander off to some distant place; fate has turned you around. Woe is me! What is this longing for Hellas which some wretched folly and the instructions of your father Phrixos have implanted in you? His last instructions before death were bitter pains for my heart. Why should you go to the city of Orchomenos—whoever this Orchomenos may be?—chasing after the inheritance of Athamas and deserting your mother in her distress?'

So she spoke. Last of all, Aietes appeared at the door, and Eidyia too, Aietes' wife, came out when she heard Chalkiope. In an instant the whole court was filled with noise. Many slaves prepared a large bull, others used bronze axes to cut up wood for fires, and others boiled water for washing. No one relaxed their efforts to serve the king.

Meanwhile Eros came unseen through the bright air, moving busily like the gadfly which attacks young heifers and which oxherds call *myops*. He quickly reached the foot of the door-post in the vestibule; he strung his bow, and selected from his quiver a new arrow destined to bring much grief. From there he swiftly crossed the threshold unobserved, peering sharply around. He crouched down low at Jason's feet, fitted the arrow-notch to the bowstring, and stretching the bow wide in his two hands shot straight at Medea. Her spirit was seized by speechless stupor. Eros darted back out of the high-roofed palace with a mocking laugh, but his arrow burned deep in the girl's heart like a flame. Full at Jason her glances shot, and the wearying pain scattered all prudent thoughts from her chest; she could think of nothing else, and her spirit was flooded with a sweet aching. As when a woman heaps up twigs around a burning brand—a poor woman who must live from working wool—so that she might have light in her dwelling at night as she sits very close to the fire, and a fierce flame spurts up from the small brand and consumes all the twigs, just so was the destructive love which crouched unobserved and burnt in Medea's heart. At one moment her soft cheeks were drained of colour, at another they blushed red, the control of her mind now gone.

When the servants had prepared a banquet for them and they had refreshed themselves in warm baths, they gladly satisfied their spirits with food and drink. Then Aietes urged his daughter's sons to speak and questioned them as follows:

'Sons of my daughter and of Phrixos, whom I honoured above all other guests in my palace, why do you return so quickly to Aia? Did some disaster befall you as you were hastening on your way? You did not believe me when I told you of the vast distance of your voyage. I knew because I once whirled across in the chariot of my father Helios, when he conveyed my sister Kirke* to the western land; we reached the Tyrrhenian coast where she lives to this day, very far indeed from Colchian Aia. But what is the point of stories? Tell me clearly what got in your way, and also who these men are who accompany you, and where you left the hollow ship.'

At these questions Argos was afraid for the expedition of the son of Aison and sought to soothe Aietes with his answer, speaking on behalf of his brothers, as he was the oldest:

'Aietes, fierce storms soon ripped apart our ship, and as we huddled clinging to a plank in the blackness of night a wave threw us on to dry land on the island of Enyalios. Some god brought us to safety, for we did not even come across those birds of Ares which used in former times to build their nests on the deserted island; these men who had disembarked from their ship the day before had driven them off. Moreover, they had been kept on the island by the mind of Zeus, which took pity upon us, or by some stroke of fate, since they gave us food in abundance and fresh clothes as soon as they heard Phrixos' glorious name and your own. It is indeed to your city that they are travelling, and if you wish to know the reason for the expedition, I shall not conceal it from you. This man has been sent here on a hopeless quest by someone, a king, who wishes to thrust him out of his homeland and his possessions, because his courage far surpasses that of all the other descendants of Aiolos. He claims that the family of the Aiolidai will not escape from the bitter wrath of

implacable Zeus, from his anger and from the appalling pollution
and punishment arising from Phrixos until the fleece comes to
Hellas.* Their ship was built by Athena Pallas,* and it is nothing
like the ships which Colchians have: the worst of all was ours which
was completely broken apart by the violence of water and wind.
Their ship, on the other hand, holds firm in its bolts, even if storm
winds from every direction should assault it. It runs equally well
before the wind and when the crew ply the oars with the vigorous
strength of their arms. Collecting in it all the best heroes of the whole
Achaian land, he has come to your city, after wandering to many
cities and over great stretches of the grim sea, in the hope that you
will grant him the fleece. However you decide, so shall it be. He has
not come to use violent force, but wishes to pay fair recompense for
the gift; I have told him of the Sauromatai* who are such a hostile
threat to you, and he will subdue them to your control. If, as is no
doubt the case, you desire to learn of the names and lineage of these
men, I shall inform you in every particular. This man, for whose
sake all the others gathered for the expedition from Hellas, is called
Jason, son of Aison the son of Kretheus; if indeed he is a descendant
of Kretheus, then he is related to us through our father, as both
Kretheus and Athamas were sons of Aiolos, and Phrixos in turn was
a son of Athamas the son of Aiolos. As for this man, you may have
heard of a son of Helios called Augeias; this is he at whom you are
looking. This man is Telamon, child of the most glorious Aiakos,
and Aiakos' father was Zeus himself. In the same way all the other
comrades who have joined together are the sons or grandsons of
immortals.'

With these words Argos sought to win Aietes over, but the king
was furious at what he heard and his spirit rose up high in anger. He
replied in a rage—his wrath was directed most at Chalkiope's sons,
for he thought that it was to help them that the Argonauts had
come—and under his brows his eyes flashed with emotion:

'Get far away at once from my sight, you villains, and take your
tricks with you! Quick, out of our land, before someone suffers
wretchedly for this story of a fleece and Phrixos! You come here from
Hellas, in league with others, not for a fleece, but to gain my throne
and royal power. If you had not already eaten at my table, I would
have cut out your tongues and chopped off both your hands and sent

you packing with only your feet left, to prevent you making any other attempt in the future, and because you told such lies about the blessed gods.'

So he spoke in his rage, and deep down the spirit of Aiakos' son swelled high. His heart within him longed to answer back with deadly words, but the son of Aison checked him, and himself first answered gently:

'Aietes, please stay calm. This expedition has not come to your city and palace for the reason you apparently suppose; we did not even wish to come here. Who would be so reckless as to choose to cross so great a stretch of sea to take another man's possession? But I have been sent by fate and the chilling command of a wicked king. We beg you to grant us this favour. I shall carry report of you as of a god through all of Hellas, and we are keen to offer you a swift requital in war, whether it is the Sauromatai or some other people whom you wish to subdue to your control.'

His gentle words tried to win over the king, but Aietes' heart in his chest was uncertain as he pondered whether he should attack and slay them on the spot or whether he should make trial of their might. Upon reflection the latter course seemed preferable and he answered Jason as follows:

'Stranger, why give me a long story covering every detail? If in truth you are descendants of the gods, or at least are not my inferiors in coming here to take the possessions of others, I shall give you the golden fleece to take away, if you so desire—when I have tested you. In the case of excellent men I am not grudging, as you say the ruler of Hellas is. The test of your strength and courage will be a challenge which my own hands accomplish, deadly though it is. I have two bulls which graze the Plain of Ares; their hooves are bronze and flames flash from their mouths. I yoke them and drive them through Ares' tough ploughland, four measures great; with the plough I quickly cut through the whole field to the end, and into the furrows I throw not the seed of the grain of Demeter, but the teeth of a terrible serpent which give rise to a crop like in body to armed warriors. As they rise up all around to menace me I cut them down and harvest them with my spear. In the morning I yoke the bulls, and I cease the harvest when it is evening. If you accomplish this task as I do, on that very same day you may carry away the fleece to the palace of

your king. Do not however harbour any hopes that I shall give it
before this. It would not be seemly for a man of noble birth to yield
to an inferior.'*

So he spoke. Jason sat silent where he was, his eyes fixed on the
ground before his feet, unable to speak, at a loss as to how to deal
with his wretched situation. For a long time he turned over and over
what he should do: it was impossible to accept with confidence,
as the challenge seemed overwhelming. At last he replied to the
king:*

'Aietes, you have every right to place this hard constraint upon
me. Therefore I shall risk the challenge, terrible though it is, even if
I am fated to die; for there is nothing worse for men than the cruel
necessity which forces me to come here at the behest of a king.'

Thus he spoke, distraught at the helplessness of his position. The
king answered the distressed man with bitter words:

'Be off to your men, since you wish to undertake the task. If,
however, fear prevents you from lifting the yoke on to the bulls, or if
you shrink back from the deadly harvest, I shall see that every
precaution is taken to make anyone else shrink from attacking his
betters.'

Such were his straightforward words. Jason sprang up from his
chair and with him came Augeias and Telamon. Argos followed him
without his brothers, as he signalled to them to stay behind there for
the time being. So they left the hall, and among them all the son of
Aison stood out for his divine beauty and grace. The young girl kept
her eyes on him, looking sideways behind her shining veil, and she
wondered at him; her heart smouldered with pain, and her mind
fluttered after his departing footsteps, creeping like a dream. Thus
they went out of the palace deep in depression. Chalkiope quickly
retreated to her chamber with her sons to avoid Aietes' anger, and
Medea also followed her. All the many cares that the Loves* stir up
tossed about in her spirit. Everything still danced right before her
eyes—how he looked, the clothes he wore, how he spoke, the way he
sat on the chair, how he walked towards the door. As she pondered
she thought that there could never have been another such man. In
her ears rang his voice and the honeyed words he spoke. She feared
for him, lest the bulls and Aietes together should destroy him, and
she grieved as though he were already dead and gone. Down her

cheeks flowed soft tears of the most awful pity in her anguish for him. She wept softly and sobbed in lamentation:

'Alas, why do I feel this grief? Whether he will die as the very best of all heroes or quite worthless, let him perish! Ah, if only he could have escaped safe . . . Please, lady goddess, daughter of Perses,* let this happen, let him escape death and return home. But if it is his fate to be killed by the bulls, may he first know that I at least take no pleasure in his awful destruction.'

So the young girl's mind was tortured by love's cares. For their part, the men returned by the same road on which they had come from the plain and, when they had left the city and its people behind, Argos addressed Jason as follows:

'You will not approve, son of Aison, of the plan which I will now propose, but we can hardly refuse to attempt it in our wretched plight. There is a young girl—you have already heard me tell you how Hekate, daughter of Perses, inspires her powers with magic drugs; if we can win her over, I do believe that we need no longer worry about defeat in the contest. I am however very much afraid that my mother may not support me in this. Nevertheless I will go back again to ask her, since all of us together have the same destruction hanging over us.'

His words were intended to help, and Jason answered:

'If this seems to you a good plan, then, my friend, I have nothing against it. Be off and with wise words beg your mother to stir herself to action. Slim indeed are our hopes, if we must entrust our safe return to women.'

So he spoke and before long they reached the marsh. Their comrades were delighted to see them and questioned them; in his distress the son of Aison answered them:

'My friends, the very heart of cruel Aietes is set against us in irrevocable anger; no purpose would be served either by me telling you everything or by your asking it. He says that he has two bulls which graze the Plain of Ares; their hooves are bronze and flames flash from their mouths. He has ordered me to use them to plough a field four measures great. He will give me seed from a dragon's jaws which will send up earth-born warriors with bronze weapons; I must slay them on that very same day. Without demur I accepted the challenge, since nothing better could be devised.'

These were his words. To everyone the task seemed impossible;
for a long time they sat in silence, unable to speak, and gazed at each
other, depressed by the hopelessness of their wretched plight. At last
Peleus addressed the assembled heroes with words of encouragement.

'It is time to consider what we will do, though I do not think that
deliberation will help us as much as the strength of our arms. If,
heroic son of Aison, you have in mind to yoke Aietes' bulls and are
keen for the task, then you should keep your promise and make
yourself ready. If, however, your heart does not have very full
confidence in its manly courage, then neither stir yourself to it nor sit
here seeking some other man from among us: I shall not hold back,
since the worst grief that can befall is death.'

So did the son of Aiakos speak. Telamon's heart was stirred and
he leapt up in eagerness for the task; so too did proud Idas, and also
the two sons of Tyndareos. With them also was the son of Oineus,*
placing himself among men in their prime, though there was not yet
any sign at all of his first soft beard; so great was the strength
bursting in his spirit. All the others gave way and kept silence. Argos
then addressed those who longed for the challenge as follows:

'This, my friends, is indeed the last resort. I think, however, that
my mother will be able to supply us with the help which we require.
Therefore, keen as you are, please remain a little longer on the ship
as before, since it is better to hold back than recklessly to bring a
miserable end upon yourselves. There is a young girl who lives in
Aietes' palace; the goddess Hekate has taught her extraordinary
skills in handling all the drugs which the dry land and the boundless
waters produce. With these she charms the blast of unwearying fire,
stops still the flow of crashing rivers, and puts bonds on the stars and
the holy paths of the moon. As we were coming here along the road
from the palace we thought of her, in the hope that her sister, my
mother, could persuade her to aid us in our challenge. If you too
think this a good plan, then on this very day I shall go back to
Aietes' palace to make the attempt; perhaps my attempt will have
god's help.'

So he spoke, and the gods sent them a sign of their favour. A timid
dove fled from the assault of a hawk and dropped in terror from the
sky into the lap of the son of Aison, while the hawk impaled itself on

the ship's sternpost. Mopsos at once explained the omen for all of them as follows:

'The will of the gods, my friends, has sent you this sign. There is no better way to interpret it than that we should by every possible means seek to persuade the maiden. I do not believe her unmindful of us, if indeed Phineus declared that our safe return would depend upon the goddess Kypris, and hers is this gentle bird which has escaped death. As my heart within me foresees on the basis of this omen, so I pray it may turn out. My friends, call upon Kythereia to help, and without delay follow Argos' advice.'

The young men approved his words, remembering Phineus' instructions. Only Idas, son of Aphareus, leapt up and, shouting in a terrible rage, cried out:

'Shame! It is women who have accompanied us here on this voyage; they call on Kypris to aid us. With your eyes no longer on the great strength of Enyalios but on doves and hawks, you hang back from challenges. Get away, worry not about matters of warfare, but rather how your prayers can deceive cowardly girls.'

Such were his violent words. The assembled comrades muttered together in low tones, but no one spoke out against him, and he sat down in fury. Jason at once sought to encourage them by revealing his intentions:

'Since we are all agreed, let Argos go off from the ship; we shall move from the river and openly tie our ropes to the land. It is no longer right to hide as though we cowered away from battle.'

So he spoke, and without delay he sent Argos off to return quickly to the city. Under instructions from the son of Aison the others drew up the anchor-stones and rowed to a berth a little out from the marsh.

Aietes lost no time in convening an assembly of the Colchians away from the palace, where they had always met in the past, to plan awful treachery and woes for the Minyans. He promised that as soon as the bulls had torn apart the man who had undertaken to carry out the dangerous challenge, he would break up the clump of trees above the wooded hillside and burn the ship, crew and all, so that those who laid insolent schemes would be made to splutter out their wretched presumption. He would never even have received in his palace the suppliant Phrixos, son of Aiolos, desperate though his need was and despite the fact that he surpassed all other guests in courtesy and piety, had not Zeus himself sent down Hermes from heaven with the message that Phrixos should receive a kindly welcome. All the more would pirates who had come to his land not be allowed to sit in peace for long; their only interest was getting their hands on other people's possessions, hatching trecherous deceit and ransacking the herdsman's yards with cowardly attacks. To himself* Aietes reflected that Phrixos' sons would pay a fair requital: they had come back in league with a gang of villains to deprive him of his royal power and honour without undue effort on their part. This accorded with a grim oracle he had once received from his father Helios, that he must beware of the crafty treachery and schemes of his own family and of destruction which came in many guises. (For this reason in fact he had dispatched them to the Achaian land in accordance with their wishes and their father's instruction—a long journey!). He had no fear at all that his daughters or his son Apsyrtos might devise some hateful scheme; rather, these grim dangers were the work of Chalkiope's family.

So in his anger he revealed his terrible plans to the people, and threatened them violently if they did not keep a close watch on the ship and its crew, so that no one should escape destruction. In the meantime, Argos had returned to Aietes' palace and sought by all manner of arguments to persuade his mother to beg Medea for her help. She herself had already been pondering how to do this, but was afraid in her heart lest either her approach should perhaps be mistimed and fruitless because Medea was scared of her father's deadly anger, or their deeds be laid bare to full view if her sister complied with her entreaties.

The young girl found respite from her grief in exhausted sleep which came over her as she lay stretched on the bed. At once she was disturbed by deadly dreams, deceitful ones such as visit someone in distress. She imagined that the stranger undertook the challenge, not at all because he wanted to recover the fleece—it was not for that that he had come to Aietes' city—but to take her back to his own home as his properly wedded wife. In her dream she herself easily accomplished the challenge of the bulls, but her parents scorned their promise because they had challenged him, not their daughter, to yoke the bulls. From this arose a bitter dispute between her father

and the stangers, and both allowed her to choose whatever outcome
her mind desired. Without thought of her parents she immediately
chose the stranger. Her parents were seized by unbearable grief and
cried aloud in their anger; with their scream sleep left her, and she
sprang up, quaking with fear and gazing wildly all around the walls
of her room. With a struggle she gathered again the spirit in her
breast and spoke in sobs of lamentation:

'Alas, how frightening are these grim dreams! I fear that this
expedition of heroes may cause some terrible disaster. How the
stranger has set my heart fluttering! Let him woo an Achaian girl far
off among his own people: maidenhood and my parents' home
should be my concern! All the same, however, I shall banish shame
from my heart and, no longer remaining apart, I shall test my sister
to see whether she will beg me to offer help in the contest, panicked
as she is for her sons. This will quench the bitter pain in my heart.'

So saying, she raised herself and opened the doors of her chamber;
she was barefoot, and wearing only her dress. She longed to go to her
sister, to cross over the threshold into the court. For a long time she
remained there in her ante-chamber: shame would not allow her to
go further. Then she turned around and went back in again, but
then came out again, and then hid away inside again; her feet
carried her this way and that, all to no purpose. Whenever longing
gripped her, shame kept her inside; when she was held back by
shame, reckless desire pushed her on. Three times she tried, and
three times she stopped short; on the fourth time she whirled around
and collapsed face down on her bed. As when a bride* in her bed-
chamber mourns for the young husband to whom her brothers and
her parents gave her, and from prudent shame she does not yet mix
with all the maidservants, but sits grieving in the inmost recess of
the house; her husband has been killed by a blow of fate before the
two of them have enjoyed to the full the delights each offers. Though
she burns inside, she makes no noise as she weeps bitterly and stares
at her widowed bed, lest the married women mock and laugh at her.
Like her did Medea lament. In the midst of her mourning she was
seen by a serving-girl, her young attendant, who suddenly appeared.
The girl immediately reported to Chalkiope, who was sitting with
her sons devising ways of winning over her sister. Without a second
thought, Chalkiope responded to the maid's unexpected report; in

amazement she rushed to the chamber in which the young girl lay in her distress, both of her cheeks scratched in mourning. When Chalkiope saw her eyes confused with tears, she said to her:

'Alas, Medea, why do you shed these tears? What is wrong? What bitter grief has upset your heart? Has a god-sent sickness seized hold of your body, or have you heard of some deadly threat which our father has made against me and my sons? How I wish I did not look upon this palace of our parents and this city, but lived at the edge of the world where no one had even heard of the name of the Colchians!'

So she spoke. Medea's cheeks grew red, and for a long time maidenly shame held her back, though she longed to reply. Words rose to the very tip of her tongue, but then flew back again deep into her chest; often they rushed up to her lovely mouth to be uttered, but then went no further and were never spoken. Finally she did speak, and with cunning, for the bold Loves* buffeted hard against her:

'Chalkiope, my heart is blown around with terrible anxiety for your sons; I am afraid that our father will soon destroy them, and the stangers as well. Just now while I was dozing in a brief sleep I saw awful dreams—may some god bring them to naught, and may you not suffer a bitter grief for your sons.'

Her words were designed to test whether her sister would take the lead in asking her to help her sons. A terrible, unendurable pain washed over Chalkiope's heart at the fear which Medea's words caused; she answered as follows:

'It is with these very things in mind that I myself have come to you, in the hope that you will work with me to devise some way of helping my sons. But swear by Earth and Heaven that you will keep to yourself whatever I say and that you will be my partner in action. By the blessed gods, by you yourself, and by our parents, I beg you not to allow them to be crushed miserably in a wretched death; otherwise, may I die together with my dear sons and return a hateful Fury from Hades to pursue you ever after.'

So she spoke, and her tears rolled down in floods. With both arms she clasped Medea's knees and let her head drop into her sister's lap. Both lamented piteously, one and then the other, and a shrill wailing rose through the palace as they grieved in their despair. Medea was then the first to speak, addressing her distraught sister:

'What remedy can I offer, poor sister, with your talk of hateful curses and Furies? Would that it really was in my power to save your sons! Be witness the great oath of the Colchians—which you yourself bid me swear—great Heaven and Earth beneath, mother of the gods, that you will not lack whatever strength I possess, if what you ask can be achieved.'

Chalkiope answered these words as follows:

'Could you not bring yourself to devise some trick or ruse by which the stranger, who himself also asks for your help, could accomplish the challenge, for my sons' sake? Argos has come from him with this very purpose, urging me to test whether you will help. When I came here, I left him for the moment in my room.'

So she spoke. Medea's heart within her leapt for joy, her beautiful face grew flushed, and a mist descended over her in the warmth of her delight. She replied to her sister as follows:

'I shall act, Chalkiope, in whatever way you desire and however will please you. May my eyes not behold the bright dawn and may you not endure the sight of my life for much longer, if I place anything before the safety of you or your sons; they are my brothers, dear members of my family, and my young friends. So too I declare that I am both your sister and your daughter, since your mother often used to tell me that when I was a baby you took me to your breast just like your sons. Go then, but shroud my service in silence, so that I may accomplish my promise without our parents realizing. In the morning I shall go to the temple of Hekate with drugs to act as charms against the bulls, and I shall give them to the stranger who is the cause of this strife.'

At this Chalkiope left the chamber and told her sons of the help offered by her sister. Medea, now left alone, was prey again to shame and hateful fear, because she was devising such help for a man behind her father's back.

The night was now drawing darkness across the earth. Sailors on the open sea looked from their ships towards Helike and the stars of Orion, the traveller and the gatekeeper were already longing for sleep, and an exhausted slumber embraced a mother whose children had died; through the city no dogs barked, no noise resounded—the darkening gloom was gripped by silence. But Medea had not been overtaken by sweet sleep. In her desire for the son of Aison many cares kept her awake; she feared the mighty strength of the bulls, which were bound to destroy him in a miserable death in Ares' field. Often her heart fluttered wildly in her breast. As when a sunbeam, which is reflected out of water that has just been poured into a bowl or a bucket, dances inside a house and darts this way and that as it is shaken in the rapid swirl, so did the young girl's heart quiver in her breast. From her eyes flowed tears of pity, and within her the pain wore her away, smouldering through her flesh, around her fine nerves and deep into the very base of the neck where the ache and hurt drive deepest, whenever the tireless Loves shoot their pains into the heart. At one moment she thought that she would give him the drugs as charms against the bulls; then she would not, but would herself face death; then she would not die and would not give the drugs, but with calmness would endure her misery just as she was. Full of doubt she sat down and said:

'Alas, which of these miseries am I to choose? My mind is utterly at a loss, nor can I find any way to stop the pain: it burns constantly, always the same! Would that I had first been killed by Artemis' swift arrows before I saw him, before Chalkiope's sons reached the Achaian land.* From there a god or some Fury brought them here to cause me much weeping and grief. Let him die in the contest, if it is his fate to perish in the ploughland! For if I devised aid with my drugs, how could my parents fail to notice? What could I say? What trick, what concealed plan can help them? Shall I meet him alone, without his companions? Ah, I do not imagine that even his death will stop the terrible ache; that is just when he will bring me pain, when he no longer lives! Away with shame, away with fine reputation! My efforts shall save him, and then he may go off safe wherever he wishes; on that very day, when he has accomplished the task, may I find death, either hanging myself from the ridge-beam or swallowing drugs which crush out life. But even after my death they will mock and reproach me in the future; the whole city will scream of my fate far off, and wherever they go the Colchian women will speak of me and accuse me of shamelessness, 'she who cared so much for a foreign man that she died, who disgraced her home and her parents in giving way to her lust'. Of what disgrace will I not be accused? Alas, for my mad folly! Much better would it be to end my life here in my room on this very night, in a death without explanation, and thus to escape all the bitter accusations before doing these awful, unimaginable things.'

With those words she fetched the casket in which she kept her many drugs—some beneficent, some destructive. She placed it on her knees and wept, soaking her lap with the ceaseless tears which gushed forth as she bitterly lamented her fate. She longed to select drugs which waste life and to swallow them. Already she was releasing the straps of the casket in her desire to take them out, unhappy girl; but suddenly a deadly fear of hateful Hades came into her mind, and for a long time she sat unmoving and speechless. All the delightful pleasures of life danced before her; she remembered the countless joys which the living have, she remembered her happy friends, as a young girl would, and the sun was a sweeter sight than before, now that she really began to ponder everything in her mind. She put the casket back from her knees; Hera caused her to change her mind,* and she now had no doubts as to how to act. She longed for the new dawn to rise at once so that she could give him the protecting drugs as she had arranged and could meet him face to face. Often she pulled the bolts back from her door, hoping to catch the gleam of dawn, and very welcome was the light scattered by the early-born, which caused everyone to stir throughout the city.

Argos had told his brothers to remain there in the city, to learn the girl's intentions and plans; he himself went back before them to the ship.

As soon as the maiden saw the first glow of dawn, she put up her fair hair, which through neglect had slipped down to hang loose about her, and rubbed her cheeks which were stained with tears; she anointed her body with a fragrant oil, put on a brilliant robe with elegantly curved clasps, and over her divinely sweet head she threw a silver-white veil. There in the palace she hurried about without a thought for the countless griefs which were right in front of her and the others which were destined to confront her in the future. She had twelve maidservants of her own age who all slept in the vestibule of her fragrant chamber, as they did not yet share a husband's bed; she told them quickly to yoke mules to a wagon so that she might travel to Hekate's glorious shrine. While the maids were preparing the wagon, she took from the hollow casket a drug which men say is called 'the drug of Prometheus'. The man who with nocturnal sacrifices gains the favour of Daira, the only born,* and then anoints his body with this drug, will be invulnerable to blows from bronze and will not yield to blazing fire, but for that day will be invincible in might and strength. It sprang up new-formed when the flesh-tearing eagle caused bloody ichor from the suffering Prometheus to drip to the ground on the Caucasian crags. Its flower rises on twin stalks a cubit high; in colour it resembles the Korykian crocus,* and the root in the earth is like newly-cut flesh. Like the dark moisture from an oak on the mountains, she had gathered its sap in a Caspian shell* to work her magic, after having bathed seven times in ever-flowing water, and seven times having summoned up Brimo,* nurse of children, Brimo the night-roamer, the infernal, the queen of the dead, in the thick gloom of night dressed in black robes. Beneath her the dark earth roared and shook as she cut the Titan's root; the son of Iapetos himself groaned as his spirit writhed in pain. This was the drug which she took out and placed in the fragrant band which was wound around her heavenly breasts.

Leaving the palace she mounted on the swift wagon, and with her mounted two maidservants, one on each side. She herself took the reins and in her right hand grasped the well-fashioned whip. As she drove through the city, the other maidservants held on to the back of the wagon-car and ran along the broad road, holding up their fine tunics as far as their white thighs. As when after bathing at the sweet waters of the Parthenios,* or in the river Amnisos,* the daughter of Leto stands in her golden chariot and drives her swift deer through the hills to accept a distant offering of rich sacrifice, and with her go her companion nymphs, some gathering from the very spring of Amnisos, others leaving the groves and the mountain-peaks with their many streams; around her the wild beasts whimper and fawn in fear. Like this did they hasten through the city, and all around the people made way for them, avoiding the eyes of the royal maiden. When she had left behind the solid city roads, she drove through the plains and reached the shrine; eagerly stepping down from the wagon, she spoke to her maids as follows:

'I have made a terrible mistake, dear friends, and I did not realize that I should not go out among the foreign men who roam our land. The whole city is upset and does not know what to do; that is why none of the women who used to gather here every day have come to the shrine. But since we are here and no one else will appear, come on, let us play happy games to our hearts' content and pick lovely flowers from the soft grass, and then we will return home at the usual time. Moreover, today you might take home many fine presents if you approve what I have in mind. Argos has been talking to me to try to win me over—so too Chalkiope herself—keep what I tell you to yourselves in silence, lest my words reach my father's ears! They are asking me to save the stranger—whoever he is who has undertaken to meet the bulls—from his deadly challenges, in return for gifts. I went along with what they said and I have told him to come to meet me face-to-face, alone without his companions; we can therefore divide up any gifts he brings amongst ourselves, and we can give him a drug, more dangerous than the one he expects. Only, when he comes, please stand away from us!'

So she spoke and they were all delighted by her deceptive scheme.

Argos led off the son of Aison, alone without his companions, as soon as he heard from his brothers that Medea would go in the morning to the sacred shrine of Hekate, and he guided him through the plain. With them went Mopsos, son of Ampykos, skilled in interpreting the appearances of birds, and skilled in giving good advice to those who travelled with him. Never in all the previous generations, neither among all the descendants of Zeus himself nor among all the heroes who were sprung from the blood of the other immortals, had there been such a man as on that day Jason was made by Zeus' wife, both to look upon and to hear speaking. Even his companions as they stared were amazed at how he shone with beauty and grace. The son of Ampykos was delighted with their trip, no doubt already foreseeing how everything would turn out.

Along the path through the plain, near the shrine, is a poplar tree with marvellously thick foliage in which chattering crows often nested. As they passed, a crow shook its wings high up in the branches and spoke mockingly through the will of Hera:*

'This prophet deserves no renown: he cannot even grasp with his mind what children know, that a young girl will not speak a sweet word of love to a young man if there are other people there to disturb them. Off with you, wretched prophet with your wretched under-standing! Neither Kypris nor the gentle Loves in affection breathe inspiration upon you.'

These were the crow's hard words. Mopsos smiled when he heard the divine-sent voice of the bird and said:

'Son of Aison, you go on to the goddess' shrine where you will find the girl. She will be very accommodating to your request, thanks to Kypris who will help you in the challenges, as indeed Phineus, son of Agenor, has already told us. As for us, Argos and myself, we shall not accompany you, but we shall wait in this very spot until you return. You go on alone, beg her, and win her over with subtle words.'

This was his sound advice, and both the others immediately approved it.

Despite the games, Medea's spirit could not be distracted to other thoughts. Whatever game she played, none gave her pleasure or kept her amused for long, but she kept breaking off, unable to concentrate. Nor could she keep her eyes fixed on the crowd of maidservants, but constantly she turned her face away and peered into the distance along the paths. Often indeed did her heart within her breast seem to shatter, whenever she was unsure whether what she heard was the rapid sound of a foot or of the wind. Soon, however, he appeared to her as she desired, like Sirius leaping high from Ocean; it rises brilliant and clear to behold, but to flocks it brings terrible misery. Just so did the son of Aison approach her, brilliant to behold, but his appearance roused the sickening weariness of desire. Her heart within her breast dropped, her eyes grew misty, and a hot flush seized her cheeks; she had no strength at all to move her legs, but her feet were held fast beneath her. In the meantime all the maidservants had withdrawn from them. The pair then faced each other, silent, unable to speak, like oaks or tall firs, which at first when there is no wind stand quiet and firmly rooted on the mountains, but afterwards stir in the wind and rustle together ceaselessly. Just so were this pair destined to have much to say under the inspiration of Love's breezes. The son of Aison realized that some divinely-sent affliction was upon her, and with soft words he addressed her as follows:

'Why, maiden, are you so afraid of me, when I am alone? I am not an insolent boaster, as other men are, nor was I when I lived previously in my homeland. My lady, do not be too shy in front of me, either to ask or to say without prompting what is on your mind. Since we have come here with friendly intentions towards each other, in a holy place, where the gods do not permit sin, speak and question me openly. Do not deceive me with sweet words, now that you have promised your sister to give me the drugs which will provide me with strength. I beseech you, by Hekate herself and your parents and Zeus who holds his hand over guests and suppliants: I have come here, both your suppliant and your guest, forced by necessity to clasp your knees; without you I shall not accomplish the grievous challenge. In return for your help I shall show my gratitude to you in the future, as is right and appropriate for those who live a long way away, by spreading your name and your glorious repute. So also the other heroes will sing your praises on their return to Hellas, as will the heroes' wives and mothers, who now no doubt sit on the sea-shore and mourn for us; it is in your power to scatter their bitter pains. Once upon a time another kindly maiden, Ariadne* daughter of Minos, rescued Theseus from terrible challenges; her mother was Pasiphae, daughter of Helios. When Minos' anger had soothed, she embarked upon Theseus' ship and left her homeland; the very immortals loved her, and as her sign in the middle of the sky a crown of stars, which men call 'Ariadne's Crown', revolves all night long among the heavenly constellations. Thus will the gods show gratitude to you also, if you save so great an expedition of heroic men; and to judge from your appearance I would guess that your character is both gentle and kindly.'

Such were his flattering words. She turned her eyes aside and smiled a heavenly sweet smile; her heart melted as she soared in his praise, and she looked up directly into his face. She did not know what to say first, but she wanted to pour out everything together in one stream. Without hesitation she took the drug from her fragrant breast-band, and his hands grasped it quickly and joyfully. She would have drawn off her whole soul from her chest and granted it to him in the thrill of his need for her; such was the love which flashed its sweet flame from his fair head and snatched the bright sparkle of her eyes. Her senses grew warm and she melted away as the dew of roses fades as it grows warm in the early rays. At one moment they both stared coyly at the ground, at the next they cast glances at each other, smiling with desire, their faces lit up. Finally, the young girl found the strength to address him as follows:

'Listen now to the help I will devise for you. After you have gone

to collect from my father the deadly teeth from the dragon's jaw for
sowing, then wait for midnight which divides the night in two. Bathe
in the stream of a river which is never still and, alone, without
others, dress in dark robes and dig a circular pit. Over it slit the
throat of a female sheep and burn it whole, heaping high a pyre on
the very edge of the pit. Make appeasement to Hekate, the only-
born, daughter of Perses, by pouring in libation from a cup the
works of bees in their hives. When you have honoured the goddess in
accordance with my instructions, then retreat back from the pyre.
Let no footfall or barking of dogs cause you to turn around, lest you
ruin everything and do not yourself return to your companions in
the condition you should. In the morning soak this drug and anoint
your naked body with it, as though it were an unguent. Your body
will possess boundless might and great strength, and you will think
yourself the equal not of men, but of the immortal gods. What is
more, sprinkle your spear, shield and sword with the liquid. Then
the spear-points of the earth-born men will not pierce you and the
irresistible darting flame of the deadly bulls will not harm you. You
will not be like this for long, but only for that one day; nevertheless,
do not hold back from the contest, and here is a further good piece of
advice which I shall give you. When you have yoked the powerful
bulls and with strength and courage ploughed the whole hard field,
the crop of earth-born will rise up in the furrows as the dragon's
teeth are sown into the dark earth; when many of them have sprung
from the field, then without being seen throw a heavy stone among
them. Like fierce dogs fighting for food, they will kill each other over
the stone; then make straight to join battle with them. If you do this,
you will carry the fleece away from Aia back to Hellas, far into the
distance; but go wherever you wish, wherever you want to go when
you have set sail from here.'

So she spoke and then fixed her eyes in silence on the ground
before her feet; warm tears flooded her lovely cheeks as she wept
because he was going to travel over the sea, far away from her. She
looked up again into his face and addressed pained words to him,
grasping his right hand; for shame had now left her eyes:

'If ever you return home safe, remember the name of Medea, as I
shall remember you, though you are far away. Please tell me this:
Where is your home? When you leave here, where will you cross the

sea in your ship? Will you pass near wealthy Orchomenos or the
island of Aiaie? Tell me about the young girl, whom you called the
glorious daughter of Pasiphae, the one who is my father's sister.'

So she spoke, and as the young girl wept, deadly love crept over
Jason also, and he replied as follows:

'Neither at night nor during the day do I think I shall ever forget
you when I have escaped death, if indeed I escape safe to the
Achaian land, and Aietes does not throw some worse challenge in
front of me. But if it would please you to learn of my country, I shall
tell you; I too am strongly urged by my spirit to this. There is a land
surrounded by steep mountains and very rich in sheep and cattle;
there Prometheus son of Iapetos fathered noble Deukalion who first
built cities and constructed shrines to the immortals, and first ruled
over men.* The people of the area call this land Haimonia.* In it is
Iolkos, my city, and there too are many other cities, and no one there
has even heard the name of the island of Aiaie. Moreover the story is
that Minyas*—Minyas of the family of Aiolos—set out from there
and founded the city of Orchomenos which borders the Kadmeians.
But why should I tell you all these empty stories, of my home and
far-famed Ariadne, daughter of Minos? This is the brilliant name by
which that lovely maiden of whom you asked me was called. As
Minos then reached agreement with Theseus about her, so I would
wish that your father would come to terms with me.'

So he spoke, seeking to calm her with his gentle words. But the
most terrible pains gripped her heart, and in her grief she addressed
him sorrowfully:

'In Hellas, no doubt, honouring agreements is a fine thing; but
among men Aietes is not as you describe Minos, Pasiphae's
husband, nor am I the equal of Ariadne. Therefore do not speak of
friendly hospitality. Only, when you reach Iolkos, remember me,
and I—despite my parents—will remember you. From far away
may a rumour or a message-bearing bird reach me when you forget
me; or may swift gusts of wind snatch me up and carry me over the
sea to Iolkos so that I may reproach you to your face and remind you
of how it was thanks to me that you escaped. On that day may I
appear an unexpected guest at the hearth of your palace!'

Thus she spoke as piteous tears poured down over her cheeks. He
then broke in and addressed her:

'Leave those gusts flapping aimlessly, my poor friend, and your message-bearing bird as well—your talk is as idle as the wind. If you reach that area and the land of Hellas, you will be honoured and respected among women and men; they will pay court to you reverently like a god, because it was thanks to you that their sons returned home safe, and their brothers, kinsmen, and husbands in their prime were saved from disaster. In our lawful marriage-chamber you shall share my bed, and nothing will separate us in our love until the appointed death enshrouds us.'

So he spoke. Her spirit within was flooded at his words, but she shuddered to contemplate the terrible things she had done. Poor girl! Not for long would she refuse to live in Hellas! So was Hera planning, that Medea of Aia should abandon her native land and reach holy Iolkos to bring disaster upon Pelias.

Already the maidservants were glancing at them from a distance in silent suffering; very soon it would be past the time when the young girl would have to return home to her mother. But she would not yet have had any thought of return, for her spirit took delight in his beauty and winning speech, had not the son of Aison prudently broken the silence:

'It is time to depart, lest the sun go down first and some outsider get to know of everything; on another occasion we shall come here to meet each other.'

This then was the limit to which they probed each other with gentle words; after this they separated. Jason went off rejoicing to his companions and his ship, and Medea returned to her maidservants. They all came up close to meet her, but she did not see their approach, for her soul was flying aloft amidst the clouds. By themselves her feet mounted the swift wagon; with one hand she grasped the reins, and with the other the ornate whip for driving the mules, which set off in haste towards the city and the palace. When she returned, Chalkiope, distraught for her sons, questioned her; but the helpless Medea, her emotions awhirl, neither heard what was said nor had the will to reply to her questions. She sat on a low stool at the foot of her bed, resting her cheek to one side on her left hand; behind her eyelids her eyes were moist, as she pondered in what an evil deed she had chosen to share.

When the son of Aison had rejoined his companions in the spot

where he had left them, they set off to return to the main group of
heroes, and he gave them a full account. Together they arrived at
the ship, and when the others saw them they greeted and questioned
them. Jason told them all of the young girl's schemes and showed
them the powerful drug; alone of the companions only Idas sat
apart, biting back his anger. Happily and quietly the others took
their ease for the moment, because night's darkness prevented
further action. At dawn, however, they sent to Aietes to request the
seed; two men went, the warrior Telamon, and with him Aithalides,
glorious son of Hermes. Their expedition was not fruitless: on their
arrival King Aietes gave them the terrible teeth of the Aonian
dragon* with which the contest was to be accomplished. At Ogygian
Thebes the dragon, guardian of the spring of Ares, had been killed
by Kadmos* when he came in search of Europa; there too Kadmos
settled, having been guided by the cow which the oracle of Apollo
had revealed to him to lead his journey. The Tritonian goddess
knocked the teeth from the dragon's jaws and divided them equally
between Aietes and the dragon's slayer himself. Kadmos son of
Agenor sowed his teeth in the plains of Aonia and settled there a
race born from the earth, all those who had been spared by the spear
in the harvest of Ares. The others Aietes then gave willingly to the
Greeks to take to the ship, since he did not imagine that Jason would
bring the challenge to completion, even if he managed to yoke the
bulls.

In the distance the sun was sinking beneath the dark earth,
beyond the furthest peaks of the western Aithiopians, and night was
placing the yoke upon her horses; besides the ship's ropes the heroes
prepared their beds. Not Jason, however. As soon as the bright stars
of Helike, the Bear, had slipped down, and the air was perfectly still
through the heavens, he went to an empty place, like a furtive thief,
with everything he needed, which he had prepared in advance
during the day. Argos had fetched him a ewe and milk taken from a
flock, but the rest he took from the ship itself. When he found a place
set apart from men's paths, open to the skies in the midst of pure
water-meadows, he first of all bathed his tender body in the holy
river as ritual demanded, and then dressed in the dark robe which
Lemnian Hypsipyle once gave to him, to remind him of their sweet
love-making. After this he dug a trench a cubit long in the earth and

made a heap of cut wood; then he slit the sheep's throat over the pit and stretched its body over the fire in accordance with the rite. He lit the wood by putting in fire at the bottom, and poured out over it a mingled libation, calling upon Brimo Hekate to assist him in the contest. Having summoned her, he retreated. Hearing the call, the dread goddess came from the furthest depths to accept the sacrifices of the son of Aison. Around her head was a garland of terrible snakes entwined with oak-branches, and her torches flashed out a blinding brightness; all around her was the piercing bark of hellish dogs. All the fields trembled at her approach; the marsh-dwelling nymphs of the river who dance around that meadow of the Amarantian Phasis screamed aloud. The son of Aison was seized by fear, but even so he did not turn around as his feet carried him back to find his companions; already early-born Dawn was scattering her light as she rose above the snowy Caucasus.

Around his chest Aietes had put on a stiff breastplate which Ares had given to him after killing Phlegraian Mimas* with his own hands. On his head he placed a golden helmet, four-bolted; its gleam was like the encircling brilliance of Helios when he first rises from Ocean. Aloft he brandished his shield many hides thick; aloft too his terrible spear, irresistible—none of the heroic men could have withstood it, once they had left Herakles far behind, who alone could have clashed with him in battle. Phaethon brought up his father's sturdy chariot and swift horses so that he could mount; he stepped up, took the reins in his hands, and drove out of the city along the broad wagon-path towards the contest; with them went a great crowd of his people. In the manner of Poseidon* when he proceeds in his chariot to the Isthmian Games, or to Tainaron, or to the water at Lerna, for indeed the grove of Hyantian Onchestos—and often indeed he processes with his horses to Kalaureia, and Haimonian Petra—or woody Geraistos. Like this was the sight of Aietes, leader of the Colchians, as he went on his way.

In the meantime Jason had followed Medea's instructions. He soaked the drug and sprinkled it over his shield and his stout spear and all around the sword. His comrades tested the weapons with violence, but they were unable to bend that spear even a little; unbroken as before, it remained firm in their strong hands. The anger of Idas, son of Aphareus, had not abated, and he beat at the

end of the spear with his great sword, but the sword-edge bounced
back like a hammer from an anvil. The heroes all gave shouts of joy in
their confidence of success in the contest. Then Jason sprinkled the
drug over himself: a mighty force entered him, inexpressible,
without fear, and his two arms moved freely as they swelled with
bursting strength. As a war-horse, longing for the fray, paws the
ground prancing and neighing, its neck held up proudly and its ears
forward, just so did the son of Aison exult in the strength of his
limbs. This way and that he sprang through the air, shaking in his
hands the bronze shield and ash-spear. You would say that storm-
lightning was darting down through the dark sky as it flashed in
patterns again and again out of clouds destined to bring the blackest
rain-storm. Not for long were the Argonauts to refrain from the
contest. They quickly took their proper places on the benches and
hastened towards the plain of Ares. It was opposite the city, further
up-river by the same distance as the winning-post which a chariot
must reach is from the starting-gate, whenever the kinsmen of a king
who has died hold games for runners and horsemen. There they
found Aietes and all the massed Colchians, the latter standing on the
Caucasian heights, while the king paced about along the bank of the
river.

As his companions secured the ropes, the son of Aison was already
on his way to the contest, armed with spear and shield; he had leapt
from the ship, taking with him both the brilliantly gleaming bronze
helmet full of sharp teeth and his sword strapped around his
shoulders. His body was naked, and in different ways he resembled
both Ares and Apollo of the golden sword. Looking around the
ploughland, he saw the bronze yoke for the bulls and next to it the
plough of tough adamant, all in a single piece. He drew close to
them and stuck his mighty lance into the ground by its pointed end
and put down the helmet to rest against it. Carrying only his shield
he advanced further, following the countless tracks of the bulls.
They have some hidden lair in the earth, where their strong pens are
thick with murky smoke; from there, they both rushed forth
together, exhaling glowing fire. Fear seized the heroes at the sight,
but Jason planted his feet firmly apart and withstood their charge as
a rough rock in the sea withstands the waves whipped up by
ceaseless storms. He held his shield in front of him to block their

path; they snorted and crashed with their great horns against the shield, but their charge could not at all lift it into the air. As when the tough leather bellows of blacksmiths penetrate the pierced furnaces and cause sparks to dash out as they stoke the deadly fire, but then rest from their blowing and the fire crackles fiercely as it leaps up from below, just so was the noise as fiery flame flashed forth from the bulls' mouths, and burning heat enveloped Jason, striking him like the lightning bolt; but the maiden's drugs protected him.

He grabbed the right-hand bull by the end of its horn and, using all his mighty strength, dragged it over to the bronze yoke; he then brought it to its knees with a swift kick against its bronze hoof. In the same way he brought the other one down on to its haunches with a single, quick strike. He threw away his broad shield and, with his feet firmly planted right and left, he held both bulls down, one on each side of him, their front knees pressed into the ground, while he bent straight ahead through the flames. Aietes was amazed at the man's strength. Meanwhile, as had been arranged long in advance, the sons of Tyndareos came up to him, lifted the yoke from the ground and gave it to him to throw on the bulls. He bound it tightly on their necks, and then raising up the yoke-pole he placed it between the bulls and attached it to the yoke by means of its sharp end. The other two then retreated out of the fire back to the ship. Jason however recovered his shield and put it on his back; he then grasped hold of the stout helmet, which contained the sharp teeth, and his irresistible spear, with which he pricked the centre of the bulls' flanks, as a labourer uses a Pelasgian goad.* With a firm hand he guided the handle which had been fashioned from adamant and joined securely to the plough.

At first the bulls showed their savage anger by exhaling a fierce blast of glowing fire; their breath rose like the groan of buffeting winds which cause terrified sailors to take in the great sail. Not long afterwards, however, the bulls set off under the constraint of the spear. Behind them, the hard field broke up as it was split by the combined efforts of the mighty bulls and the strong ploughman. Along the furrows made by the plough great fragments of earth, as large as a man could carry, broke off with a terrible rasping. Jason followed behind, his powerful foot pressed down on the end of the ploughshare.* He scattered the teeth into the freshly ploughed land well away from himself, constantly turning around to make sure that the deadly crop of the earth-born did not attack him before he was ready. In front of him the bulls pressed their bronze hooves into the earth as they struggled. At the time when only the third part of the day which began at dawn is left, and exhausted labourers call for the swift arrival of the sweet hour at which they can release the oxen, then the field had been ploughed by the tireless ploughman, though it was four measures great, and the bulls were released from the plough. He shooed them away so they could escape over the plain, and went back to the ship, as he saw that the furrows were still empty of the earth-born warriors. His comrades gathered round to encourage him. With his helmet he then drew water from the flowing river to quench his thirst; he flexed his knees to keep them supple and filled his great heart with martial spirit. He was eager for the fray, like a wild boar which sharpens its tusks against men who hunt it and streams of foam flow to the ground from its angry mouth.

The earth-born were now springing up all over the ploughed field. The enclosure of Ares the man-destroyer bristled with stout shields and sharpened spears and shining helmets; the gleam flashed through the air, reaching all the way from the earth to Olympos. As when, after a heavy snowfall, wind gusts suddenly scatter the wintry clouds in the gloom of night, and all the stars of heaven shine brilliantly in the darkness; just so did the earth-born shine as they rose from the earth. Jason remembered the advice of crafty Medea: he picked up from the plain a great round rock, a terrible disc of Ares Enyalios—four strong men would not have been able to lift it even an inch from the ground—but he took it up easily and, darting forward, hurled it a great distance into their midst. Then he stealthily crouched down behind his shield, confident in the outcome. The Colchians gave a great roar, like the roar of the sea as it thunders against sharp rocks; but Aietes was struck dumb in amazement at how the great disc had been thrown. Like fierce dogs the earth-born leapt upon it and destroyed each other with a terrible screaming. Under their own spears they fell to earth, their mother, like pines or oaks which have been shaken loose by wind squalls. As a fiery star quivers upward in the heaven trailing a furrow of light behind it—a wondrous sign to men who see it shoot through the dark air with a brilliant gleam—just so did the son of Aison rush upon the earth-born, wielding the naked sword-blade which he had drawn from his sheath.

He cut them down wherever he met them. Many had risen into the air only as far as the stomach and the side—half of them still hidden in the earth*—others had reached the knees, others had just got to their feet and others still were already running to the battle. As when there is war between neighbouring peoples and a farmer fears that the enemy will ravage his fields before the harvest: he snatches up his well-curved sickle which has just been sharpened and hurriedly cuts the crop before it is fully ripe, not waiting until harvest-time for it to be dried by the rays of the sun; just so did Jason cut the crop of the earth-born. The furrows were filled with blood as irrigation-channels fill with streams from a well. The earth-born fell, some face-first, their teeth biting the broken earth, others on their backs, others resting on their arms and sides, looking like beached sea-monsters. Many were struck before they had lifted their feet clear of the earth and that part of them which had reached the upper air lay on the ground, sinking under the weight of their soft heads. It is no doubt like this when a fierce storm from Zeus causes young shoots in the vineyard to bend to the ground, broken at the roots. The labour of the farm-workers is wasted, and the farmer who owns the land is seized by despair and bitter grief. Just so then did grievous pain grip King Aietes' mind; he went back to the city accompanied by the Colchians, plotting how he might thwart them with all speed. Nightfall came, and Jason's task was at an end.

BOOK 4

You yourself, goddess, tell of the suffering and thoughts of the Colchian girl, you Muse, child of Zeus; within me my mind whirls in silent helplessness, as I ponder whether I should call it the mad, sickening burden of desire or a shameful panic which caused her to abandon the tribes of the Colchians.

Together with the leading men of the people Aietes spent all night in his palace devising treachery which would bring certain death to the Argonauts; his heart raged with anger at the outcome of the hated contest, and he did not for a moment imagine that it had been accomplished without his daughters' help. Into Medea's heart, however, Hera cast most grievous fear: she took fright like a gentle fawn which has been startled in the thickets of a deep wood by the baying of dogs. All of a sudden she was sure that her assistance was no secret and that at any moment she would meet utter destruction. She was scared of what her servants knew. Fire filled her eyes, and in her ears was a terrible roaring; often she felt her throat, often she screamed in pain and lamentation, pulling her hair out by its roots. There and then the young girl would have killed herself with poisons, before her due time and bringing Hera's plans to naught, had not the goddess made her decide to flee in terror with Phrixos' sons. In her chest her fluttering heart was calmed and, changing her plans, she emptied out the whole casket of drugs and placed them all in the folds of her dress. She kissed her bed and both sides of the double door to her chamber, and ran her hand over the walls; she cut off a long lock of her hair, and left it in her room for her mother as a memorial of her virginity. In a voice of grief she lamented:

'As I go I leave you this flowing lock, mother, to take my place. Farewell—this is my wish as I depart on a very distant journey; farewell, Chalkiope and all my home! Stranger, would that the sea had torn you in pieces before you reached the Colchian land!'

So she spoke, and tears poured down from her eyes. Like a young girl, recently separated by fate from her homeland, who was torn* as a prisoner from a rich house and who has not yet tasted wearying labour, but unused to wretchedness and the work of slaves, she goes in terror into the harsh control of a mistress; this was how the lovely girl rushed from her home. The door-bolts yielded to her of their own accord: they sprang back at the rapid sound of her magic incantations. On naked feet she ran through the narrow streets; with her left hand she held up her robe above her eyes to conceal her forehead and lovely cheeks, and with her right she lifted the hem of her tunic off the ground. Swiftly she passed in terror out of the walls of the broad city by a lonely path; none of the guards recognized her and she escaped unseen. She intended to make straight for the ship; she knew the roads well, as often in past days she had roamed in search of corpses and poisonous roots in the earth, as women who work in drugs do. Her heart trembled and quaked with fear. The daughter of Titan, the goddess Moon, was just rising from the horizon and saw her in her mad haste; she rejoiced with malicious pleasure as she reflected to herself:

'I'm not the only one then to skulk off to the Latmian cave, nor is it only I who burn with desire for fair Endymion.* Ah! How many times have your treacherous incantations caused me to hide when my mind was full of love, so that in the gloom of night and without disturbance you could work with your drugs in the way that brings you pleasure. But now you yourself, it would seem, are a victim of a madness like mine; a cruel god has given you Jason to cause you grief and pain. Be off then and for all your cleverness learn to put up with a misery that will bring you much lamentation.'

So she spoke, but Medea's feet carried her on quickly in her haste. With relief she climbed the rising banks of the river when she saw opposite the glow of the fire which the heroes kept burning all night long as they celebrated the outcome of the contest. In a shrill voice she called loudly through the darkness from her side of the river to Phrontis, Phrixos' youngest son. He and his brothers, together with the son of Aison himself, realized that it was the maiden's voice; their companions were struck with silent amazement when they understood the full truth of the matter. Three times she cried out, and three times Phrontis shouted back at the urging of the group; in the meantime the heroes rowed quickly in her direction. They had not yet cast the ropes from the ship to the opposite bank when Jason leapt swiftly on to the dry land from high on the deck; after him Phrontis and Argos, two of the sons of Phrixos, also jumped to the ground. With both arms she embraced their knees and said to them:

'Friends, save me in my wretchedness, and save yourselves too from Aietes! Everything that we did is in the open—the situation cannot be salvaged! Let us flee on the ship before he has the chance to mount his swift horses. I shall give you the golden fleece by putting to sleep the dragon which guards it. You, stranger, before your companions here call the gods to witness the undertakings which you gave me, and once I have travelled far from my home here do not turn me into an object of scorn and disgrace because I have no one to protect me!'

So she spoke in her grief, and the son of Aison's heart rejoiced greatly. He gently raised her from where she had fallen to embrace his knees and spoke to her with warm words of encouragement:

'Dear girl, may Olympian Zeus himself, and Hera goddess of marriage, who shares Zeus' bed, witness my oath that I shall make you my lawful wedded wife in my home, when we return safely to the land of Hellas.'

With these words he straightaway took her right hand in his. She bade them row their swift ship without delay to the sacred grove, so that they could thwart Aietes by spiriting the fleece away while it was still night. They hastened to carry out her instructions as soon as they had been spoken. They embarked at once and pushed the ship away from the land; there was a great din as the heroes went with all speed at their oars. Medea rushed back and stretched her hands out towards the land in helpless despair, but Jason spoke to her encouragingly and supported her in her distress.

At the time when huntsmen shake the sleep from their eyes— huntsmen who trust in their dogs and never sleep all through the night so that the light of dawn should not wipe away the tracks of the animals and their scent, as it strikes the ground with its bright rays—at that time the son of Aison and the maiden stepped from the ship on to the grassy spot called 'the Ram's Bed', where the ram first bent its weary knees after the journey with the Minyan son of Athamas on its back. Near there was the smoke-blackened base of the altar which Phrixos of the race of Aiolos had once established to Zeus Phyxios* when he sacrificed that marvel covered in gold, as he had been instructed by the kindly words of Hermes who came to

meet him. It was there that Argos advised the heroes to deliver
Jason and Medea. They followed a path in the direction of the
sacred grove, looking for the huge oak on to which the fleece had
been thrown, like a cloud which blushes red in the flaming rays of
the rising sun. Directly in front of them the dragon stretched out its
vast neck when its sharp eyes which never sleep spotted their
approach, and its awful hissing resounded around the long reaches
of the river-bank and the broad grove. It was heard by those who
dwelled in that part of the Colchian land which lies very far from
Titan Aia, beside the streams of the Lykos; this river breaks off from
the crashing Araxes and unites its sacred stream with that of the
Phasis to flow as one into the Caucasian sea. Women who had
just given birth woke in terror, and in panic threw their arms
around the infant children who slept in their arms and shivered at
the hissing. As when vast, murky whirls of smoke roll above a forest
which is burning, and a never-ending stream spirals upwards from
the ground, one quickly taking the place of another, so then did that
monster uncurl its vast coils which were covered with hard, dry
scales. As it rolled towards them, the maiden fixed it in the eye* and
called in a lovely voice upon Sleep, the helper, the highest of the
gods, to bewitch the beast; she invoked too the queen, the night-
wanderer, the infernal, the kindly one,* to grant success to their
enterprise. Behind her followed the son of Aison, terrified. Already
under the spell of the song the dragon was relaxing the ridge of its
earth-born coils, and it stretched out its numberless spirals, as when
a black wave rolls weak and noiseless on a gentle sea. Even so,
however, it lifted high its terrible head, seeking to enwrap them both
in its deadly jaws. With a fresh-cut sprig of juniper which had been
dipped in a potion, Medea sprinkled powerful drugs over its eyes
while she sang, and all around sleep was spread by the overwhelming
scent of the drug. Just where it was, its jaw dropped to the earth and
far into the distance its countless spirals were stretched out through
the thick wood.

Then Jason removed the golden fleece from the oak at the
maiden's instruction. She stayed where she was, rubbing the beast's
head with the drug, until Jason gave the order to turn back towards
the ship, and they left the deep-shaded grove of Ares. As when a
young girl catches in her fine dress the gleam of the full moon

hanging high over her bedroom under the roof, and her heart is
delighted at the sight of the lovely radiance; just so then did Jason
rejoice as he lifted the great fleece in his hands, and over his fair
cheeks and forehead the sparkle of the wool threw a blush like flame.
It was the size of the skin of a yearling heifer or one of the deer which
huntsmen call 'achaiineai',* golden all over, and heavy with its thick
covering of fine fleece. As he walked, the ground in front of his feet
sparkled brilliantly. Sometimes he carried it draped over his left
shoulder, and it reached all the way from the top of his neck to his
feet; sometimes he rolled it up and stroked it in his hands, very
fearful lest some man or god would cross his path and take it away.

Dawn was spreading over the earth as they rejoined the group.
The young men stared in wonder at the great fleece which shone like
Zeus' lightning. Everyone approached in his eagerness to touch it
and hold it in his hands; but the son of Aison restrained them and
threw a freshly woven robe over the fleece. He lifted up the young
girl and settled her at the stern of the ship, and then addressed them
all as follows:

'No longer hold back, my friends, from the return to your
homeland: the object for which we undertook this terrible voyage
and for which we laboured and suffered has been successfully
accomplished by the maiden's skills. With her consent I shall take
her home to be my lawful wife. She has brought noble aid to all of
Achaia and to you yourselves: keep her safe! Aietes, I imagine, will
come with a great force to prevent us reaching the sea from the river.
Therefore each second man through the length of the ship should
stay on his bench and ply the oars, while the others protect our
return by holding out their ox-hide shields as a powerful barrier
against enemy missiles. Now we have in our hands the fate of our
children, our dear country, and our aged parents; upon our success
rests whether Hellas will reap despair or great glory!'

With these words he put about himself the weapons of war, and
the others gave a great shout of eagerness. Jason drew his sword
from its sheath and cut the ropes at the ship's stern. Clad in his
armour he took his place near the maiden, beside Ankaios, the
steersman. The ship raced forward in the men's haste to row out of
the river without delay.

Medea's love and what she had done was already fully known to proud Aietes and all the Colchians. They gathered under arms in their meeting-place, as numberless as the waves of the sea raised high by a winter wind or the leaves in a dense forest which drop to the ground in the month when the trees are stripped—who could count them? Like this were the vast hordes who thronged the river banks yelling with enthusiasm for the fray. On his finely wrought chariot Aietes was resplendent with the horses which Helios had given him; they ran like the blasts of the wind. In his left hand he raised up his circling shield, in the other a huge torch, and beside him lay his mighty spear, pointed forward. Apsyrtos held the chariot-reins in his hands. Already, however, the ship was cutting through the open sea in front of it, driven forward by the strength of the rowers and the current of the great river as it swept down to its mouth. In his grievous distress the king raised his arms to Helios and Zeus, and called them to witness the wrongs he had suffered. He shouted terrible threats against his whole people: if they did not bring back his daughter there and then, finding her either on land or still in the boat on the swell of the open sea, so that he could sate his anger which demanded revenge for all that had happened, they would take the full weight of his rage and distress on their heads and be taught a lesson.

So spoke Aietes. On that same day the Colchians drew down their ships, placed the equipment on board, and on that same day they put out to sea. You would have said it was a huge family of birds whirring over the sea in flocks rather than a vast naval expedition.

The goddess Hera caused the wind to blow strongly so that Aiaian Medea should reach the Pelasgian land with all speed, to bring disaster upon the house of Pelias. On the third morning they tied their stern-cables to the Paphlagonian shore at the mouth of the river Halys, for Medea had told them to disembark and offer propitiatory sacrifices to Hekate. All that was done as the maiden prepared the sacrifice—let no one know, may my heart not urge me to sing of it!—I forbear from telling. From that day, however, the shrine which the heroes built to the goddess on the shore stands still visible to later generations. In that spot Jason and all the other heroes recalled that Phineus had said that they would follow a different route on the way back from Aia, but no one had any idea what it was. Argos, however, responded to their need:

'Our destination was Orchomenos, by the route which that truthful prophet whom you recently encountered warned you to travel. For there is another way for ships, which the priests of the immortals who were born of Thebe, daughter of Triton,* discovered. Not yet did all the constellations whirl around the heaven, not yet could enquirers learn of the sacred race of the Danaans. Only the Apidanean Arkadians* existed, Arkadians, who are said to have lived even before the moon, eating acorns in the mountains. At that time the Pelasgian land was not ruled over by the glorious descendants of Deukalion; Egypt, mother of the men of earlier times, was called Eeria,* rich in crops, and Triton* was the name of the broad-flowing river by which the whole of Eeria is watered—as heavy rain from Zeus never drenches it—and whose streams cause crops to shoot up in the fields. The story is that a man* set out from there to travel through the whole of Europe and Asia, trusting in the might, strength, and boldness of his armies. In the course of his progress he founded numberless cities, some of which are still inhabited, and some not, for long ages have passed since then. Aia at least remains intact even to this day, together with the descendants of those men whom this conquerer settled in Aia. Moreover, they preserve writings of their ancestors, pillars on which are shown all the paths and boundaries of the sea and the land for those who are going to travel in a circuit. There is a river, the remotest branch of Ocean, broad and very deep and navigable by a merchant ship; men who have traced it a great distance call it the Istros.* For a long space it cuts its path as a single river through a vast territory, for its sources bubble up far away in the Rhipaian mountains beyond the blast of Boreas, but when it reaches the boundaries of the Thracians and the Scythians, it splits in two: one stream empties here into the eastern sea; but behind it the other branch flows through the deep gulf which rises up from the Trinakrian sea which lies along your land, if indeed it is true that the Acheloos comes forth in your land.'*

So he spoke, and the goddess granted them a favourable omen; at the sight of it all shouted in approval that they should take this path. Out in front of them a furrow of radiant light in the heavens marked the path they must take. They left Lykos' son there and joyfully sailed across the sea with billowing sail, their eyes fixed on the mountains of the Paphlagonians. They did not go round past Karambis* since both the breezes and the gleam of heavenly fire stayed with them until they reached the great stream of the Istros.

Some of the Colchians travelled out through the Dark Rocks at the mouth of the Pontos and searched in vain; the others under the command of Apsyrtos* made for the river, which he entered through the Lovely Mouth, thus leaving the Argonauts behind. In this way he crossed the neck of the land and reached the furthest gulf of the Ionian Sea before them. This was possible because the mouth of the Istros creates a triangular island called Peuke; its long side faces the coast, whereas the narrow strip of its point faces into the river, which splits into two around the island. One mouth men call 'Narex', the other on the south the 'Lovely Mouth'. It was through the latter that Apsyrtos and the Colchians darted with greater speed than the Argonauts who travelled in the distance around the northernmost tip of the island. In the meadows the shepherds of the countryside left their vast flocks in terror at the ships, believing that what they saw were beasts emerging from the sea which teemed with monsters. For they had never before seen ships on the water— neither the Scythians who mingled with the Thracians, nor the Sigunnoi, nor the Traukenioi, nor the Sindoi who already lived around the great desert plain of Laurion.

When they had passed Mount Angouron and, far in the distance from Mount Angouron, the cliff of Kauliakos, around which the Istros splits into two to empty into the sea in both directions, and the plain of Laurion, then the Colchians emerged into the sea of Kronos and cut off every path by which the Argonauts could escape. The heroes travelled down the river behind them and came out at two nearby islands of the Brygoi which were dedicated to Artemis. On one of these there was a sacred shrine, and the Argonauts disembarked on to the other, thus avoiding Apsyrtos' great force, for as there were many surrounding islands he had stayed away from these out of reverence for the daughter of Zeus, but had packed the others with his Colchians to guard the exits to the sea.* Moreover, Apsyrtos had installed a great force on the coasts near the island as far as the river Salangon and the Nestian land.*

There the Minyans would have succumbed in grievous war, a small force overcome by a larger one. But they avoided this great strife by first reaching an agreement that since Aietes had promised them the golden fleece if they should complete his challenges, they should keep it for ever as of proper right, regardless of whether they had taken it against his will by trickery or by quite overt means, but that Medea—for this was the point of dispute—should be entrusted to the maiden daughter of Leto and separated from everyone else, until one of the kings who issue judgements should decide whether she had to return back to her father's house or follow the heroes to the land of Hellas. When the young girl had thought this all over in her mind, her heart was wracked by violent waves of bitter pain. Straightaway she called Jason aside, away from his companions, and when they were far from the others she addressed these words of lamentation to his face:

'What, son of Aison, is this plan you have devised about me? Has your success made you completely forgetful? Do you care nothing for all you said when hard pressed by necessity? Where are your oaths by Zeus, protector of suppliants? Where have all the sweet promises gone? It was these which made me abandon my homeland, the reputation of my house, and even my parents, everything which was most important to me! This is not how I should have behaved—from shameless desire! Far from my home I drift alone over the sea with the gloomy halcyons, all because of your sufferings, because I wanted you in safety to complete the tasks of the bulls and the Earth-born. Last of all, when my help was no longer a secret,* my mad folly even won you the fleece, and I poured deadly shame over all women. For this I tell you that I follow you to the land of Hellas as your daughter, wife, and sister: in everything now protect me willingly! Do not leave me bereft and far away as you pay court to kings, but defend me come what may. Consider the agreement and the sacred accord, to which we both pledged ourselves, valid for ever. If not, then right now use your sword to slash here, through the centre of my throat, so that my wantonness can receive its fitting reward. Cruel man! How shall I come into my father's sight, if this ruler to whom you have both turned over this cursed agreement of yours decides that I belong to my brother? My reputation will be very glorious indeed! What revenge, what grim and horrible fate will I not suffer for the terrible things I have done! You, however, will return safely as your heart desires. May the all-ruling wife of Zeus, on whom you pride yourself, not bring this to fulfilment! I pray that when you are worn out with your sufferings you will one day remember me, and that fleece of yours will vanish into the darkness like a dream. May my Furies drive you straight from your homeland, because of what I have suffered through your heartlessness. What I say the gods will not leave unaccomplished—it cannot fall idly to the ground—for you have broken a very solemn oath, pitiless one! But not for much longer will you sit here happily and laugh at me—for all your agreements!'

So she spoke, seething with grim anger. She longed to set fire to the ship, to destroy everything before their eyes, and then throw herself into the consuming flames. Jason took fright and sought to soothe her fury:

'Calm down, poor lady. I too take no pleasure in this, but we are looking for some way to put off the battle, so large is the horde of the enemy blazing around us because of you. All who inhabit this area are keen to help Apsyrtos, so that the Colchians can take you back home to your father, as if you had been plundered in war. If we join battle, we will all perish in hateful death, and the pain will be even worse for you if our deaths leave you an easy prey for them. But this agreement is a trick by which we will lead Apsyrtos to destruction. For the local peoples will not be so hostile to us in their desire to please the Colchians, when the leader who is your guardian and brother is not there; I too shall not shrink from facing the Colchians in battle, if they do not allow me to pass through.'

So he spoke, trying to soothe her, but her reply was deadly:

'Listen carefully now. This too we must plan cunningly, after my shameful acts, in view of my first mad folly and the evil plans that a god made me carry out. Your task is to ward off the Colchian spears in battle, but I shall cajole that man into coming into your hands. Soften him with splendid gifts, in the hope that I can persuade the heralds when they depart to make him come quite alone to hear what I have to say. If this plan satisfies you, then I have no objection—do the killing and raise war with the Colchians.'

So the two of them reached an agreement and prepared a terrible deceit against Apsyrtos. They sent many gifts of friendship, including the holy, purple robe of Hypsipyle. The divine Graces themselves had woven this for Dionysos on sea-girt Dia;* he gave it

to his son Thoas who in turn left it for Hypsipyle who offered it to
the son of Aison to take away as a splendid friendship gift, together
with many other wonderful things. You could never satisfy your
sweet desire either by touching or gazing upon it. An ambrosial
scent hovered over it ever since the time when the Nysaian lord
himself, tipsy with wine and nectar, lay upon it as he pressed against
himself the lovely breasts of the maiden daughter of Minos, whom
Theseus once abandoned on the island of Dia after she had followed
him from Knossos. Medea entrusted her message to the heralds, to
lure Apsyrtos to come, as soon as she reached the goddess' temple in
accordance with the agreement, and the dark gloom of night was
spread around; he would help her devise a trick by which she might
take the great golden fleece and return again to Aietes' house, for the
sons of Phrixos had forcefully compelled her when they handed her
over to the strangers. Together with this deceitful message, she
sprinkled alluring drugs through the air and breezes; from a great
distance they could attract a wild animal down from a towering
mountain.

Reckless Eros, great curse, greatly loathed by men, from you come
deadly strifes and grieving and troubles, and countless other pains
on top of these swirl up. Rear up, divine spirit, against my enemies'
children as you were when you threw hateful folly into Medea's
heart.

How then did she crush Apsyrtos in bitter death when he came to
see her? This is the next stage of my song.

When they had left Medea in the temple of Artemis in accordance
with the agreement, the two sides separated and returned in their
own ships to their respective camps. Jason however hid in ambush
to await the arrival of Apsyrtos and then of his companions.
Deceived by the terrible promises, Apsyrtos quickly crossed the
swell of the sea in his ship and stepped on to the holy island in the
dead of night. Alone, he went straight to find his sister and spoke to
her to test whether she would plan treachery against the strangers,
like a young child testing a winter torrent which not even grown men
will cross. The two of them had just reached agreement on all the
details, when the son of Aison leapt from his cunning ambush, the
naked sword-blade raised in his hand. The maiden turned her eyes
away and covered her face with her veil so that she should not have

to look upon the blood which marked her brother's death by the sword-blow. As the slaughterer at a sacrifice kills a great, horned bull, so did Jason strike down his prey near the temple which the Brygoi who live on the mainland opposite had built to Artemis. In the vestibule of the temple he sank to his knees, and as his life ebbed away, the hero caught up in both hands the dark blood from the wound; with it he stained red Medea's silver veil and robe though she turned away. With disapproving eye the pitiless Fury, subduer of all, saw clearly the deadly deed they had done. The hero, son of Aison, cut off the dead man's extremities; three times he licked the blood, and three times he spat the pollution out from his teeth, as is the proper way for slayers to expiate treacherous murders.* He buried the corpse in the ground while it was still fresh; to this day those bones lie among the Apsyrteis.*

As soon as they saw in front of them the glow of the torch which the maiden raised as a sign for their approach, the other heroes brought their ship alongside the Colchian ship, and wiped out the Colchian crew, as hawks ravage flocks of doves or savage lions rush into stalls and scatter a large herd of sheep. Not a single one of them escaped death, but like fire the Argonauts overran and destroyed the whole group. Jason appeared at the end, eager to assist, but they did not need his help and indeed were already becoming concerned about him.

After this they sat down to consider the best plan for the rest of the voyage, and the young girl joined their deliberations. Peleus was the first to speak:

'I bid you right now, while it is still night, embark upon the ship and row in the opposite direction to that which the enemy control. My guess is that, when they have a clear view of everything in the morning, there will be no consensus in favour of seeking to pursue us further. Without their leader, they will break apart in bitter quarrels. The passage will be easier for our return when they have been split in two.'

So he spoke, and the young men approved the words of the son of Aiakos. They quickly embarked and rowed with all their strength until they reached the holy island of Elektris, the last of the islands, near the mouth of the river Eridanos.* When the Colchians realized that their leader had been killed, they hastened to search for the *Argo* and the Minyans over the whole area of the sea of Kronos, but Hera restrained them by terrible lightning flashes from the sky. In the end—for they had come to loathe the thought of living in the Kytaian land in their terror of Aietes' cruel anger—they scattered far and wide to settle permanently. Some of them went to the very same islands where the heroes had stopped, and they live there bearing the name of Apsyrtos. Others fortified a town beside the dark depths of the Illyrian river, among the Enchelees, where the tomb of Harmonia and Kadmos lies.* Others dwell in the mountains which bear the name Keraunia,* ever since the lightning-bolts [keraunoi] of Kronian Zeus prevented them from crossing to the island opposite.

When the heroes believed that they could return safely, they emerged and tied their ropes to the land of the Hylleans.* Many islands stood out in the sea and made sailing between them difficult. The Hylleans no longer as before plotted unfriendly acts against them, but in fact themselves devised a route for the Argonauts and received as reward a great tripod of Apollo. When the son of Aison came to holy Pytho to make enquiries about this very voyage, Phoibos had given him two tripods for the long journey upon which he had to go. It was fated that any land in which these tripods were dedicated would never be laid waste by an enemy invasion. For this reason the tripod lies hidden in that land to this day: it is near the lovely city of the Hylleans and is buried deep in the ground so that mortals will never be able to see it. The heroes did not find King Hyllos still alive there, whom beautiful Melite had borne to Herakles in the land of the Phaeacians. Herakles had come to the halls of Nausithoos* and to Makris, nurse of Dionysos, to cleanse himself of the foul blood-guilt of his children; there he fell in love with the daughter of the river Aigaios, the naiad Melite, and lay with her, and she bore mighty Hyllos. When he left boyhood behind, he did not wish to dwell in the same island under the proud gaze of Nausithoos the king, and so he gathered together a force of the autochthonous Phaeacians—for the hero Nausithoos assisted him in the expedition—and he went towards the sea of Kronos. He settled where the city later stood; the Mentores killed him as he sought to defend his grazing cattle.

How is it, goddesses, that beyond this sea, in the Ausonian land

and the Ligurian islands called Stoichades,* many clear traces of the *Argo*'s voyage appear? What necessity and need took them so far away? What winds directed them?

When the tall body of Apsyrtos crashed to the ground in death, Zeus himself, the king of the gods, was no doubt seized by anger at what they had done. He devised that they should be cleansed of the blood of the murder by the skill of Aiaian Kirke, and return home after enduring numberless sufferings. None of the heroes knew this, but they were quickly pursuing their distant course after leaving the land of the Hylleans. They left behind all the Liburnian islands* which had recently been occupied in succession by the Colchians— Issa, Dyskelados, and lovely Pityeia. After these they went past Kerkyra, where Poseidon settled the daughter of Asopos, lovely-haired Kerkyra, far from the land of Phlius where love had caused him to snatch her away. From out at sea sailors see that this island is everywhere black from dark forests and call it 'Black Kerkyra'.* Rejoicing in the warm breeze, they next passed Melite* and steep Kerossos,* and then, far across the sea, Nymphaie, where Queen Kalypso,* daughter of Atlas, lived; they also thought they saw the Keraunian mountains in misty outline. It was then that Hera realized Zeus' plans for them and his great anger. So that they might complete the voyage, she roused winds from the opposite direction which swept them back towards the rocky island of Elektris. As they rushed along, there was a sudden shout from the plank of the hollow ship which Athena had fashioned from an oak of Dodona and set in the middle of the keel. It spoke with a human voice, and deathly fear seized them as they heard the voice and heavy anger of Zeus. It said that they could not escape from their suffering on the vast ocean and the terrible storms until Kirke had cleansed them for the pitiless murder of Apsyrtos. It ordered Polydeukes and Kastor to pray to the immortal gods to grant them passage into the Ausonian sea, where they could find Kirke, the daughter of Perse and Helios.

Thus did the *Argo* shout in the darkness. The sons of Tyndareos leapt up and, raising their hands to the immortals, prayed for everything as they had been instructed. The other Minyan heroes were gripped by despair, but the *Argo* sped far on, carried by its sail. They entered the remotest part of the stream of the Eridanos, where once Phaethon,* half-consumed by fire, fell from Helios' chariot into the waters of the deep marsh, after the blazing thunderbolt had struck him in the chest. To this very day the marsh exhales a heavy vapour which rises from his smouldering wound; no bird can stretch out its fragile wings to fly over that water, but in mid-flight it falls dead in the flames. Around the lake the unhappy Heliades,* encased in their slender poplars, grieve in moaning lamentation. Bright drops of amber fall to the ground from their eyes; on the sand these are dried by the sun, and when the waters of the dark lake wash over the shores, as they are driven by the breath of the groaning wind, then the swelling current rolls all the amber into the Eridanos. The Celts' tale, however, is that it is the tears of Leto's son Apollo which are carried by the whirling currents. He is said to have wept countless tears at the time when he reached the holy race of the Hyperboreans, after leaving glittering heaven in the face of his father's threats; he was angry because of the son whom noble Koronis had borne to him in rich Lakereia beside the streams of the Amyros.* This then is how the story goes amongst those people. The heroes desired neither food nor drink, nor did their minds have any thought of delights. The days they spent worn out and exhausted, weighed down by the foul smell which rose from the small branches of the Eridanos as Phaethon's corpse steamed; at night they heard the piercing sound of the Heliades' shrill lamentation. As they wept, their tears were carried on the waters like drops of oil.

From there the Argonauts entered the deep stream of the Rhodanos* which joins the Eridanos; at the meeting of the waters the torrent surges and roars. The river rises in the remotest recess of the earth, where are the gates and halls of Night; on leaving there, part of it thunders forth on the shores of Ocean, part again enters the Ionian sea, and another part issues through seven mouths into the vast gulf of the Sardinian sea.* From this river they rowed into the storm-filled lakes which spread out over vast distances in the land of the Celts. There they would have met a wretched fate, for a tributary stream led to the gulf of Ocean and in ignorance they were going to enter it; they would not have returned safely. But Hera leapt down from heaven and screamed from the top of the Herkynian rock;* all the heroes alike quaked with fear at her voice, for the great sky resounded with a terrible roar. The goddess caused them to turn back, and they found the route along which a safe return lay. After a long journey they reached the coasts of the sea, travelling unharmed through the midst of the massed tribes of the Celts and Ligurians; the goddess Hera aided them by pouring a deep mist around them on every day of their journey. They emerged through the central mouth of the river and disembarked on to the Stoichades islands, safely arrived thanks to the sons of Zeus.* For this reason permanent altars and rites are established in their honour, and that was not the only voyage over which they watched as protectors, but Zeus entrusted to them also the ships of men who came after. Leaving the Stoichades they crossed to the island of Aithalia* where they used pebbles to wipe off all the sweat that their labours had produced, and pebbles bearing the mark of the sweat are still found all over the beach. There too are discs and marvellous remnants* of these men at the place called 'the Harbour of the *Argo*'.

From there they quickly passed over the swell of the Ausonian sea, their gaze fixed on the coasts of Tyrrhenia. They reached the famed harbour of Aiaie* and at once moored the ship's ropes to the shore. There they found Kirke purifying her head in the flowing salt waters because she had been much disturbed by dreams during the night. All the chambers and courts of her house seemed to drip with blood, and flame consumed all the drugs with which it had been her habit till then to bewitch any stranger who arrived; she herself doused the raging fire with the blood of a slaughtered victim which she gathered up in her hands, and this put an end to her deathly fear. Because of this dream she had gone to purify her hair and clothes in the flowing waters of the sea as soon as she woke with the arrival of dawn. Her beasts*—which were not entirely like flesh-devouring beasts, nor like men, but rather a jumble of different limbs—all came with her, like a large flock of sheep which follow the shepherd out of the stalls. Similar to these were the creatures which in earlier times the earth itself had created out of the mud, pieced together from a jumble of limbs, before it had been properly solidified by the thirsty air or the rays of the parching sun had eliminated sufficient moisture. Time then sorted these out by grouping them into proper categories. Similarly unidentifiable were the forms which followed after Kirke and caused the heroes amazed astonishment. As soon as each of them looked at Kirke's statuesque form and into her eyes, they realized without difficulty that she was the sister of Aietes.*

When she had dismissed the fears caused by her night dreams, she immediately went back towards her house and, signalling softly with her hand, she offered a treacherous invitation to them to follow her. The son of Aison told all the other Argonauts to remain where they were and ignore her, but he took the Colchian maid with him. The two of them followed the path which Kirke had taken until they reached her palace. In her ignorance of why they had come, she bade them be seated upon sumptuous chairs; but silent and unable to speak they rushed to take position at the hearth as is proper for wretched suppliants. Medea buried her face in her hands, and Jason planted in the ground the great hilted sword with which he had killed Aietes' son. Neither raised their lowered eyes to look directly at Kirke, but she immediately understood that they were suppliants who had committed sinful murder. Therefore she respected the ordinance of Zeus, Protector of Suppliants, whose anger against murderers is as great as the help he offers them, and she performed the sacrifice* by which suppliants who have committed outrage are cleansed when they make their request at the hearth. First of all, to expiate a murder which could not be undone, she stretched over them the offspring of a sow whose teats still swelled with milk from just giving birth, and slitting its throat she soaked their hands with blood. Then she made other propitiatory offerings, calling upon Zeus the Purifier, the Avenger of Murder, the Respecter of Supplications. Her Naiad servants who had prepared everything for her carried all the impure waste out of the house, while at the hearth Kirke burnt cakes and, without wine,* made propitiatory offerings and prayers; she prayed that the anger of the awful Furies might be calmed, and that Zeus might be well disposed and kindly towards both of them, whether it was the blood of a stranger or of a kinsman which stained the hands of her anguished suppliants.

When everything had been properly done, she raised them up and sat them on polished chairs, and herself sat nearby facing them. At once she asked them in detail about the reason for their voyage and why they had thus come to her land and home to take up a suppliant position at her hearth. As she wondered about this, the dread memory of the dreams entered her mind, and as soon as she saw the young girl lift her eyes from the floor, Kirke longed to hear her speaking her own language: the whole race of Helios was easy to identify upon sight, because their eyes threw out into the far distance sparkling rays which glittered like gold. In reply to her detailed questions the daughter of cruel-minded Aietes gave a full and gentle response in the Colchian language. She told her of the expedition and the heroes' travels, of all their efforts in the tough challenges, how her anguished sister had persuaded her to act falsely, and how she had fled away with the sons of Phrixos from fear of her father's violence. Of the murder of Apsyrtos she did not speak, but Kirke's mind was not deceived. Even so she felt pity for Medea's tears and spoke to her as follows:

'Poor girl, it is truly a wretched and shameful journey in which you are involved. I do not think that you will long escape the bitter anger of Aietes. Soon he will come even to the territories of the land of Hellas to take vengeance for the murder of his son, for your deeds have been unspeakable. Since, however, you are my suppliant and belong to my family, I shall bring no further evil upon you, now that you have come here. Leave my house, go with this stranger— whoever this unknown man is whom you have carried off behind your father's back. Do not remain at my hearth to supplicate me, for I shall never approve what you have plotted and your shameful flight.'

At her words Medea was seized by a terrible grief and wept in lamentation, covering her eyes with her robe. She shook with fear as the hero took her by the hand and led her out of the hall to the entrance; then they left Kirke's house.

Their departure was noted by the wife of Zeus son of Kronos; Iris informed her when she saw them leaving the hall, for Hera had told her to watch out for their return to the ship. Hera then gave her a further mission:

'If ever, my dear Iris, you have carried out my instructions, do so now! Be off please on your swift wings and bid Thetis come up out of the sea to visit me here; I have need of her. After that go to the shores where the bronze anvils of Hephaistos are beaten by the heavy hammers: tell him to dampen the blasts of fire until the *Argo* is safely beyond them. Then go to Aiolos—Aiolos who rules over the winds which the air creates. Tell him too what I have in mind: he is to calm every gust that blows in the air, and no breeze is to chop up the sea; but a favourable Zephyr should blow until the Argonauts reach the Phaeacian island of Alkinoos.'

So she spoke, and without delay Iris leapt down from Olympos and, stretching wide her light wings, cut through the air to dive into the Aegean sea at the spot where Nereus' house is situated. First she went to Thetis, reported to her as Hera had planned, and bade her travel to see the goddess. Next, she journeyed to Hephaistos and made him lay down his iron hammers forthwith; his grimy bellows ceased to blast. Thirdly, she went to Hippotes' glorious son, Aiolos. She then gave her swift knees a rest from travelling after delivering her final message to Aiolos, while Thetis left Nereus and her sisters behind and rose from the sea to visit the goddess Hera on Olympos. Hera made her sit beside her and revealed her purpose:

'Listen now, noble Thetis, to what I wish to say. You know what great honour I have in my heart for the heroic son of Aison and the others who aid him in his task, and how I brought them safely through the journey between the Planktai,* where terrible gusts of fire roar and the waves seethe around the harsh reefs. Now, however, they must travel past the great rock of Skylla and the terrible whirlpool of Charybdis. Come—ever since you were a baby I have brought you up and cherished you beyond all other goddesses who dwell in the sea, because you were not wanton enough to lie in Zeus' bed though he desired you—his mind is always on such things, whether it be immortals or mortals he wants to sleep with!— but out of respect for me and because your heart was afraid, you rejected him. He then swore a mighty oath that no immortal god would ever call you his wife. Despite this, and though you were unwilling, he kept his eyes on you, until the revered Themis told him in detail how you were fated to bear a son greater than his father; though he was still keen, he left you alone out of fear that some rival would rule over the immortals and so that he could preserve his power for ever. I gave you the best of all mortal men to be your husband,* so that your marriage might please your heart and you might bear children; I called all the gods together for the marriage-feast, and I myself raised the marriage-torch aloft in my hands, because of that gentle honour you paid to me. Come now—I will tell you something which will certainly prove true. When your son goes to the Elysian plain—the son who at this moment is looked after by the Naiads in the territory of the centaur Cheiron and who sorely misses your milk*—then he is to become the husband of Aietes' daughter, Medea. Help your daughter-in-law, mother-in-law as you are, and Peleus too! Why is your anger so firmly set? He made a mistake; even gods make mistakes. Upon my instructions Hephaistos will, I feel sure, leave off his fiery blasts, and Aiolos, son of Hippotes, will hold back the swift gusts of wind, except for the gentle Zephyr, until they reach the harbours of the Phaeacians. You too help them to travel safely. Only the rocks and violent waves induce fear, but you and your sisters can overcome these. Do not allow them in their powerlessness to fall into Charybdis, lest she suck them all down and sweep them away, or to pass by the hated cave of Skylla—savage Ausonian Skylla whom night-wandering Hekate bore to Phorkos, she whom men call Krataiis*—lest she leap upon them with her terrible jaws and destroy the flower of the heroes. Keep the ship in that narrow channel which avoids destruction.'

So she spoke, and Thetis answered her as follows:

'If in truth the fiercely blazing fire and the furious wind-storms will cease, then indeed would I confidently promise to save the ship, even if the waves oppose us, provided that the Zephyr blows gently. Now it is time to set off on this distant journey to my sisters who will help me, and to the place far away where the ship's ropes are fastened, so that in the morning the men will be minded to pursue their return.'

With these words she leapt down through the air and plunged into the whirls of the dark-blue sea. She called to her sister Nereids to help her, and when they heard they all gathered round. She told them of Hera's instructions and quickly dispatched them all towards the Ausonian sea. Swifter than a sparkle of light or the rays of the sun when it rises above the limit of the earth, she nimbly sped off through the water until she reached the Aiaian shore of the Tyrrhenian mainland. She found the Argonauts beside their ship, amusing themselves by throwing the discus and shooting arrows. She moved closer, and touched the fingers of Peleus, the son of Aiakos; he was her husband, and to no one else was she manifest and visible, but his eyes alone beheld her. She spoke to him:

'No longer remain sitting on the Tyrrhenian shore, but in the morning untie the cables of the swift ship in obedience to Hera who offers you her help. In accordance with her instructions the Nereid maidens are all hastening to assist in bringing the ship safely

through the rocks which are called Planktai; for this is the route
which fate has allotted to you. When you see me there with the
others, do not point me out to anybody but keep this to yourself, lest
you anger me even more than your thoughtless action angered me in
the past.'

With these words she dived back into the depths of the sea and
disappeared. Peleus was pierced by bitter grief as she had not visited
him since she abandoned their bed-chamber in her anger over
glorious Achilles who was still a baby. In the dead of night she
would constantly put burning fire around his mortal flesh, and
during the days she anointed his tender limbs with ambrosia, to
make him immortal and to keep hateful old age away from his body.
But Peleus leapt from his bed and saw his dear son gasping in the
flames; at this sight he let out a terrible scream—foolish man! When
Thetis heard, she snatched out the crying baby and dropped him to
the floor and, in form like a breath of wind, she sped from the house
like a dream and leapt into the sea in her anger. After this she did
not return. Peleus' mind was now gripped by helpless despair, but
even so he relayed all of Thetis' instructions to his comrades. They
stopped what they were doing and finished their games at once;
having prepared their supper and beds, they dined and then settled
down for the night in the usual way.

When light-bringing Dawn struck the edge of heaven, they left the
land to go to their benches as a fresh Zephyr blew down. In joyful
mood they drew up the anchors from the bottom, made ready all the
rest of the tackle in its proper place, and hauled up high the sail
which was held tight by the ropes from the yard. A moderate wind
carried the ship forward, and soon they saw the lovely island of
Anthemoessa* where the clear-voiced Sirens, daughters of Acheloos,
destroyed all who moored beside them with the enchantment of their
sweet songs. Beautiful Terpsichore, one of the Muses, bore them
after sharing Acheloos' bed, and once they had looked after the
mighty daughter of Deo,* while she was still a virgin, their voices
mingled in song. When the Argonauts came, however, they looked
in part like birds and in part like young girls. They kept a constant
look-out from their perch in the lovely harbour: many indeed were
the men whom they had deprived of their sweet return, destroying
them with wasting desire. For the Argonauts too they opened their

mouths in pure liquid song as soon as they saw them. The men made
ready to throw the ship's cables to the shore, and would have done
so, had not Thracian Orpheus, the son of Oiagros, taken up his
Bistonian lyre* in his hands and played a fast rendition of a quick-
rolling tune, so that its resounding echo would beat in their ears, thus
blurring and confounding the other song. The lyre overpowered the
virgin voices, and the ship was carried forward by the combined
efforts of the Zephyr and the lapping waves which came from astern;
the Sirens' song became quite unclear. Nevertheless, alone of the
comrades, the noble son of Teleon had already leapt into the sea
from his polished rowing-bench; Boutes' heart had been softened by
the pure song of the Sirens, and he swam through the surging swell
to gain the shore, poor fool! There and then the Sirens would have
taken away his chance of safe return, but out of pity the goddess
Kypris who rules over Eryx snatched him from the swirling water,
and in her kindness she brought him safely to dwell upon Cape
Lilybaeum.*

In deep grief they left the Sirens behind, but worse dangers,
destructive of ships, waited to confront them. On one side could be
seen the glassy rock of Skylla, on the other Charybdis' whirlpools
roared ceaselessly. In another part the Planktai Rocks resounded to
the great surge of the waves, where until then blazing flame had
leapt up from the high peaks far above the boiling rock. The air was
thick with smoke and you could not have seen the rays of the sun;
although Hephaistos had paused from his labours, the sea still
bubbled with hot vapour. From everywhere gathered all the maiden
Nereids to help them. From behind the ship glorious Thetis placed
her hand upon the blade of the rudder to guide them through the
Planktai. As when in sunny weather a school of dolphins leaps
around a ship as it hurries forward, sometimes appearing in front,
sometimes behind and sometimes alongside, and the sailors rejoice;
so the many Nereids frolicked in front of the *Argo* and leapt around
it, while Thetis controlled their route. Just as they were about to
crash against the Planktai, the nymphs lifted their hems up to their
white knees and swiftly took up positions at regular intervals above
the very rocks and the breaking surf on either side. The surge was
knocking the ship off course, and all around the high, rough waves
seethed against the rocks, which at one moment soared to the

heavens like great cliffs, and at the next sunk to reach the bottom-most depths of the sea as the vast mass of wild swell washed over them. As when near a sandy beach young girls divide themselves into two groups and roll up the folds of their tunics to the tops of their legs to play with a round ball—each one in turn receives it from another and throws it high up into the air so that it does not fall to the ground; in this way the Nereids passed the speeding ship from one to the other, lifting it high above the waves, never letting it touch the rocks, while the raging water boiled all around. Upright on the very top of a sheer rock stood the ruler himself, Hephaistos, watching the Nereids as he rested his heavy shoulder on the handle of a hammer; high above in the gleaming heaven the wife of Zeus stood and watched also—so great was her fear that she threw her arms around Athena.

For the length of time by which the day is extended in spring, they laboured to heave the ship through the roaring rocks. Once they were through, the sailors rushed on their way, driven again by the wind; swiftly they passed the meadow of Thrinakia,* nurse of the cattle of Helios, while the Nereids plunged into the depths like diving birds, after carrying out the instructions of Zeus' spouse. From close at hand the Argonauts heard the bleating of sheep and the lowing of cattle drifting through the air. The sheep were herded through dew-filled woods by Phaethousa, youngest daughter of Helios, who held a silver crook in her hand, while Lampetie had charge of the cattle and followed after them brandishing a staff of glittering orichalk.* The Argonauts watched the cattle grazing beside the waters of the river, spread out through the plain and marshy meadow; not a single one was dark in colour, but all were like milk and proudly carried their horns of gold. During the day they sailed past the cattle; in the following night, they joyfully traversed the great open sea until once again early-born Dawn cast out her light for the travellers.

At the head of the Ionian strait, set in the Keraunian sea, is a large and fertile island,* where is buried, so the story goes (your gracious pardon, Muses! it is against my will that I relate a story told by men of earlier generations), the sickle with which Kronos pitilessly cut off his father's genitals. Others say that it is the reaping scythe of chthonian Demeter, for Demeter once took up residence in that land and, out of love for Makris,* taught the Titans how to harvest the rich crop. From that time the sacred nurse of the Phaeacians has been named Drepane ['Sickle'], and so too the Phaeacians themselves are born from the blood of Ouranos. After being held back by many wearying adventures, the *Argo* was carried by the winds across the Thrinakian sea to the Phaeacians. Alkinoos and his people welcomed them warmly with sacrifices pleasing to the gods and the whole city smiled with delight upon them; you would have said that their joy was for their own sons. Amongst the throng the heroes themselves rejoiced as though they had disembarked in the very middle of Haimonia.* Soon, however, they would have to arm for battle, for right close at hand appeared a huge force of Colchians who had travelled down through the mouth of the Pontos and between the Dark Rocks in search of the heroes. Their unconditional demand was the handing over of Medea to be returned to her father; otherwise with grim determination they threatened a terrible conflict then and there which would later be continued by an expedition led by Aietes. Despite their thirst for war, King Alkinoos held them back, for he wanted to resolve this violent strife without fighting.

Gripped by deadly fear, the young girl offered many pleas to the comrades of the son of Aison, and many times she touched the knees of Arete, wife of Alkinoos:

'I beg you by your knees, queen! Show kindness to me! Do not give me over to the Colchians to be taken back to my father! You too belong to the mortal race whose minds are very quick to embrace disaster through minor errors; so it was that prudence and reason deserted me—it was not through lust. Be witness the holy light of Helios, be witness the rites of the night-wandering daughter of Perses, against my will did I leave my home in the company of foreign men; it was hateful fear which persuaded me to think of fleeing—I had made a mistake, there was no other possible plan! My virgin's belt remains unstained and untouched, just as it was in my father's house. Take pity on me, lady, and try to win over your husband. May the immortals grant you both a life of fulfilment and all splendour, children,* and the glory of an unravaged city.'

These were her pleas as she wept at Arete's knees. To each of the heroes in turn she pleaded as follows:

'It is because of you and the tasks you had to confront, you who are by far the greatest of all heroes, that I am prey to this terror; it was thanks to me that you yoked the bulls and reaped the deadly harvest of earth-born men, and through me that you will return safely to Haimonia with the golden fleece. I am the one who has lost country and parents, who has lost her home and everything which is delightful in life; but you will again dwell in your country and your homes because of me, and you will see again the sweet sight of your parents. From me, however, bitter fate has taken all splendours, and I must wander with strangers, an object of hate. Be fearful of your agreements and oaths, be fearful of the Fury who protects suppliants and of the revenge of the gods, should I fall into Aietes' hands to be put to death in the most horrible pain. No temples, no strong tower, no other means of defence is mine other than you alone. Wretched men, without feelings or pity—you do not even feel shame in your hearts when you see me in my helplessness stretching out my arms at the knees of a foreign queen! But when you wanted to get the fleece, you would have fought with the whole Colchian people and with cruel Aietes himself; now you have forgotten your courage, when the Colchians are isolated and cut off.'

So she begged them, and all at whose knees she fell sought to encourage her and calm her grief; in their hands they brandished their sharp spears and drew their swords from their sheaths, and promised that their help would be unstinting should the verdict be erroneous. As she lay in despair among them, night which brings men rest from labours came on, spreading quiet over the whole world. But sleep brought Medea no rest at all. In her breast her aching spirit whirled like a spindle turned in the night by a toiling woman whose orphaned children cry all around her; her husband is dead, and as she weeps at the awful fate which has seized her, tears drip over her cheeks. Like her, Medea's cheeks grew wet as her heart writhed in the piercing pain of grief.

In the city King Alkinoos and Arete, the queenly wife of Alkinoos, were in their palace as before, and as they lay in bed in the gloom they discussed what to do about the young girl. As a wife speaking to her lawful husband, Arete addressed him with pressing words of affection:

'Please, dear husband, for my sake save the young girl who has suffered so much from the Colchians, and bring help to the Minyans. Argos is close to our island, and so are the men of Haimonia. Aietes' home is nowhere near us; we do not even know who he is, we merely hear of him. The pleas of this poor young girl have broken my heart: do not, my lord, hand her over to the Colchians for them to take her back to her father's palace. She made a mistake when she first gave him the magical drugs against the bulls; soon after that, she tried to cure one ill by another—as we often do in our foolishness—and she fled from the bitter anger of her violent father. According to my information, Jason is from that moment bound by great oaths to make her his lawful wife in his palace. Therefore, dear husband, do not consent to make the son of Aison break his oath and do not allow a father with seething anger in his heart to commit horrible outrages against his child. Parents are too prone to sternness with their children. Look at what Nukteus planned to do with fair Antiope;* look at the sufferings endured by Danae* on the sea because of her father's wickedness; recently, and not far away, the violent Echetos* pierced his daughter's eyes with bronze pins and her life wastes away in grief-filled doom as she grinds bronze in a dark hut.'

So she pleaded with her husband, and his wife's words warmed his heart and he answered as follows:

'I too, Arete, would for the maiden's sake like to help the heroes and use force to drive off the Colchians. I am afraid, however, of outraging the straight justice of Zeus, nor is it to our advantage to ignore Aietes, as you say. No king is greater than Aietes, and if he so wanted he could pursue his quarrel in Hellas, far away though he lives. Therefore I must produce a judgement which all men will consider excellent; and I shall not conceal it from you. If she is a virgin, I direct that she be conveyed back to her father; if, however, she is sharing a husband's bed, I shall not separate her from her spouse, nor shall I hand over to its enemies any child she may be carrying in her womb.'

With these words sleep instantly enfolded him. Arete took full note of his careful words, and straightaway she leapt out of bed and hurried through the palace; with her rushed her serving-women, bustling after their mistress. She quietly summoned her herald and cleverly told him to tell the son of Aison that she urged him to have intercourse with the young girl and not to bother pleading with King Alkinoos. He himself would go out to deliver the judgement to the Colchians, that if she were a virgin he would return her to her father's house, but if she were sharing a husband's bed he would no longer seek to cut her off from a love sanctioned in marriage.

When she finished, the herald swiftly left the palace in order to pass on to Jason Arete's welcome news and the plans of god-fearing Alkinoos. He found the Argonauts awake and under arms beside their ship in the harbour of Hyllos near the city, and reported the whole message. The heart of every hero rejoiced, for his words were very pleasing to them. Without delay they prepared a mixing-bowl of wine in honour of the blessed gods, as is proper, and with correct ritual brought sheep to the altar. On that very night they made ready the young girl's marriage-bed in the sacred cave where once had dwelt Makris, the daughter of wise Aristaios,* who discovered the works of bees and the rich juice of the olive, gained through much labour. On Abantian Euboia it was she who first received in her lap the Nysaian son of Zeus,* and who wet his dry lips with honey when Hermes had brought him from the flames; Hera saw and in her anger chased Makris out of the whole island. She then took up residence far away in the holy cave of the Phaeacians and provided the inhabitants with extraordinary wealth. There it was that they prepared a great couch; over it they threw the radiant golden fleece so that the wedding should be honoured and become the subject of song. The Nymphs gathered flowers of many colours and brought them cradled in their white breasts. All were surrounded by a radiance like that of fire—so bright was the sparkling glow from the tufts of golden wool. In their eyes the fleece lit a sweet longing; but despite their desire, all were too shy to place their hands upon the fleece. Some were called the daughters of the river Aigaios, others haunted the peaks of the mountain of Melite, others were wood-nymphs from the plains; Zeus' wife, Hera herself, had roused them to come, to bring honour to Jason. That holy cave is called to this day 'the Cave of Medea'; it was there that they stretched out fragrant cloths and brought the marriage of Jason and Medea to fulfilment. The Argonauts brandished the spears of war in their hands, lest an enemy force should launch an unexpected attack before the ceremony was completed; they garlanded their heads with thickly-leaved sprays and to the pure rhythms of Orpheus' lyre they sang the marriage-hymn at the entrance to the nuptial chamber. It was not in the territory of Alkinoos that the heroic son of Aison had wished to marry, but in the house of his father after his safe return to Iolkos; this too had been Medea's intention, but necessity forced them to lie together at that time. It is a fact that we tribes of suffering men never plant our feet firmly upon the path of joy, but there is ever some bitter pain to keep company with our delight. Thus it was that they too, though warmed by sweet love-making, were fearful whether Alkinoos' judgement would come to fruition.

As dawn rose, its ambrosial rays dissolved the dark night through the sky; the island's shores and, in the distance, the dewy paths across the plains smiled. In the streets there was a busy din: the inhabitants stirred throughout the city, as did the Colchians far away on the edge of the promontory of Makris. Without delay Alkinoos came out to reveal his decision about the girl in accordance with the agreement. In his hand he held the golden staff of legal authority with which he administered straight justice to the people in the city; after him in their several groups came the leading men among the Phaeacians, dressed in the armour of war.

All the women left the city fortifications in order to see the heroes, and with them gathered the country folk on hearing the news, for Hera had spread about a truthful rumour of what had happened. One brought a ram specially chosen from the flock, another a heifer which had not yet been put to work; others placed amphoras of wine near the cave for mixing with water, and the smoke of sacrifices swirled near and far. As you would expect, the women brought cloths upon which much labour had been expended, and gifts of gold and, moreover, jewellery of all kinds, such as adorns new brides. They were struck with wonder at the sight of the handsome form of the glorious heroes, and among them the son of Oiagros who beat the ground in rapid time with his glittering sandal to the tuneful sound of his lyre and his song. Whenever the Argonauts sang of marriage, all the nymphs blended their voices with them in the lovely wedding-hymn. At other times the nymphs sang and danced by themselves in a circle, in your honour, Hera;* for it was you who put into Arete's mind the idea of revealing Alkinoos' careful decision.

As soon as Alkinoos had declared the terms of his straight judgement and the fulfilment of the marriage had been announced, he continued to arrange matters in precisely the same way and was not affected by deadly fear or the grim wrath of Aietes, for with unbreakable oaths he had bound both sides to abide by the verdict. When therefore the Colchians realized the futility of their request and Alkinoos ordered them either to respect his ordinances or to remove their ships far from his harbours and country, they pleaded with him to receive them as allies, since they were frightened of their king's threats. For a long time then they lived on the island among the people of Phaeacia; but when in the course of time the Bakchiadai, who were originally from Ephyra, took up residence there, the Colchians went to the mainland opposite the island, and from there they were to move to the Keraunian mountains of the Amantes, and to the Nestaioi and Orikos.* These things, however, happened in the long passage of the ages. There to this day the altars which Medea established in the shrine of Apollo Nomios receive annual sacrifices in honour of the Moirai and the Nymphs. As the Minyans departed Alkinoos gave them many gifts, and many too were Arete's, and moreover she gave twelve Phaeacian servants to be Medea's attendants.

On the seventh day they left Drepane. At dawn the weather was clear and a strong breeze blew; they sailed quickly on, propelled by the strength of the wind. It was not yet fated, however, for the heroes to step upon the Achaian land: first they must undergo further sufferings on the borders of Libya. Already they had left behind the gulf named after the Ambracians, already—the sail spread wide— the land of the Kouretes* and the chain of narrow islands together with the Echinades themselves were behind them, and the land of Pelops had just come into view. Then the North Wind came in a deadly gust and swept them off course towards the Libyan sea; for nine whole nights and as many days it drove them until they were deep within Syrtis* from where ships can no longer return once they have been forced into this gulf. All around are stagnant shallows, all around clumps of seaweed cover the depths, and over them the wave's foam washes noiselessly. As far as the eye can see stretches sand; there is no movement of animal or bird. They were driven very rapidly by the tide—for the water here often retreats from the

mainland to rush back and thunder violently against the shores—
into the furthest recess of the coast where only the base of the keel
was still covered by water. They leapt from the ship, and grief seized
them as they viewed the sky and the wide stretches of land like the
sky, which disappeared into the distance without break. They could
see no source of fresh water, no path, no herdsmen's yard far off in
the distance; everything was in the grip of perfect calm. In their
anguish they would question each other:

'What land is this proud to be? Where have the winds driven us?
Would that we had neglected our deadly fear and had had the
courage to travel the same route through the Rocks! Indeed it would
have been better to journey against Zeus' decree and perish while
attempting some great exploit. Now what can we do if the winds
force us to remain here for even a very short time? How emptily
stretches the coast of this vast land!'

Such were their words. Then the steersman Ankaios addressed his
distraught companions; he too was helpless in the face of their
wretchedness:

'Surely the most awful death awaits us; there is no way to escape
disaster. Now that we have been thrust ashore into this desert, we
shall have to endure the most terrible sufferings, even if offshore
winds come up. As I gaze all around, a sea of shallows meets my
eyes in every direction, endless water broken up as it runs over the
white sand. This holy ship would long ago have been most wretchedly
shattered far off from the shore, but the tide lifted it up and brought
it here. Now the tide hurries back to the open water, and all that is
left is this swirling foam: we cannot sail over it, it barely covers the
ground. Therefore I declare that we have lost all hope of continuing
our voyage and of returning safely. Let someone else show their
skill—anyone who wishes to travel back is welcome to sit at the
tiller. But it is not at all Zeus' will to bring about the day of our
return after our labours.'

Thus he spoke as he wept, and all who were knowledgeable about
ships agreed with the despairing man. All their hearts went cold and
the colour drained from their cheeks. As when men roam through a
city like lifeless ghosts, awaiting the destruction of war or plague or a
terrible storm which swamps the vast lands where cattle work;
without warning the cult statues sweat with blood and phantom

groans are heard in the shrines, or in the middle of the day the sun draws darkness over the heavens and through the sky shine the bright stars: like this did the heroes then wander in aimless distress along the stretches of the shore. Soon the gloom of evening descended upon them. They threw their arms around each other in sorrowful embrace and wept as they took their leave; each would go off alone to collapse in the sand and perish. They separated in all directions, each to find a solitary resting-place. They covered their heads with their cloaks and lay all night long and into the morning, with no nourishment at all, waiting for a most pitiful death. In one group all the young girls lamented beside the daughter of Aietes. As when young birds which cannot fly have fallen from their nest in a hollow rock and utter shrill cries in their lonely desolation, or as when beside the banks of the fair-flowing Paktolos* swans raise their song and all around the dewy meadow and the fair streams of the river throb with sound, just so did the girls let their blonde hair trail in the dust and all night long they moaned in piteous lamentation.

There and then they would have all departed from life, the best of heroes with their task uncompleted, leaving no name or trace by which mortal men might know of them; but as they wasted away in helplessness, the heroines, guardians of Libya,* took pity on them. Once when Athena had leapt resplendent from her father's head, it was they who welcomed her and bathed her in the waters of Lake Triton. It was the middle of the day; all around the rays of the sun at their fiercest were burning Libya. The heroines stood beside the son of Aison and gently lifted his cloak from his head. He shrank back and turned his eyes away in awe of the goddesses, but they remained visible to him alone and addressed the panicked man with kindly words:

'Unhappy man, why are you so downcast and despairing? We know that you and your comrades went to gain the golden fleece; we know every detail of all your sufferings, all the extraordinary things you have endured on land and sea in your wanderings over the ocean. We are the shepherd goddesses of the land, endowed with human voice, the heroines, guardians and daughters of Libya. Rise up, and no longer groan in distress like this! Stir your comrades! As soon as Amphitrite releases the speeding chariot of Poseidon, then pay fair requital to your mother for all she has suffered in carrying you in her belly for so long; in this way you will return safe to the holy Achaian land.'

So they spoke, and disappeared just where they had been standing at the very moment that their voices ceased. Jason sat on the ground and, looking all around, he said:

'Be gracious, glorious goddesses who inhabit the desert! As for our return, I cannot at all understand your words. I shall indeed gather my comrades together and tell them in the hope that we may find some indication of how we may return; it is better to rely on the counsel of many.'

With these words he sprang up and, filthy with dust, shouted over the wastes to his companions, like a lion which roars as it seeks its mate through the forest; at the sound of its deep voice the mountain-glades far away resound, and the cattle in the fields and the herdsmen of the cattle shudder with fright. But Jason's voice did not terrify the Argonauts, as it was a comrade calling to his friends. They all gathered round him, their heads lowered in despair. He sat the grieving men down together with the women near where the ship lay, and gave them a full report of what had happened:

'Listen, friends. As I lay in grief, three goddesses stood over my head very close to me; they were dressed in goatskins from the top of their necks around their backs and waists, just like young girls.* With light hands they uncovered my head by drawing back my cloak, and they told me to get up and to come to rouse you. We must pay a generous requital to our mother for all she has suffered in carrying us in her belly for so long, whenever Amphitrite looses the speeding chariot of Poseidon. My mind is completely at a loss to understand this divine utterance. They said that they were heroines, the guardians and daughters of Libya, and claimed to know thoroughly every detail of all we have already endured on land and on sea. After this I could no longer see them in that place, but some mist or cloud suddenly concealed them from my sight.'

So he spoke, and they were all amazed at his words. Then the Minyans received the most wonderful sign. From the sea towards the land sprang a monstrous horse, a giant creature, its neck covered with a golden mane and held aloft; it shook the dripping foam from its body and quickly sprinted off, its legs flowing like the wind. At once Peleus joyfully addressed his gathered comrades:

'I declare that the chariot of Poseidon has just now been loosed by the hands of his dear wife; our mother I interpret to be none other than the ship itself, for it has constantly had us in its belly and has suffered pain in our grievous adventures. With unbreakable strength and unwearying shoulders let us lift her up and carry her into the heart of the sand-filled land in the direction in which the swift horse's legs carried it. It will not lose itself in a dry place, but I believe that its steps will reveal some gulf of the sea which lies above us.'

So he spoke, and his excellent plan pleased them all. This tale is the Muses', I sing obedient to the daughters of Pieria. This report too I heard in all truth that you, much the greatest sons of kings, by your strength and by your courage placed the ship and all that your ship contained aloft upon your shoulders, and carried it for twelve whole days and an equal number of nights through the sandy deserts of Libya. Who could tell of the suffering and wretchedness which was the fate of those men as they laboured? Truly they were of the blood of the immortals, such was the task which the violent constraint of necessity forced them to undertake. As they carried the ship ever forwards, so it was that with joy they entered the waters of Lake Triton far away and placed it down from their sturdy shoulders.

Then like crazed dogs they rushed around in search of a spring, for a parching thirst oppressed them in their exhausted suffering. They did not roam in vain, for they reached a holy place where still on the previous day Ladon, a serpent born from the earth, guarded golden apples in the territory of Atlas; around him the Hesperid nymphs* used to sing in their lovely voices as they worked. Now, however, the snake had been destroyed by Herakles, and it lay against the trunk of the apple tree; only the tip of its tail still moved freely, as it sprawled lifeless from its head to the end of its dark spine. The arrows had left the angry poison of the Lernaian hydra in its blood, and flies withered on the rotting wounds. Nearby, the Hesperides lamented in shrill voices, their silvery hands placed on their fair heads. All the heroes approached, and instantly the Hesperides became dust and earth as they rushed up. Orpheus understood this divine wonder and sought to win them over with his prayers:

'O beautiful and kindly divinities, be gracious, powerful ones, whether you are counted among the goddesses of heaven or of the underworld, or are called shepherd nymphs. Come, nymphs, sacred offspring of Ocean,* in answer to our need show yourselves clearly to us, goddesses, and reveal some source of water in a rock or some holy spring bubbling up from the earth, with which we may douse the ceaseless fire of our thirst. If ever we sail back safe to the Achaian land, then among the foremost goddesses we shall offer you in gratitude countless gifts of libations and feasts.'

This was his urgent plea to them. They soon took pity on the grief-stricken men, and first of all they sent up shoots from the earth; tall stalks burgeoned up from the shoots, and then flourishing young trees grew upright to a great height above the ground. Hespere became a poplar, Erytheis an elm, and Aigle the sacred trunk of a willow. From these trees as they were, they changed back again precisely to their earlier forms—an amazing marvel! With gentle words Aigle replied to them in their need:

'A very great help indeed in your sufferings was the visit of that most vile man, whoever it was who took away the life of the snake which kept watch, and carried off the golden apples of the goddesses. Bitter is the grief he left behind for us. Yesterday some man came, most foul in his violence and his appearance, his eyes blazing under his fierce brow, quite pitiless! He wore the skin of a giant lion, untreated and untanned; he carried a thick olive branch and a bow, with which he shot and killed this creature here. He too came with a raging thirst, as you would expect of someone travelling the land on foot. He dashed about all over here looking for water—which he was unlikely to see! But there is here a certain rock near Lake Triton and—whether he had the idea himself or was inspired by a god—he kicked it violently at the bottom, and a great stream of water flowed out. Pressing both arms and his breast to the ground, he drank a vast quantity from the cleft in the rock, until, flat on the ground, he had filled the pit of his belly like a grazing beast.'

So she spoke, and as soon as Aigle showed them the direction of the welcome spring, they joyfully ran off to find it. As when a swarm of earth-boring ants mass around the narrow entrance to their hole, or when countless flies throng near a small drip of sweet honey with insatiable energy, just so then did the whole group of Minyans rush

around that spring in the rock. One no doubt happily said to
another through wet lips:

'A true wonder! Though he is far away, Herakles has saved his
comrades who were worn out by thirst; if only we could find him on
his travels as we traverse the broad land.'

Such were their words and as answer* those who were prepared
for this task rushed off, scattering in different directions to seek for
the man, for his footprints had disappeared as the sands shifted with
the winds during the night. The two sons of Boreas took off, trusting
to their wings, as did Euphemos, confident in the lightness of his
feet, and Lynkeus whose sharp eyes could see great distances, and
Kanthos sprinted off also, to make five in total. He was sent on that
search-party by divine fate and his own courage, for he wished to
gain accurate information from Herakles as to where he had left
Polyphemos, son of Eilatos; it meant much to him to ask in detail
about his comrade. But after founding a glorious city among the
Mysians, Polyphemos had gone across the great continent in search
of the *Argo*, for he longed to rejoin the expedition. Finally he reached
the land of the Chalybes who dwell by the sea; there Fate brought an
end to his life and a tomb was built for him under a tall, white
poplar, very close to the edge of the sea. As for Herakles, Lynkeus
alone at that time thought that he saw him far away across the vast
land, as a man sees or imagines he sees the moon through a mist at
the beginning of a new month. On returning to his comrades he told
them that no other searcher would catch up with him on his travels
again. The others then returned—swift-footed Euphemos and the
two sons of Thracian Boreas whose labours had been as empty as
the wind.

Kanthos, in Libya the deadly Keres* overtook you. You came
upon grazing flocks followed by their shepherd. In defending his
sheep which you wished to take back to your comrades who were in
need, he hurled a stone at you and killed you. No weakling was
Kaphauros,* the grandson of Lykoreian Phoibos* and of the chaste
maiden Akakallis, whom once Minos sent away to Libya when she
was carrying the heavy seed of the god, though she was his daughter. ·
She gave birth to a glorious son for Phoibos, whom men call
Amphithemis and Garamas. Amphithemis then lay with a nymph of
Triton who bore him Nasamon and strong Kaphauros who at that

time killed Kanthos in defence of his flocks. He however did not
escape the angry hands of the heroes when they learned what he had
done. The Minyans then lifted up the corpse and brought it back
and buried it in the earth as they grieved. The sheep they carried off
back to their companions.

There on that same day pitiless fate overtook Mopsos, son of
Ampykos. His prophetic skill did not help him escape the bitterness
of his allotted end, for death cannot be bought off. Lying in the sand
and trying to avoid the midday sun was a terrible serpent. It was too
sluggish to bite of its own accord, nor would it directly attack
someone who retreated from it. But the moment that any of the
living creatures which the fruitful earth nourishes is infected with its
black poison, then the length of their path to Hades is not even a
cubit, not even if Paian—if the gods permit me to say this openly—
should administer drugs, when once its fangs have sunk in. When
godlike Perseus Eurymedon—for his mother gave him this name as
well—flew over Libya, bringing to the king* the head of the Gorgon
which he had just cut off, all the drops of dark blood which fell to the
ground gave rise to the race of those serpents. Mopsos stepped on
the very tip of the snake's spine with the sole of his left foot; as it
writhed around in pain it left the mark of its bite in his flesh,
squarely between the tibia and the leg-muscle. Medea and her
servant-girls fled, but Mopsos calmly felt the gory wound where the
pain was not too severe.* Poor man! Already beneath his skin
numbness was undoing his joints and a thick mist descended over
his eyes. Very soon his heavy limbs collapsed onto the ground, and
he grew cold beyond remedy; his comrades and the heroic son of
Aison gathered around him, struck dumb by his terrible fate. For no
time at all was his body to lie exposed to the sun, for at once the
poison began to rot his flesh within and the hair on his body grew
moist and fell away. In all haste they at once used bronze picks to
dig a deep grave, and both they and the young girls cut locks of hair
as they wept for their dead comrade who had suffered piteously.
Three times they went around his tomb in armour, granting him his
proper share of burial rites, and then they heaped up earth over him.

When they embarked on the ship, a southerly wind was blowing
over the sea, and they tried to work out where there might be
channels which would enable them to leave Lake Triton; for a long

time they were without a plan and roamed all day without purpose. As when a snake winds on its tortuous path under the fiercest blast of the sun's heat, and as it hisses it turns its head this way and that, and its eyes blaze with rage like sparks of fire until it can slip into its hole through a crack in the ground; just so did the *Argo* long wander as it searched for a navigable channel out of the lake. Finally Orpheus bade them offer up outside the ship the great tripod of Apollo, as a propitiation to the local gods for their return. Therefore they disembarked on to the land and set up Phoibos' gift. Wide-ruling Triton appeared to them in the form of a young man; he picked up a clod from the earth and offered it to them as a gift of friendship, saying:

'Receive this, my friends, since I have with me here and now no truly wonderful gift to offer those I meet. If you are searching for the channels into this sea, as men who are travelling in a foreign land often must do, I shall tell you. My father Poseidon has made me knowledgeable about this sea, and I rule over the coast. If, though you come from far away, you have heard of a Eurypylos,* born in Libya which nurses wild beasts, then I indeed am he.'

So he spoke. Euphemos willingly stretched out his hands to grasp the clod and replied to him as follows:

'If by chance, O hero, you know of Apis* and the sea of Minos, reply truthfully to our questions. For it is not of our choosing that we have come here, but northerly storms drove us to the borders of this land, and we have carried our ship aloft through the vast territory to the waters of this lake, suffering grievously under its weight. We do not know in which direction to sail out in order to reach the land of Pelops.'

Thus he spoke. Triton stretched out his arm and with these words showed them the open sea and the deep mouth of the lake far off in the distance:

'There is the passage into the open sea, where the still, deep waters are most darkly coloured; on both sides is the gleam of curling white breakers, and between the breakers is a narrow channel through which you can row. That sea continues out through the mist, beyond Crete, to the divine land of Pelops. When you have left the lake for the swell of the sea, then set your course close in with the coast on your right until it turns northwards. When the coast

bends around the other way, then you may safely sail off from the
headland which juts out. Go joyfully, and let no wearying grief come
over you—your limbs burst with youth to meet the challenges
ahead.'

These were his kindly words. They quickly embarked in their
eagerness to row out of the lake, and full of enthusiasm they pressed
forward. In the meantime Triton took up the great tripod and
appeared to slip into the lake. No one saw him after this, so suddenly
did he vanish with the tripod. Their hearts warmed with pleasure
because of the propitious meeting with one of the blessed gods. They
told the son of Aison to sacrifice to him the choicest of all their flocks
and to praise the god with prayers. Without delay he quickly
selected the animal, lifted it over the stern and slit its throat, praying
in these words:

'Divine being, whoever you are who appeared at the edge of this
lake, whether you are Triton, the wonder of the sea, or whether the
daughters of the water call you Phorkys or Nereus, be gracious and
grant us the completion of our return, as our hearts desire.'

As he prayed he cut the throat and allowed the animal to drop
down from the stern into the water. Out from the depths appeared
the god visible in his true form. As when a man prepares a swift
horse for the broad arena of the games, and he clutches the obedient
animal's shaggy mane as he trots alongside it; the horse follows him,
its neck held proudly aloft, and as it champs on one side, then the
other, the foam-covered bit clinks all around its mouth: like this did
the god take hold of the keel of the hollow *Argo* and lead her out into
the sea. From the top of his head to his belly, and all around his back
and his waist, his body was exactly like the glorious form of the
blessed gods, but beneath his flanks spread in two directions the
long, forked tail of a sea-monster. The surface of the water was
lashed by his spines whose points divided in curving needles like the
horns of the moon. He led them all the way until he had brought
them to the sea, and then suddenly he dived into the deep vastness;
all the heroes gave a shout when their eyes beheld this extraordinary
marvel.

In that place is 'the harbour of the *Argo*' and traces of the ship and
altars to Poseidon and Triton, since they took a pause during that
day. At dawn, however, they spread wide the sail and, with the same

desert land on their right, they ran on before the breezes of the Zephyr. On the following morning they caught sight both of the jutting headland and of the recess of the sea lying beyond it. Suddenly the Zephyr dropped and the bright south wind blew up; their hearts rejoiced at the sound of its coming. At the time when the sun has set and the homing-star* which brings rest to long-suffering ploughmen has risen, then the wind dropped in the dark night; they took down the sail and let down the long mast, and vigorously plied their well-planed oars all night and the next day and the night which followed that day. Rocky Karpathos appeared next far off, and from there they were to cross over to Crete which rises above all other islands in the sea.

Bronze Talos* broke rocks off a great cliff and prevented them from attaching their cables to the land when they ran into the sheltered harbour of Dikte. Among the generation of demi-gods he was the last survivor of the bronze race of men born from ash-trees, and the son of Kronos gave him to Europa to watch over the island by travelling three times a day around it on his bronze feet. His whole body and all his limbs were of unbreakable bronze, but below the ankle-tendon there was a vein which carried blood, and the thin membrane covering it held the key to his life and death. Though they were worn out and exhausted, the heroes quickly rowed the ship back from the land in fright. They would have been carried far from Crete in their wretchedness, bearing the burden of thirst and pain, had not Medea spoken to them as they shrank back from the island:

'Listen to me. I believe that alone I can destroy this man for you—whoever he is—even if his whole body is made of bronze, provided that his life is destined to reach an end. Use gentle oar-strokes to hold the ship here out of range of the rocks, until he yields to destruction at my hands.'

So she spoke. They removed the ship from the danger of the missiles and held it with the oars while waiting to see what unexpected plan she would carry out. She held up a fold of her purple robe over her two cheeks and moved towards the stern-deck; the son of Aison took her hand and guided her passage between the benches. Then in her incantation she sought to win over the magic help of the Keres,* devourers of the spirit, swift dogs of Hades which prowl through all the sky and are set upon mortal men. Three times did she beseech and call upon them with incantations, and three times with prayers. Her mind set upon evil, she cast a spell upon bronze Talos' eyes with her malevolent glances; against him her teeth ground out bitter fury, and she sent out dark phantoms in the vehemence of her wrath.*

Father Zeus, my mind is all aflutter with amazement, if it is true that death comes to us not only from disease and wounds, but someone far off can harm us, as that man, bronze though he was, yielded to destruction through the grim power of Medea, mistress of drugs. As he was heaving up great boulders to prevent the Argonauts from reaching anchorage, he knocked his ankle on the sharp point of a rock, and from it flowed ichor like melting lead. Not for much longer did he remain standing on the top of the jutting cliff. Like a mighty pine tree high up in the mountains which woodcutters left half-chopped by their sharp axes when they went down from the forest, and at night it first shakes in the wind-blasts, but then topples over, broken off at the base; just so for a while did he sway from side to side on his unwearying feet, but then collapsed strengthless with a thunderous crash.

During that night, then, the heroes' camp was on Crete. After it, as the glow of dawn was just appearing, they established a shrine to Minoan Athena, drew water, and embarked in order to be able to row around the headland of Salmonis* with all possible speed. Suddenly, however, as they raced over the great expanse of the Cretan sea they were terrified by the darkness which men call *katoulas*;* no stars penetrated the deadly darkness, no beams of the moon; down from the heavens spread a black emptiness, or it was some other gloom rising up from the furthest depths. They had no idea whether they were moving in Hades or over the waters. They handed over their hopes of return to the power of the sea, helpless to control where it might lead them. Jason, however, raised up his hands and in a loud voice called upon Phoibos, summoning him to save them. In his despair tears flowed down; countless were the offerings he promised to provide, many at Pytho, many at Amyklai, many to Ortygia.* Son of Leto, you heard his prayer and swiftly descended from heaven to the two Melantian rocks which lie in the open sea. You leapt to the top of one and held aloft your golden bow in your right hand; in all directions it shone with a gleaming brilliance. Before their eyes a small island of the Sporades appeared, near the little island of Hippouris; there they threw out the anchor-stones and made a stop. Soon came the light of dawn's rising, and in a shady grove they made a glorious sanctuary and altar of stones in Apollo's honour, and they called upon Phoibos with the title 'Gleamer' because of the gleam which had been visible afar off. The rugged island they called Anaphe ['Appearance']* because Phoibos had caused it to appear to them in their wretchedness. They made sacrifices of the kind which men might be expected to make on a deserted shore. When Medea's Phaeacian servants saw them pouring libations of water over the burning wood, they could no longer hold their laughter within their breasts, as they had constantly seen sacrifices of cattle in great numbers in the palace of Alkinoos. The heroes were delighted with their jesting and in turn mocked them with unseemly words, and this kindled a sweet exchange of abuse and mutual wrangling. As a result of the heroes' merry-making, the women still compete with the men in this way on the island whenever they offer propitiatory sacrifices to Apollo the Gleamer, guardian of Anaphe.

After they had untied their ropes from that island also, blessed with fair weather, Euphemos then remembered a dream he had had in the night, as he paid honour to the glorious son of Maia.* He dreamed that the divine clod* was in his arms at his breast and was nourished by white drops of milk, and from the clod, small though it was, came a woman looking like a young virgin. Overcome by irresistible desire he made love to her, but lamented as though he had bedded his own daughter whom he had nursed with his own milk. She, however, consoled him with gentle words:

'I am of the race of Triton, I, my friend, am your children's nurse, not your daughter, for my parents are Triton and Libya. Entrust me to the maiden daughters of Nereus so that I may dwell in the sea near Anaphe. Later I shall go towards the sun's rays, when I am ready for your descendants.'

So Euphemos remembered this in his heart and told the son of Aison. He then pondered in his mind the oracles of the Far-Worker and suddenly cried out:

'Ah! Most glorious is the fate which awaits you. If you throw the

clod into the sea, the gods will fashion from it an island, where the
future sons of your sons will dwell, since Triton presented you with
this piece of the Libyan land as a gift. It was no other immortal than
he who gave it to you when he met us.'

So he spoke, and Euphemos did not ignore the dream-interpretation
of the son of Aison, but rejoicing at this foretelling he cast the clod
into the deep. From it arose an island, Kalliste, the holy nurse of the
sons of Euphemos. Once upon a time they lived on Sintian Lemnos,
but were driven out of Lemnos by the Tyrrhenians and went to
Sparta to settle in the land. When they left Sparta, Theras, the noble
son of Autesion, led them to the island of Kalliste, and you, Theras,
gave the island your name. But these things happened long after
Euphemos.*

From there they swiftly crossed the vast open sea and, leaving it
behind, put in at the shores of Aegina. There they engaged in a
playful contest to see who could be the first to draw water and return
to the ship, for both need and a stiff breeze enjoined haste. To this
day, the sons of the Myrmidons carry full amphoras on their
shoulders, as they compete with marvellously light feet for victory in
games.

Be gracious, heroes, children of the blessed gods, and may these
songs be from year to year ever sweeter for men to sing. For now I
have reached the glorious conclusion of your struggles, since no
other challenge confronted you as you sailed up from Aegina, nor
did wind-storms block your path, but undisturbed you sailed past
the coast of the Kekropian land* and past Aulis* within Euboia and
the cities of the Opuntian Lokrians,* and gladly you stepped out on
to the shores of Pagasai.

EXPLANATORY NOTES

BOOK I

3 *a country man*: i.e. both 'a fellow Thessalian' and 'from the country (as opposed to the city)'. The poet here reproduces the ambiguity of oracular utterance.

the Anauros: a Thessalian river which flowed into the Gulf of Pagasai not far from Iolkos.

Athena: on the earlier poetic versions of the myth see Introduction, pp. xxi–xxii. The role of Argos, son of Arestor, was not in fact a regular part of the tradition, and the *Argo* was often said to be the work of Argos, son of Phrixos; Apollonius may be teasing us with the fact that he will have two characters bearing this significant name.

the Pimpleian height: conceived as part of the mountain range of Pieria, and particularly associated with the Muses, cf. Callimachus, *Hymn to Delos*, 7.

Zone: west of the mouth of the Hebrus (modern Evros) in north-east Greece.

Bistonian Pieria: the Bistones were a tribe of southern Thrace, whereas Pieria is north of Mount Olympos; Apollonius is probably conflating variant traditions, in a way typical of Alexandrian poetry.

Peiresiai: a Thessalian town, where the Apidanos and the Enipeus come together to flow into the Peneios.

4 *Lapiths*: legendary Thessalian race of noble heroes whose battle with the centaurs was frequently represented in art.

Phylake: a Thessalian town near (Phthiotic) Thebes to the west of the Gulf of Pagasai.

Pherai: Thessalian town (modern Velestino) north-west of Iolkos. Mount Chalkodonion is perhaps Kara Dagh which rises near the town.

Alope: town near the Malian Gulf opposite the north coast of Euboia. The Amphryssos flowed north towards the Gulf of Pagasai, cf. Virgil, *Georgics*, 3. 2.

Gyrton: Thessalian town north of Larissa.

heavy fir-trees: the Lapith Kaineus was invulnerable to attack, and so was only brought down when the Centaurs buried him alive under a hail of trees.

Titaresian Mopsos: Mopsos' grandfather was Titaron, and the Titaressos was a Thessalian river equated by Strabo with the Europos, which flows through Tempe.

Xynias: The Dolopes lived in central Greece between Aitolia and Thessaly; Lake Xynias lies north-west of the town of Lamia.

Opous: Locrian town on the west side of the Euboian Gulf.

5 *the giver himself*: The position of these verses suggests that Apollonius is thinking of Euboian Oichalia, to the east of Eretria. For Eurytos's mad challenge to rivalry in archery with Apollo cf. *Odyssey*, 8. 226–8.

the Attic island: Salamis in the Saronic Gulf.

the land of Kekrops: Attica, so named after the first legendary king of the land.

Tainaron: the southernmost point of the Peloponnese, sacred to Poseidon (cf. 3. 1241), and said to be the site of an entrance to the Underworld.

a fruitless journey: there is doubt about the text. Theseus and Perithous journeyed to the Underworld in an unsuccessful attempt to carry off Persephone; Theseus was subsequently rescued by Herakles. Accounts differed as to whether or not Theseus had been an Argonaut, and here Apollonius explains his absence through a typical synchronization of different myths.

Siphai: Boiotian town on the coast of the Corinthian Gulf.

Tritonian Athena: here the epithet most naturally refers to a Lake Triton in Boiotia, cf. 3. 1183, 4. 260.

Araithyrea: a town near Nemea in the north-eastern Peloponnese, later renamed Phlious from the eponymous Argonaut listed here. The Asopos flows into the sea just east of Sikyon.

6 *Iphiklos*: cf. *Odyssey*, 11. 287–97. The seer Melampous used his prophetic skills to secure for his brother Bias the cattle of Iphiklos, which King Neleus had demanded as the price for marriage to his daughter Pero. As a result of his success, Melampous was imprisoned in Iphiklos' cattle-stalls until his marvellous powers secured his release.

so we learn: the poet thus alludes to the fact that previous accounts differed widely over whether or not Herakles had taken part in the expedition, cf. n. on 'we know' below, p. 143.

Lyrkeian Argos: Lyrkeia was a mountain region north of Argos.

Erymanthian marsh: the capture of a monstrous boar from the Arcadian region of Mount Erymanthos and the river of the same name was one of the traditional labours of Herakles. Lampeia was part of the Erymanthos range.

we know: an ironical marker of how different genealogies have here been moulded to the poet's purpose.

Idmon: Apollonius exploits an etymology of the prophet's name as 'knower'.

son of Leto: Apollo.

the house of Tyndareos: the introduction of the Dioskouroi leaves deliberately unclear whether their paternity is to be ascribed to Zeus, to Tyndareos, or, as in Pindar, *Nemean* 10, to both.

Arene: on the west coast of the Peloponnese north of Pylos. For the juxtaposition of the Dioskouroi and the sons of Aphareus cf. Theocritus 22.

the tight corners of war: Periklymenos was given the power of metamorphosis by Poseidon, but was eventually killed by Herakles with Athena's help, cf. Hesiod, fr. 33 MW.

7 *Apheidas*: a legendary king of Tegea, son of Arkas (the eponymous hero of Arcadia) and father of Aleos.

Mainalian bear: Mainalos was the name of an Arcadian mountain and town.

Aigialos: probably conceived as the area of northern Achaia running west from Sikyon, cf. *Iliad*, 2. 573–5.

Tainaron: cf. above, p. 142.

Imbrasian Hera: Parthenia was an ancient name of Samos, and the Imbrasos was a Samian river originally called Parthenios; Hera had important links with Samos in both mythology and cult.

Kalydon: Aitolian town west of Naupaktos.

Olenian Lernos: Olenos, an Aitolian town named by Homer (*Iliad*, 2. 639), is of uncertain location.

8 *land of Kekrops*: Attika, cf. above, p. 142. The story of the rape of Oreithyia is most famously recounted by Plato in the *Phaedrus* (229b–c). The Ilissos flows around Athens to the south; Apollonius here etymologizes its name as 'winding, whirling' (*elissein*).

Erginos: The identity of these Thracian sites is uncertain.

Minyas: this legendary king was associated with both Boiotian Orchomenos and Thessalian Iolkos, and Apollonius will subsequently explain the connection (cf. 3. 1091–5).

the coast: Apollonius envisages Pagasai as the port of Iolkos, cf. Strabo, 9. 5. 15.

10 *Eileithyia*: goddess of childbirth, long since identified with Artemis.

13 *Aisonis*: an unidentified Magnesian town; the phrase may, however, merely be a periphrasis for Iolkos.

Ortygia: Delos, cf. 4. 1705.

14 *the sons of Aloeus*: the giants Otos and Ephialtes who sought to attack Olympos by piling Pelion upon Ossa, but were killed by Idmon's father, Apollo, cf. *Odyssey*, 11. 305–20.

15 *He sang*: Orpheus sings a cosmological song of strife and unity, to reflect the quarrel we have just witnessed and to introduce the idea of the voyage as a representation of the growth of civilization, cf. Introduction, p. xxiii. The quarrelsome Idas was in fact eventually killed by Zeus' thunderbolt, as the end of the song hints.

Ophion and Eurynome: Apollonius uses not only Hesiod's *Theogony*, but also a theogony of Pherecydes of Skyros, according to which Kronos and Rheia were preceded by the Titans Ophion (or Ophioneus) and his wife Eurynome.

the Diktaian cave: we are probably to think of Mount Dikte on Crete.

Kyklopes: children of Ouranos and Gaia, who became the makers of Zeus' weapons, cf. Hesiod, *Theogony*, 139–46.

16 *in the water*: according to some traditions, the *Argo* itself refused to carry Herakles because he was too heavy.

Ismenos: Theban river, site of an important cult of Apollo.

best of all men: this passage alludes to the tradition, not adopted by Apollonius, that the *Argo* was the very first ship. For the divine audience for the *Argo* cf. the opening of Catullus 64.

Itonian Athena: the most famous cult of this Athena was in Boiotia, but Apollonius is here probably referring to Thessalian Iton (or Itonos), an inland town on the west of the Pagasitic Gulf. There is a variant reading 'Tritonian Athena'. cf. above, p. 142.

17 *headland of Sepias*: south-eastern tip of the Pelion peninsula opposite Skiathos.

Peiresiai . . . Dolops: these Magnesian places cannot be identified (for another Peiresiai cf. 1. 37). The scholiast tells us that Dolops was a son of Hermes.

'*Sailing of the* Argo': Apollonius appears to place 'Aphetai' on the eastern side of the Magnesian peninsula; 'Aphetai' means 'launching', 'letting go'.

storms: there may well be textual confusion here, as the geography of these verses seems out of sequence. Meliboia, Homole, and Eurymenai are imagined as towns on the north coast of Thessaly.

Amyros: this river did not in fact flow into the sea, but into Lake Boibe.

Myrine: that the shadow of Mount Athos (1,935 m.) could reach Myrina, modern Kastro on the west coast of Lemnos, was often noted in antiquity, cf. Pearson's note on Sophocles fr. 776; the distance involved is some 45 miles.

Sintian island: the Sinties were early inhabitants of Lemnos.

18 *Thoas*: Thoas' father was Dionysus, and the nymph Oinoe too has a name connecting her with the wine-god. Sikinos is a small island in the Cyclades to the west of Ios.

works of Athena: i.e. weaving, the traditional occupation of women.

Aithalides: Hermes granted his son undying memory (cf. Teiresias) and alternating life on earth and among the dead (cf. the Dioskouroi); this figure was taken up by the Pythagoreans who saw his soul as eventually passing into Pythagoras himself.

Acheron: a river in Epiros, believed to be one of the entrances to the Underworld. The name is then more widely used as that of one of the rivers of the Underworld (cf. *Odyssey*, 10. 513).

19 *the Keres*: Spirits of death, cf. 4. 1665. Polyxo jokes that death is unwilling to take someone as old and decrepit as herself.

20 *straightaway now*: a significant variation on Hypsipyle's 'without fear' (1. 707); the messenger knows what is on the women's minds.

the Itonian goddess: cf. above, p. 144.

the Kyklopes: cf. above, p. 144.

Amphion and Zethos: the legendary founders of Thebes, who traditionally represent two opposing lifestyles: Amphion the life of culture and the intellect, Zethos the life of physical struggle.

21   *Kytherean goddess*: Aphrodite, whose adultery with Ares is related in
      Odyssey 8.

      the Teleboans: Originally from Acarnania, the Teleboans stole the
      cattle of Elektryon, king of Mycenae. Elektryon's sons were later
      avenged by Amphitruo, Elektryon's son-in-law and mortal 'father' of
      Herakles. 'Taphians' is here used as an alternative name for the
      Teleboans, Taphos being one of the small islands (the Echinades) off
      the coast of Acarnania.

      Pelops: any suitor for the hand of Hippodameia, daughter of
      Oinomaos the king of Pisa (Olympia), had to survive a test. The
      suitor took the girl in his chariot and drove off with Oinomaos in
      pursuit; when the king caught up, he killed the suitor. According to
      some versions, Pelops bribed Myrtilos, the king's charioteer, to
      'doctor' the king's chariot and was thus successful.

      Tityos: Zeus hid Tityos' mother in the ground from fear of Hera's
      jealousy, so that Tityos appeared to have double parentage. For his
      attack upon Leto cf. *Odyssey*, 11. 576-81.

      Itonian Athena: cf. above, p. 144.

      Mainalos: cf. above, p. 143.

      the bright star: Hesperos, the evening star, associated with love and
      marriage, cf. Catullus 62.

23   *son of Hera*: Hephaistos.

24   *a child*: legend in fact told of two sons of Jason and Hypsipyle, Euneos
      and Thoas, cf. the fragmentary remains of Euripides' *Hypsipyle*.
      Euneos was king of Lemnos at the time of the Trojan War (cf. *Iliad*, 7.
      467-9).

      ask me to stay: this is merely a guess at the sense of a very obscure and
      possibly corrupt phrase.

25   *the island of Elektra*: Samothrace, the site of the famous mysteries of the
      Kabeiroi, which were at least partly concerned with safety at sea.

      the 'Black Sea': not the modern Black Sea, but rather the Gulf of Saros
      between Thrace and the Chersonnese.

      Athamas' daughter: Helle. Her stream is the Hellespont.

      Rhoiteian headland: at the entrance to the Hellespont on the Asian
      (eastern) side.

      Dardania . . . Pityeia: towns on the eastern coast of the Hellespont.

a steep island: the triangular peninsula on the eastern side of the modern Gulf of Erdek on the north Turkish coast. See map.

26 *the 'Beautiful Harbour'*: ancient Artake to the west of Kyzikos.

the *Far-Worker*: Apollo.

the Ionian sons of Neleus: a reference to the later possession of the peninsula by settlers descended from the inhabitants of Pylos in the Peloponnese. Neleus, father of Nestor, was the ancestor of the Pylian dynasty.

the 'Closed Harbour': an artificial haven on Kyzikos' western side.

27 *a Pelasgian war-force of Makrians*: the Makrians were neighbours and enemies of the Doliones.

28 *were also killed*: the translation of this passage aims to reproduce the style of the original in which, in imitation of some Homeric catalogues, verbs for killing and death are varied in a very mannered way.

son of Oineus: Meleager.

29 *halcyon*: a mystic bird of legend, often identified with the kingfisher.

the god: probably Rheia, the Great Mother.

the 'Thracian Harbour': Kyzikos' eastern harbour.

Aisepos . . . Adrasteia: when looking westwards the Argonauts see the Aisepos (the modern Gönen) and the town of Adrasteia, probably at the mouth of the R. Granikos. For the 'Nepeian Plain' at Adrasteia cf. Callimachus fr. 299 (= *Hecale*, fr. 116 Hollis).

30 *Titias and Kyllenos*: two of the 'Idaian Daktyls' of Crete, the assistants of the Great Mother, said here to be the children of an otherwise unknown Anchiale.

Oiaxian: Cretan, from Oaxes, a town on the island.

Aigaion: a giant buried by Poseidon in Phrygia.

32 *a ploughing-ox*: Apollonius alludes to a story told also in the *Aitia* of Callimachus in which Herakles killed an ox of Theiodamas, king of the Dryopes, in order to feed his son Hyllos. Apollonius' version seems to refer also to the previous *aition* of Callimachus, a similar story in which Herakles asked a Lindian peasant for food and, when he refused, killed and ate one of his oxen.

Pegai: lit. 'springs'.

34 *Glaukos*: a minor marine divinity, here revealing the truth on behalf of Nereus, 'the old man of the sea'.

35   *the name of their river*. i.e. Kios, near modern Gemlik.

    Trachis: an ancient city in southern Thessaly, closely connected with the sagas of Herakles.

BOOK 2

36   *with whom she had lain*: alternatively, Amykos' mother was one of the nymphs called 'Meliai' ('ash-trees') and her name was Bithynis. The title 'Genethlios' ('generative') implies that Poseidon was the creator and protector of the Bebrykians.

    the best man: this formula calls attention to the absence of Herakles, best of all boxers.

37   *Typhoeus*: a snake-headed monster, child of earth, and the last unsuccessful challenger to the supremacy of Olympian Zeus; cf. Hesiod, *Theogony*, 820–80.

    the darkness of evening: the evening star was particularly associated with erotic power and marriage.

38   *Aner*: the text is quite uncertain; something may be missing.

39   *a laurel tree*: the text is again uncertain.

    Therapnaian son of Zeus: Polydeukes. Therapne, near Sparta, was the site of important shrines of the Dioskouroi and their sister Helen.

40   *over the clouds*: text uncertain.

    the Harpies: rapacious 'snatchers', as their name (from *harpazein*) implies; they are represented with the characteristics of both winds and birds.

42   *Floating Islands*: it is unclear where Apollonius placed these islands. They were traditionally identified with the Echinades off the southern tip of Acarnania, or placed further out in the Ionian Sea, but in view of the Harpies' final destination in Crete, Apollonius may have conceived them as Aegean islands.

    Styx water: the 'hateful' river of the Underworld. For the special sanctity of such an oath cf. Hesiod, *Theogony*, 775 ff.

44   *then proceed*: Phineus describes the voyage eastwards along the southern shore of the Black Sea in the dry style of Ionian ethnography. For the detailed itinerary see the map, and cf. above p. xxiii.

    the Black Promontory: a headland to the east of the Rhebas, modern

Riva (see map), usually identified with the modern Kara Burun, which has the same meaning.

Thynias: also called Apollonia, the modern Kefken Adası.

Acherousian headland: Baba Burun on the Turkish coast. Lykos' city is at the site of Heraclea, modern Ereğli.

Enetean Pelops: the epithet means 'Paphlagonian', as the Enetoi were a local tribe (cf. *Iliad*, 2. 852); Pelops is more usually considered a Lydian.

Karambis: the modern Kerempe, west of Sinope.

Halys: the modern Kızıl Irmak, which flows into the Black Sea east of Sinope.

Iris: the modern Yeşil Irmak.

Thermodon: the modern Termeçay.

45 *a rugged island*: Apollonius clearly imagines the island of Ares to be not very far west of Trebizond.

the Kytaian land: Colchis. Kyta was believed to be a Colchian town (cf. Kutaisi in Georgia).

46 *the Kyprian goddess*: Aphrodite.

the Diktaian crag: Mount Dikte on Crete was sacred to Zeus.

the Early-Born: Dawn.

47 *the Etesian winds*: the name means 'annual'.

Peneios: the great river flowing through Thessaly, which is here, as often, called Haimonia.

48 *the Hill of Myrtles*: this lay to the west of Kyrene and was the site of a cult of Apollo 'of the myrtles', cf. Callimachus, *Hymn to Apollo*, 91.

Agreus and Nomios: 'of the countryside' and 'pastoral'.

the islands of Minos: the Cyclades over which Minos ruled, cf. Thucydides, 1. 4. The rising of Sirius, the 'dog star', near the end of July marked the onset of the hottest and most pestilential season of the year.

Parrhasian people . . . Lykaon: i.e. Arcadians, Parrhasie being an area of western Arcadia. Lykaon was the great Arcadian founder and first king.

far from his own land: text and interpretation of this striking simile are very uncertain. Many have wished to link it to the story of the poet's exile from Alexandria, cf. Introduction p. xvi.

the Inhospitable Sea: an alternative name for the euphemistic designation of the Black Sea as 'Hospitable' (*Euxeinos*).

50 *with soft words*: Jason tests the heroes, as Agamemnon tested the Greek army in *Iliad* 2 with near-disastrous consequences.

51 *without concealment*: the sense is not certain.

Kolone: the location of this is uncertain. For the Rhebas cf. above, p. 148.

amphilyke: a Homeric *hapax* which Apollonius seems to associate with 'Lycian' Apollo.

52 *Iepaiion Iepaiion*: both an epithet of Apollo and the ritual chant in his honour. Apollonius and Callimachus (*Hymn to Apollo*, 97–104) explain the title as a cry of encouragement to the god when he was killing the Delphic serpent: 'shoot (*hie*), child (*pai*), the arrow (*ion*)'.

Bistonian lyre: cf. above, p. 141.

Delphyne: a name of the serpent killed by Apollo at what then became 'Delphi'; the other name of the shrine, Pytho, was explained from the 'rotting' (*puthein*) of the serpent (*Homeric Hymn to Apollo*, 363, 371–4).

Korykian nymphs: the cave of Korykos on Parnassos was the site of an important cult of the nymphs, cf. P. Amandry, *Bulletin de correspondance hellénique*, Suppl. 9 (1984), 395–425; here the nymphs are made daughters of the Pleistos which flows below Delphi into the Corinthian Gulf.

Sangarios: the modern Sakarya.

53 *Acherousian headland*: cf. above, p. 149.

Eastern Sea: i.e. the Black Sea.

Nisaian Megarians: Nisa or Nisaia was the part of Megara, and the Megarians had important colonial links with the Pontic coast.

Soonautes: i.e. 'Saviour of sailors'.

54 *Hippolyte*: Queen of the Amazons whose talismanic belt—a gift from Ares—was coveted by Eurystheus' daughter; the king dispatched Herakles to fetch it. Cf. 2. 964–9.

Billaios: the modern Filyos Çay, which flows into the Black Sea at Hisarönü.

Hypios: the modern Melen Su, which flows into the Black Sea at Akçakoca.

55 *Nisaians*: cf. above, note on '*Nisaian Megarians*'.

56 *Imbrasian waters*: above, p. 143.

57 *the Nysaian son of Zeus*: Dionysos, whose name is thus 'etymologized'. Nysa was a city or mountain identified in many areas of the Greek world, but always as a site of Dionysiac ritual. 'Kallichoros' means 'beautiful dancing' and 'Aulion' means 'Place of Lodging'.

tomb of Sthenelos: not far to the east of Heraclea, but the exact location is uncertain.

the lovely waters: the Parthenios, 'river of the virgin', (the modern Bartın suyu) is naturally associated with the virgin Artemis. Cf. 3. 876–7.

Sesamos . . . Kytoros: coastal towns west of Karambis (Kerempe) in the area of modern Amasra.

58 *separated from Herakles*: according to the most common version, the sons of Deimachos became separated from Herakles during his expedition against the Amazons; they then settled the area around Sinope. Apollonius puns on their names: Deimachos Trikkaios suggests *kaiein* 'to burn', and Phlogios suggests *phlox* 'flame'; *-leon* is '-lion' and *-lykos* '-wolf'.

Argestes: the north-west wind. The name means 'the cleanser'.

Halys: cf. above. p. 149. For the Iris cf. above, p. 149.

Thermodon: cf. above, p. 149.

59 *Akmon*: legendary Phrygian hero and founder, brother of Doias who gave his name to the Doiantian plain.

headland of Genetaian Zeus: of uncertain location, perhaps near the modern Yasun Burun.

60 *island of Ares*: cf. above, p. 149.

61 *Arktouros*: the rising of this star at the start of autumn was a traditional harbinger of storms at sea, cf. the prologue of Plautus' *Rudens*.

62 *the two groups*: the narrative here is very abrupt, but there is no obvious sign of textual corruption.

on its own instructions: the ram itself told Phrixos what to do; the Greek could, however, mean 'on the instructions of Zeus' or 'on the instructions of Hermes' (cf. 4. 121).

Zeus Phyxios: Zeus 'the protector of those who flee' (*pheugein*).

64 *Lake Serbonis*: located, together with the 'plain of Nysa', on the borders of Egypt and Syria. Mount Kasion in Syria was one of the sites where

the battle of Zeus and Typhon (cf. above, p. 148) was placed, and Apollonius or his source is probably taking advantage of the fact that there was a homonymous Egyptian mountain. More commonly, Typhon was thought to be buried under Etna.

island of Philyra: exact location uncertain.

BOOK 3

66 *a lovely name . . . you*: the Muse Erato is associated through etymology with *eros*. In the third century the individual Muses were not yet fixed in a settled pattern of functions.

desire by bewitchment: not only is Athena a resolute virgin, but she was born not from a mother's body, but from her father's head.

67 *the Wandering Island*: one of the chain of Aeolian Islands off the north-eastern coast of Sicily, perhaps to be identified with Hiera (modern Vulcano).

chief among goddesses: Aphrodite's teasing is given an edge by the memory of how she beat Hera and Athena in the Judgement of Paris.

Ixion: Ixion conceived a passion for Hera, but Zeus fooled him with a cloud phantom in Hera's shape; he was then bound for eternity to a fiery wheel.

68 *blame myself later on*: Eros presumably hinted that he would punish his mother with a disgraceful passion, as when Zeus made her desire the shepherd Anchises (*Homeric Hymn to Aphrodite*).

69 *the Idaian cave*: Zeus' birth is often placed on Mount Ida in Crete; at 1.509 the cave was said to be on Mount Dikte.

a round ball: the description of the marvellous ball evokes the whole cosmos, which Eros controls, and also contemporary astronomical globes which depicted that cosmos.

70 *the sceptre of Hermes*: Hermes was the divine herald and protector of mortal heralds. The sceptre indicates the specially protected status of the herald.

71 *their custom*: the 'Plain of Kirke' was a familiar feature of Colchian ethnography. The burial practices which Apollonius describes provide a suitably sinister, non-Greek atmosphere for the Argonauts' entry to Colchis, and can be well paralleled in the anthropology of ancient and modern societies.

mist through the city: there is a difficult problem here about whether the mist is imagined to cover them in the city or in the plain, and textual corruption has been suspected. In the *Odyssey*, Athena conceals Odysseus in mist as he approaches Alkinoos' palace.

when the Pleiads set: the rising of the Pleiads (roughly late May) marked the beginning of the summer and their setting (roughly mid-November) the start of the cold season.

the Phlegraian plain: in Thrace, the traditional site of the battle of the Gods and Giants.

Phaethon: lit. 'the shining one'. The name is more usually given to a son, not a grandson, of Helios who crashed his father's flaming chariot, cf. 4. 596–626.

Jason and his companions: something appears to be missing from the text here.

73   *Kirke*: Apollonius' Kirke, like Virgil's, lives on the coast of Latium between Rome and Naples; cf. the modern Monte Circeo.

74   *the fleece comes to Hellas*: the syntax of this sentence is very elliptical, and may express Argos' embarrassment.

Athena Pallas: it is very unusual for the names to be given in this order, and this too may be a sign of the speaker's embarrassment.

Sauromatai: the Sarmatians, a Scythian tribe on the northern borders of Colchis.

76   *yield to an inferior*: the tyrant masks his savagery behind the traditional language of *arete*.

replied to the king: the transmitted text reads 'replied to the king with cunning [or 'profitable'] words'.

the Loves: this plural (*erotes*) not uncommonly denotes 'the forces of love', and is barely distinguishable from the singular *eros*.

77   *daughter of Perses*: Hekate.

78   *the son of Oineus*: Meleager.

80   *to himself*: like all tyrants, Aietes keeps his fears and a knowledge of a threatening oracle to himself. There is a link with the oracle foretelling doom to Pelias from 'a one-sandalled man'.

81   *as when a bride*: Medea thinks of herself as already 'married' to Jason, but he will be killed before she can derive adequate pleasure from the relationship.

82   *the Loves*: cf. above, n. on this page.

84   *reached the Achaian land*: the sons did not, of course, reach 'the Achaian land', as Medea would know if she had been listening to Argos' narrative, (rather than staring at Jason?). Fränkel proposed reading 'before the sons had been brought here by the Achaian ship'.

85   *Hera . . . mind*: Hera's role remains central—she works through a young girl's understandable terror of death—but it is characteristic of Apollonius' difference from Homer that she is only named after the human drama has been fully set out. Cf. Introduction p. xxvi–xxviii.

86   *Daira, the only born*: Hekate, 'only born' because she has no siblings. Elsewhere Daira is an Eleusinian deity associated with Persephone.

      Korykian crocus: Korykos in Cilicia (southern Turkey) was a famous source of saffron.

      Caspian shell: Apollonius imagines the Caspian linked to the Black Sea by a river system, cf. 4. 131–5.

      Brimo: 'the roarer', i.e. Hekate.

      Parthenios: cf. above, p. 151.

      Amnisos: a Cretan river, site of a shrine of Artemis-Eileithyia, cf. above p. 144.

87   *through the will of Hera*: this talking crow must be connected with two similar birds in Callimachus (*Iambus* 4 and *Hecale* fr. 260).

89   *Ariadne*: like Medea, a granddaughter of Helios. Ariadne eloped from Crete with the young Athenian hero, Theseus, but was then, as Jason omits explicitly to say, abandoned by him on the island of Naxos; there she was found by Dionysos who, after sleeping with her (cf. the ambiguous 'the very immortals loved her'), placed her bridal crown in the heavens as *Corona borealis*. This exemplum shows starkly the vulnerability of Medea's position.

91   *first ruled over men*: Deukalion was one of the traditional Greek culture heroes, credited with establishing civilization after the flood. That his father was Prometheus, now chained not far from Medea's home, increases the power of Deukalion to arouse Medea's interest.

      Haimonia: Thessaly, cf. above, p. 149.

      Minyas: cf. above. p. 144.

93   *the Aonian dragon*: the Aones were early inhabitants of Boiotia before the time of Kadmos.

      Kadmos: Kadmos was sent out from Phoenicia to search for his sister Europa who had been abducted by Zeus; the Delphic Apollo told him to abandon the search and instead to found a city at the spot to which a cow would lead him. On the site of what became Thebes he killed Ares' dragon and sowed the teeth to create his first citizens. Ogygos was believed to have been an early king in the region, but poets often use 'Ogygian' to mean 'ancient', 'revered'.

94 *Phlegraian Mimas*: a giant killed in the Battle of the Gods and Giants on the Phlegraian plain (cf. above p. 153).

Poseidon: Aietes is associated with the elemental power of the earth-shaker; a previous foe of the Argonauts, Amykos, was Poseidon's son. The Isthmian Games were held in Poseidon's precinct at Corinth; Tainaron, on the southern tip of the Peloponnese, contained a famous temple of Poseidon; Lerna in the Argolid was the site of springs sacred to Poseidon Genesios; Onchestos, called Hyantian after the early tribe Hyantes, was a special Boiotian seat of the god; Kalaureia is Poros in the Saronic Gulf where there was an ancient temple of Poseidon; Petra near Mount Olympos is here associated with, but may not in fact have been the site of, games held in honour of Poseidon Petraios; Geraistos, a promontory in southern Euboia, contained another important temple of the god.

96 *Pelasgian goad*: 'Pelasgian' means 'Thessalian', which is not only appropriate for Jason, but also points to the dialect of the gloss which Apollonius uses for 'goad'.

the end of the ploughshare: text and sense uncertain.

98 *hidden in the earth*: something seems to be missing from the text here.

BOOK 4

99 *who was torn*: text and interpretation of this simile are uncertain, but Medea's departure from her home seems to be likened to entering upon a life of slavery.

100 *Endymion*: the moon mocks Medea, recalling her own passion for the sleeping Endymion on Mount Latmos in Caria. Despite uncertainties in the text, the moon seems to recall occasions when Medea's magic powers 'brought her down' from the sky, cf. 3. 533.

101 *Zeus Phyxios*: cf. above, p. 151.

102 *fixed it in the eye*: Medea's malevolent eyes exert baneful influence over the eyes of the dragon.

the kindly one: these epithets refer to Hekate; the last, if correctly understood, will be euphemistic.

103   '*achaiineai*': the origin of this rare term is unclear; the scholiast
       associates it with a supposed Cretan city called 'Achaia'. The prose
       form is *achaines*.

105   *Thebe, daughter of Triton*: the eponymous heroine of Egyptian Thebes.

       Apidanean Arkadians: the 'pre-lunar' Arkadians are a familiar feature of
       ancient accounts of the rise of civilization. 'Apidanean' probably
       refers to 'Apis' or 'Apia', an old name for the Peloponnese.

       Eeria: probably lit. 'the misty land'.

       Triton: the Nile.

       a man: Argos' tale reflects accounts of the legendary Egyptian king
       and conquerer, Sesostris, cf. Herodotus, 2. 102–11, where Sesostris'
       conquests explain the racial affinity between Colchians and Egyptians.
       Sesostris was often seen as a kind of proto-Alexander, and thus as a
       model for the Ptolemies themselves.

       the Istros: the Danube. For the geographical conception implied by the
       speech see the maps, and cf. Introduction, p. xxiii–xxiv.

       comes forth in your land: the 'eastern sea' is the Black Sea, and the
       'Trinacrian sea' is the sea to the east of Sicily; Argos imagines the
       western branch of the Istros flowing through the Adriatic all the way
       to Sicily. The Acheloos, modern Aspropotamo, is named as the
       largest, 'most representative' of Greek rivers.

106   *Karambis*: cf. above, p. 149.

       Apsyrtos: the pursuing Colchians take the quicker of the two entrances
       to the Istros as it flows from the Black Sea to the Adriatic, and are
       therefore waiting in ambush when the Argonauts emerge.

       the exits to the sea: the Colchian ambush was set on the many islands,
       called in 4. 563 'the Liburnian islands', lying off the Croatian coast
       on the north-east edge of the Adriatic. The Bryges were an Illyrian
       tribe.

       river Salangon and the Nestian land: to the south of where the Istros is
       imagined to emerge, roughly the area between modern Zadar and
       Split.

107   *no longer a secret*: text and meaning uncertain.

108   *Dia*: the site of Dionysos' meeting with Ariadne (above, p. 154), and
       usually identified with Naxos.

110   *treacherous murders*: the cutting off of the hands, feet, nose, and ears, the
       so-called rite of *maschalismos*, both prevents vengeance from the dead

man and offers the corpse to the gods of the Underworld. The second rite of licking and spitting out the dead man's blood is intended to remove blood-guilt.

Apsyrteis: the scene of murder ends with an aetiology for the name of the current inhabitants of the island (perhaps modern Cres).

Eridanos: the Po. The island of Elektris is imagined to lie at the mouth of the Po at the very north of the Adriatic; the island owes its name to the amber (*elektron*) carried by the river, cf. 4. 605–17.

111   *Others fortified . . . Kadmos lies*: the 'Illyrian river' is to be identified with the inlet at modern Kotor south of Dubrovnik. Various legends associated Kadmos and his wife Harmonia with north-west Greece, where they were believed to have gone after their exile from Thebes; there was clearly a cult of them on this coast, cf. Dodds on Euripides, *Bacchae*, 1330–9. The Enchelees, 'eels, serpents', were an Illyrian tribe, cf. Herodotus, 6. 51.

Keraunia: the Albanian Mali i Çikës and the promontory of Kara Burun, the Roman Acroceraunia, famed as a danger to shipping.

land of the Hylleans: probably the area around modern Zadar, roughly opposite Ancona.

Nausithoos: father of Alkinoos who led the Phaeacians to settle Drepane (Corcyra). For Makris cf. below, p. 159.

112   *Stoichades*: the Îles d'Hyères off the French coast between Marseilles and Monaco.

the Liburnian islands: cf. above, p. 156.

'Black Kerkyra': not the better known Corcyra (Corfu), but modern Korčula north of Dubrovnik.

Melite: modern Mljet, off the coast from Dubrovnik.

Kerossos: unidentified island.

Kalypso: the Argonauts pass another famous site from the *Odyssey*. It is not clear where Apollonius imagined this island, which Homer called Ogygia.

Phaethon: cf. above, p. 153.

113   *Heliades*: Phaethon's sisters who were metamorphosed into poplars which wept tears of amber.

Amyros: a reference to the tale of Thessalian Koronis whose son by Apollo, Asklepios, was killed by Zeus for raising mortals from the dead, cf. Pindar, *Pythian* 3.

Rhodanos: the Rhône into which, in Apollonius' conception, the Po flows.

Ionian sea . . . Sardinian sea: i.e. the Adriatic, and the Mediterranean west of Sardinia.

the Herkynian rock: this epithet is found elsewhere attached to the mysterious mountains and forests of 'central Europe'.

114 *the sons of Zeus*: the Dioskouroi, traditional saviours of ships.

Aithalia: the island of Elba.

marvellous remnants: text and sense uncertain.

Aiaie: cf. above, p. 153 (n. on *Kirke*).

beasts: Kirke's 'mixed creatures' recall the theories of the pre-Socratic Empedocles who posited an evolutionary stage of 'separate limbs not joined together' followed by one of forms made from disparate limbs.

the sister of Aietes: the distinctive and threatening eyes of all descendants of Helios are readily visible in Kirke.

115 *the sacrifice*: i.e. sacrifices of purification from blood-guilt, cf. R. Parker, *Miasma* (Oxford, 1983), 370–4.

without wine: wine was not offered to the Erinyes (Furies).

117 *the Planktai*: a notorious interpretative problem, as Apollonius elsewhere distinguishes the Symplegades from the Planktai, and it was Athena who brought the *Argo* safely through the former. There is a serious doubt about the text.

your husband: Peleus.

misses your milk: an allusion to an etymology of Achilles' name from *a-kheilos*, 'he who did not put his lips to the breast'.

118 *Krataiis*: Scylla's mother, according to Homer (*Odyssey*, 12. 124), is here identified with Hekate, who was Scyllas's mother in other traditions.

119 *Anthemoessa*: lit. 'the flowery island'. Homer had placed the Sirens in a 'flowery meadow' (*Odyssey*, 12. 159). Apollonius clearly imagines an island somewhere near Capri, but more than one spot on the coast south of Naples was associated with the Sirens.

daughter of Deo: Persephone, whose companions before her rape by Hades were subsequently metamorphosed into the bird-like Sirens.

120 *Bistonian lyre*: cf. above, p. 141.

Cape Lilybaeum: the western tip of Sicily, modern Marsala. Aphrodite's saving intervention explains the hero-cult of Boutes there.

121   *Thrinakia*: Sicily.

      orichalk: an unidentified precious metal or alloy, perhaps fictitious.

      a large and fertile island: Corfu, called by Apollonius Drepane ('Sickle'),
      and identified as Homer's Phaeacia. For the Keraunian sea cf. above,
      p. 157.

122   *Makris*: nurse of Dionysus (cf. 4. 540); the island bore her name in
      various traditions, cf. 4. 1131–40.

      Haimonia: Thessaly, cf. above, p. 149.

000   *children*: we think especially of Nausicaa, cf. Introduction p. xxiv–xxv.

124   *Antiope*: daughter of Nukteus who pursued her for vengeance when he
      discovered that she was pregnant (by Zeus).

      Danae: exposed on the ocean with her son by Zeus, Perseus, after her
      father Akrisios discovered what had happened.

      Echetos: named by Homer (*Odyssey*, 18. 84) as a cruel king of Epirus.
      Later sources tell that he blinded his daughter for having a love affair
      and forced her to try to grind metal into flour as the means to recover
      her sight.

125   *Aristaios*: cf. 2. 498–530. For his bees cf. Virgil, *Georgic* 4.

      Nysaian son of Zeus; cf. above, p. 151.

126   *Hera*: cf. 3. 818 n.

127   *Orikos*: The subsequent history of the Colchians refers to the
      colonisation of Corcyra from Corinth (Ephyra) by the Bakchiadai.
      The Colchians move first to the mainland opposite Corcyra, and then
      north to the area around the Albanian promontory of Kara Burun (cf.
      4. 519 n.). Orikos is at the head of the bay formed by the promontory;
      the Amantes and the Nestaioi were local Illyrian tribes.

      the land of the Kouretes: Acarnania.

      Syrtis: the feared and treacherous shoals and desert wastes imagined
      to stretch around the modern Gulf of Sirte on the Libyan coast.

129   *Paktolos*: Lydian river, flowing from the Tmolus mountains to Sardis,
      and famous for gold-bearing streams.

      heroines, guardians of Libya: local rural deities, rather like protecting
      nymphs. Their appearance here is a kind of cross between an epic
      dream-sequence and the description of a desert mirage.

130   *like young girls*: an apparent reference to the fact that Libyan women
      were believed to wear tasselled goatskin tunics, very like the
      traditional dress of Athena, cf. Herodotus, 4. 189.

131 *the Hesperid nymphs*: traditional guardians of the golden apples created by the earth as a wedding present for Zeus and Hera. Their garden is variously situated, usually in the extreme west. The fetching of the apples was one of Herakles' canonical tasks.

132 *offspring of Ocean*: Orpheus seems to address them as he would like them to be: water-nymphs who will be able to relieve the Argonauts' desperate thirst.

133 *as answer*: text and sense uncertain.

      the deadly Keres: spirits of death, cf. above, p. 145.

      Kaphauros: Apollonius draws on foundation myths which linked Crete and Libya. Kaphauros' brother Nasamon is the eponymous ancestor of the Libyan Nasamones.

      Lykoreian Phoibos: i.e. Delphic, Lykoreia being the name both of the peak of Mount Parnassos and a village on the mountain.

134 *the king*: Polydektes of Seriphos who ordered Perseus to bring him the Gorgon's head.

      pain was not too severe: sense uncertain.

135 *Eurypylos*: Triton claims to be a legendary founding king of Kyrene, son of Poseidon.

      Apis: cf. above, p. 156.

137 *the homing-star*: Hesperos, the evening star which signals the end of the working day.

      Talos: a legendary Cretan giant, sometimes said to be a creation of Hephaistos, but here the last survivor of Hesiod's Bronze Age, the age before that of the demi-God Argonauts themselves.

      Keres: spirits of death, cf. above, p. 145.

138 *her wrath*: Medea puts the evil eye on Talos by sending out dangerous phantoms (*deikela*) from her eyes; the description is intended to recall 'scientific' accounts of this magical procedure.

      Salmonis: the north-east tip of Crete (modern Sidero), where there was a cult of Athena.

      '*katoulas*': Apollonius seems to associate this word with *oloos* 'deadly'; it may in fact mean 'enshrouding'.

      Ortygia: Jason names three famous Apolline sites, Delphi, Amyklai near Sparta, and Delos (here called Ortygia), cf. 1. 419. This passage is very close to Callimachus' description of the same events (fr. 18).

139 *Anaphe*: modern Anafi, next to Thera (cf. 4. 1775–64).

son of Maia: Hermes, god of dreams.

the divine clod: i.e. Triton's gift, cf. 4. 1552 ff.

140 *long after Euphemos*: a brief account of the foundation legends of Thera from which Battos eventually colonized Kyrene (cf. Pindar, *Pythian* 4). The prominence of this story at the end of the poem is important in assessing its political context, cf. Introduction, p. xi.

the Kekropian land: Attica, cf. above p. 142.

Aulis: Boiotian town on the coast opposite Euboea where the channel (the Euripus) is at its narrowest. Aulis is thus said to be 'within', i.e. dominated by, Euboia.

Lokrians: cf. above p. 142.

NAME INDEX TO THE *ARGONAUTICA*

Numbers refer to pages of the translation. There are no entries for Aietes, Argonauts, Colchis/Colchians, Jason/son of Aison, and Medea. An asterisk indicates an Argonaut.

INDEX

Oinomaos, father of Hippodameia, beaten in a chariot race by Pelops 21

Olympos, Thessalian mountain, home of the gods 15, 17, 29, 43, 50, 64, 68, 69, 97, 117

Onchestos, town in Boiotia 94

Ophion, predecessor of Kronos on Olympos 15

Opous, Lokrian town 4, 140

Orchomenos, town in Boiotia 51, 61, 62, 91, 105

Orchomenos, Boiotian hero 63, 72

Oreites, one of the Bebrykians 38

Oreithyia, mother of *Zetes and *Kalais 8

Orikos, town in NW Greece 127

Orion, constellation 31, 83

Ornytos, grandfather of *Iphitos 8

Ornytos, one of the Bebrykians 37

*Orpheus, legendary Thracian musician and singer 3, 15, 16, 25, 30, 39, 52, 57, 120, 126, 131, 135; son of Oiagros 16, 52, 126

Ortygia, see s.v. Delos

Ossa, Thessalian mountain 17

Othrys, Thessalian mountain 48

Otrere, Amazon queen 45

Ouranos, primeval sky-god 64, 122

Pagasai, port of Iolkos 8, 10, 13, 15, 140

Paian, 'Healer', title of Apollo 134

Paktolos, Lydian river 129

*Palaimonios, of Aitolia 7

Pallene, Thracian peninsula 17

Paphlagonians, Black Sea tribe 44, 54, 104, 106

Paraibios, assistant to Phineus 46–47

Parnassos, mountain of central Greece sacred to Apollo 52

Parthenia, name for Samos 7, 56

Parthenios, Pontic river 57, 86

Pasiphae, daughter of Helios and mother of Ariadne 89, 91

Pegai, spring at Kios 32

Peiresiai, Thessalian town 3

Peiresiai, town on Magnesian coast 17

Peirithous, Lapith hero 5

Pelasgians, ancient inhabitants of Thessaly 17, 64, 96, 104, 105

*Peleus, father of Achilles 5, 16, 28, 55, 56, 64, 78, 110, 118–119, 130; son of Aiakos 38, 56, 78, 110

Pelias, king of Iolkos 3, 8, 9, 10, 24, 26, 34, 50, 53, 67, 92, 104

Pelion, Thessalian mountain 12, 15, 16, 17, 63

Pellen, Peloponnesian hero 7

Pellene, town in Achaia 7

Pelopeia, sister of *Akastos 10

Pelops, eponymous hero of the Peloponnese 21, 44, 54, 127, 135

Peneios, Thessalian river 47

*Periklymenos, of Pylos 6

Perkote, town on the Hellespont 25, 26

Pero, daughter of Neleus 5

Perse, mother of Kirke 112

Persephone, daughter of Demeter, queen of the Underworld 57, 119

Perses, see s.v. Hekate

Perseus, hero who killed the Gorgon 134

Petra, Thessalian town 94

Peuke, mouth of the Istros (Danube) 106

Phaeacia/Phaeacians, inhabitants of Drepane 111, 116, 118, 122–127, 139

THE WORLD'S CLASSICS

A Select List

HANS ANDERSEN: Fairy Tales
Translated by L. W. Kingsland
Introduction by Naomi Lewis
Illustrated by Vilhelm Pedersen and Lorenz Frølich

JANE AUSTEN: Emma
Edited by James Kinsley and David Lodge

Mansfield Park
Edited by James Kinsley and John Lucas

J. M. BARRIE: Peter Pan in Kensington Gardens & Peter and Wendy
Edited by Peter Hollindale

WILLIAM BECKFORD: Vathek
Edited by Roger Lonsdale

CHARLOTTE BRONTË: Jane Eyre
Edited by Margaret Smith

THOMAS CARLYLE: The French Revolution
Edited by K. J. Fielding and David Sorensen

LEWIS CARROLL: Alice's Adventures in Wonderland
and Through the Looking Glass
Edited by Roger Lancelyn Green
Illustrated by John Tenniel

MIGUEL DE CERVANTES: Don Quixote
Translated by Charles Jarvis
Edited by E. C. Riley

GEOFFREY CHAUCER: The Canterbury Tales
Translated by David Wright

ANTON CHEKHOV: The Russian Master and Other Stories
Translated by Ronald Hingley

JOSEPH CONRAD: Victory
Edited by John Batchelor
Introduction by Tony Tanner

DANTE ALIGHIERI: The Divine Comedy
Translated by C. H. Sisson
Edited by David Higgins

VIRGIL: The Aeneid
Translated by C. Day Lewis
Edited by Jasper Griffin

HORACE WALPOLE: The Castle of Otranto
Edited by W. S. Lewis

IZAAK WALTON and CHARLES COTTON:
The Compleat Angler
Edited by John Buxton
Introduction by John Buchan

OSCAR WILDE: Complete Shorter Fiction
Edited by Isobel Murray

The Picture of Dorian Gray
Edited by Isobel Murray

VIRGINIA WOOLF: Orlando
Edited by Rachel Bowlby

ÉMILE ZOLA:
The Attack on the Mill and other stories
Translated by Douglas Parmée

A complete list of Oxford Paperbacks, including The World's Classics, OPUS, Past Masters, Oxford Authors, Oxford Shakespeare, and Oxford Paperback Reference, is available in the UK from the Arts and Reference Publicity Department (BH), Oxford University Press, Walton Street, Oxford OX2 6DP.

In the USA, complete lists are available from the Paperbacks Marketing Manager, Oxford University Press, 200 Madison Avenue, New York, NY 10016.

Oxford Paperbacks are available from all good bookshops. In case of difficulty, customers in the UK can order direct from Oxford University Press Bookshop, Freepost, 116 High Street, Oxford, OX1 4BR, enclosing full payment. Please add 10 per cent of published price for postage and packing.